S0-BBH-873

Further praise for *Power and the Idealists*

"Berman's thoughtful book is a valuable history lesson, especially for those too young to remember much about the tumultuous 1960s or '70s. He draws the curtain back on the era of the 'New Left,' a time when capitalism and American power were considered the chief culprits for the world's woes and when a global peasant revolution seemed not merely possible but something that college students could help spark. But what makes this book more than merely a collection of reminiscences of intellectual arguments from the glory days . . . is that many of these activists have assumed positions of influence in Europe. . . . Berman's most important contribution is to show how these leaders remain influenced by their old debates, especially about when and how military force should be used. . . . Illuminating."
—Derek Chollet, *Washington Post Book World*

"Remarkable. . . . Lucid. . . . If anyone can put this dispute into its historical context, it's Berman. He is not only an alumnus of the rebellion; he is the keeper of its yearbook and its funeral director. In this free-standing sequel to his superb *A Tale of Two Utopias*, he revisits the European graduating class of Rebellion High."
—Johann Hari, *New York Times Book Review*

"[An] important book for liberal internationalists . . . of critical significance for international affairs. Berman's book is, indirectly, the story of his own intellectual journey from left-wing activist to liberal interventionist: political history as picaresque tale."

—Peter Ross Range,
Democratic Leadership Council's *Blueprint*

"An extraordinarily important book on the generation of 1968 and its fortunes. We were all united by Che Guevara's conviction that as long as the world was as it was, none of us wanted to die in bed. We became divided by the conviction of some of us (including me) that the path of the legendary Che was a road to nowhere."

—Adam Michnik, editor in chief,
Gazeta Wyborcza (Warsaw)

"Not even Paul Berman's enemies would accuse him of ducking a fight. If you haven't read him yet, you have missed the bracing experience of confronting the most fluent New York intellectual writing today. *Power and the Idealists* is a follow-up to his *A Tale of Two Utopias*. But whereas the first book was a generally optimistic account of how the 1960s generation had broken restraints on human sexuality and undermined the apparently unending dictatorship of the Soviet empire, the sequel is far darker." —Nick Cohen, *New Statesman* (London)

"Paul Berman's latest book is remarkable. It is partly a collective biography, partly a work of contemporary history, and partly a political essay and argument about what has happened to the radical left over the past 30 years. It examines political and ethical issues of the utmost seri-

"The book is not about the German foreign minister from 1998 to 2005, but is rather a collective portrait of a generation of left-wing idealists. . . . Berman uses a wide array of sources to draw a fascinating and convincing picture of these idealists. He relies on speeches, debates, articles and books, and carefully notes what these '68ers said or did not say; he considers how they dealt with crises in politics and their own political lives; he examines how far they engaged in domestic politics, in revolutionary activities, in humanitarian projects. And he finds differences between all of them, but notes their common belief in morally justified actions. . . . Berman's book is thus the story of a kind of alternative elite, written with sympathy and distance. Probably this generational project—if it was one—has not yet come to an end. And its achievements in national cultures as well as in the international realm should not be underrated."

—Jost Dülffer, professor of modern history,
University of Cologne (Germany)

ousness and challenges all of us on the left at the deepest level. . . . It is also, one has to say, an extraordinarily well-written book, and hard to put down once you have started."   —Philip Spencer, Democratiya.com

"*Power and the Idealists* is the work of an extraordinary writer."   —Benjamin Kerstein, *Azure* (Jerusalem)

"An impassioned story of the revolutionary idealism of thirty years ago, and of its transfer, in some cases, to positions of power."   —Christian Rocca, *Il Foglio* (Italy)

"The sharpest chronicler of contemporary intellectual history tells the story of the illusions and crimes, the dreams and the myopia that defined this generation. Ideals and nightmares, debates and dogmas, rebellions and servilities. . . . You can quarrel with his argument. What is undeniable is that his work is one of the most lucid, valiant and provocative examinations of our intellectual pulse."   —Jesús Silva-Herzog Márquez, *La Reforma* (Mexico City)

"Personal testimony but also an effort to give coherence to a succession of sometimes confused events, this book offers a preciously valuable reflection on one of the major political phenomena of these last thirty years."
—Eric Aeschimann, *Libération* (Paris)

"An interesting, well-written and stirring book."
—*Trouw* (Amersterdam)

POWER AND THE IDEALISTS

OR, THE PASSION OF JOSCHKA FISCHER, AND ITS AFTERMATH

PAUL BERMAN

W. W. NORTON & COMPANY
NEW YORK LONDON

Copyright © 2005 by Paul Berman

Preface copyright © 2007 by Richard Holbrooke

"Who is Joschka Fischer?" by Michael Kelly copyright © 2003,
The Washington Post Writers Group. Reprinted by permission.

Frontispiece photograph copyright © 1973, Lutz Kleinhans, FAZ.
Reprinted with permission.

Book design by David Janik

Library of Congress Cataloging-in-Publication Data

Berman, Paul.
   Power and the idealists : the passion of Joschka Fischer,
   and its aftermath / Paul Berman.
      p. cm.
   ISBN 1-932360-91-3 (alk. paper)
   1. Fischer, Joschka. 2. Radicalism--Germany.
   3. Politicians—Germany—Biography. 4. Social history—
   1960–1970. 5. Social history—1970– 6. Liberalism.
   7. Radicalism.   I. Title.
   HN460.R3B473 2005
   943.088'2'092—dc22
   [B]
2005012965

ISBN 978-0-393-33021-2 pbk.

W. W. Norton & Company, Inc.
500 Fifth Avenue, New York, N.Y. 10110
www.wwnorton.com

W. W. Norton & Company Ltd.
Castle House, 75/76 Wells Street, London W1T 3QT

POWER AND THE IDEALISTS

OR,
THE PASSION OF
JOSCHKA FISCHER,
AND ITS AFTERMATH

The results of one other poll came in, quite a fascinating poll precisely because its subject went beyond Fischer himself. The subject in this instance was the generation of 1968. The radicals of that period—were they mainly "interested in power"? Or were they "idealists"? Such was the question . . .

—Chapter One

CONTENTS

PREFACE
by Richard Holbrooke

During my college years one of the books we all read was Edmund Wilson's *To the Finland Station: A Study in the Writing and Acting of History.* I never forgot it. Wilson was a great writer and literary critic, and his book was beautifully written. But his book excited me mostly because it described something unusual and extremely important: the relationship of philosophical ideas and practical events—the savage intersection where theories and personalities meet and sometimes end up changing the world, for better or for worse. Wilson described this intersection by recounting the history of socialism. He described the rise of various theories about history and economics. And he showed how Lenin and a small number of other people came along and put those ideas (altered, of course, to fit circumstances) to use in the Bolshevik Revolution, and thereby changed world history—disastrously, in that instance, as Wilson ultimately recognized.

Paul Berman is a writer in Edmund Wilson's tradition. In *Power and the Idealists*, Berman's theme, too, is the intersection of ideas and events. In some ways *Power and the Idealists* is a continuation of Wilson's classic book—a story of the political left and its evolution and its effect on world events. Berman begins with the left-wing radicals from the period half a century after Lenin's revolution—the years around 1968. A lot of us today think we know everything we need to know about 1968. In the one-line summary of history so popular in the modern media, 1968 was a crazy time. Sex, drugs, and rock and roll created a wild, irresponsible group of self-indulgent, authority-defying, flag-burning, New Left anarchists who threatened our very values, our Way of Life. This one-line summary of 1968 has energized right-wing politics ever since. Many people today still cannot abide political leaders from the center-left who, when they were young, stood anywhere near the rebellious atmosphere of that period. We have seen this in the right-wing opposition to figures like John Kerry and Bill Clinton, neither of whom was especially radical when he was young. And we have seen something very similar in Europe, where some people on the political right will never forgive political leaders like Joschka Fischer and Daniel Cohn-Bendit—who were, in fact, quite radical in their youth. The memories and myths and sometimes the misrepresentations that came out of 1968 created a fault line in American and European political life, and the fault line has aroused enmities and resentments that will last as long as the '68ers are around.

Well, some of those myths and memories cannot be denied. The stunning events of 1968 really happened—the Tet Offensive in Vietnam, the assassinations of Martin Luther King, Jr., and Robert F. Kennedy, the sometimes peaceful and sometimes destructive political demonstrations in Paris and New York and Chicago, the razor-thin victory of Richard Nixon over Hubert Humphrey, the rage that led some ultra-leftists to join the murderous Baader-Meinhof Gang in Germany two years later and led other people who should have known better to entertain some very Old Left delusions about Fidel Castro, the PLO, the Chinese Cultural Revolution, and other gods that failed. For both those who indulged (in any, or every, sense of the word) and those who did not (or say they did not), the era imprinted them for the rest of their lives.

Yet there was another legacy from 1968, which many people have failed to recognize. The events of that period led some of the participants in the New Left to argue with one another about what had happened, and the arguments produced an intellectual ferment, especially in Europe. In the years that followed, some of those veterans of the New Left became thoughtful about the disasters of their own movement—about the left-wing disasters that Edmund Wilson had begun to notice long ago in *To the Finland Station*. Some of those veterans of the European New Left, the old '68ers, sifted through their own beliefs, trying to separate the moral concerns that might have been valid from the left-wing dogmas that had turned out to be destructive and false. They began to look at world events with fresh eyes. Some moved beyond their original visceral anti-Americanism. To the astonishment of many, some of those European veterans of 1968 achieved political respectability, too, as the years went by, and their new ideas began to have an impact on the world of politics and policy. A lot of attention has been paid to modern movements of the right, such as the neoconservatives. But some of the veterans of the New Left, especially in Europe, produced their own approach to world politics, a post–Cold War way of thinking, and this new way of thinking eventually permeated the policy process—even though very few "decision-makers" in the United States and other countries have fully understood these new ideas or have even been aware that new ideas were coming into existence, or where they came from.

Paul Berman has followed all this like no one else on either side of the Atlantic, and, as a veteran himself of '68, has understood how important was the ferment among some of the European '68ers. Now he has done something quite remarkable: out of the many internal disputes within the left (Old, New, and divided), he has found a pattern and a story line that is compelling and important. He has identified the roots of an important development in post–Cold War thinking: a turn, among a small but influential group of the '68ers, away from some of the traditional left-wing and anti-American dogmas of the past in favor of a new kind of liberal antitotalitarianism. Berman told part of this story in his book *A Tale of Two Utopias: The Political Journey of the Generation of 1968* (published in 1996), which focused on the American Left, though in that book he gave some attention to Europe, as well. Now he has reached across the Atlantic to examine some of the European '68ers and their foreign policy ideas in full detail. He has described the origins and nature of the new thinking about world affairs. He has shown the powerful influence of this new thinking on attitudes and policies from Cambodia and Vietnam to the East Bloc revolutions of 1989 and the

Balkan wars of the nineteen-nineties. And he has brought the story forward into the age of Iraq.

It takes some kind of determination and skill (including archival skill, in fact, for most of his sources are unknown in the United States) to excavate these precincts. But Berman is fully up to the task. By recounting the history of a handful of people from the European '68ers, he has painted a huge canvas. He has shown how these people helped generate a postmodern approach to international affairs. His book can help policy-makers, who usually live in a hermetically sealed world of their own, to understand the origins and nature of some of their own ideas. His book could help build a broader, bipartisan consensus for an enlightened Atlantic foreign policy. Everybody knows that, on the political right, foreign-policy "realists" in the tradition of Henry Kissinger and the first President Bush have engaged in a battle for many years with the strange group of neo-cons and right-wing Wilsonians that gathered around the second President Bush. Berman shows that a parallel battle has been taking place all along on the left side of the political spectrum. He even shows some of the influence of the European left-wing debate in the United States, not just recently but from a period long before neoconservatism became a significant political current. One of the most striking anecdotes in his book is his account of Joan Baez in the nineteen-seventies—among the earliest people on the left side of American politics to recognize that if she had opposed the American involvement in Vietnam, she also had to oppose the totalitarian behavior of the North Vietnamese after they took over. Baez was roundly denounced for doing this by many of her early antiwar compatriots. But history has shown that she was right, and universal principles were on her side.

Three of the personalities in Berman's story stand out: three men (they happen to be men), each with his own fascinating history, each of whom has contributed in a different way to the development of the new ideas. Collectively their histories illuminate the larger story:

- Joschka Fischer, who has run the gauntlet from beating up a German policeman at an ultra-left rally in 1973, as shown in some dramatic photographs, to wearing three-piece suits as Germany's foreign minister during the period that extended from the Kosovo War to the wars in Afghanistan and Iraq. (When, as American ambassador to Germany in 1993, I first met Fischer, he was wearing a kind of transitional uniform consisting of a blue-jeans suit and a checkered shirt with an odd sort of tie; the three-piece suits came later, and does Berman have fun with them!) Fischer, who became Germany's most popular politician, could not have succeeded politically in the United States, given his ultra-left-wing past and those terrible photographs from long ago. But there he was at the turn of the twenty-first century, pushing his country into support of the Clinton Administration's actions in Kosovo, then a few years later confronting Donald Rumsfeld, George W. Bush's secretary of defense, in a public conference just before the war in Iraq. This took place in February 2003 in a Munich hotel ballroom, and, by chance, I was seated for a while almost directly between the two men, Fischer and Rumsfeld. That was the famous conference in which Fischer, switching from German to English, told Rumsfeld to his face, "Excuse me, I'm not convinced. This is my problem. I cannot go to the public and say, 'Oh well, let's go to war because there are reasons' and so on, and I don't believe in them." Berman captures the full import of that dramatic confrontation, which was broadcast live on German television and riveted Germany—a confrontation that even received a bit of attention in the United States, especially because, as Berman shows, Rush Limbaugh took the occasion to launch one of his demagogic right-wing radio attacks.

- Daniel Cohn-Bendit, "Danny the Red" himself, the leader of the French student uprising of 1968 but legally a German citizen, a man with friends all over Europe, whose passage through subsequent history shows an admirable consistency of beliefs and a highly self-aware sense of what can be accomplished in public life. In Berman's accounting Cohn-Bendit tends to play the role of wise, ironic commentator on the events that he has lived through.

- Bernard Kouchner, the charismatic French doctor who was also deeply involved in the 1968 demonstrations and even lent his car to Danny the Red at a crucial moment in the drama. Kouchner was originally a young member of the Old Left. But he found that the reality of such hell-holes as Biafra and Cambodia defied the easy anti-Americanism of the Old Left, and of the New Left, and of a great many French intellectuals. This restless, brilliant doctor saw that if he wanted to change the world, he had to abandon his original ideas and attack equally crimes and totalitarianism of the left and the right. Cofounding Doctors Without Borders, relentlessly pushing humanitarianism with a political face—or was it politics with a humanitarian face?—Kouchner played an immense role in shaping a new view of intervention in the internal affairs of other nations. As early as 1988, Kouchner, together with some colleagues, drew up a United Nations General Assembly resolution asserting the right to intervene in another country in case of some dreadful emergency.

Astonishingly, this passed the General Assembly—"the very first expression," as Berman points out, "of a victim's right to be represented by someone other than his own government." General Assembly resolutions carry little weight in the real world, but this one launched a movement that would end with Kouchner asserting something he called the *"droit d'ingérance"*—the "right to intervene." By the mid-nineteen-nineties, after the horrible lessons of Rwanda and Bosnia, many nations, including ultimately the United States and the members of the European Union, began to find reasons to accept this new formulation and apply it to Bosnia (1995) and Kosovo (1999), where enormous numbers of people needed to be rescued. Since policy-makers tend to be oblivious to the origins of new ideas, almost no one in Washington and few in Brussels realized that the intellectual roots of intervention in the Balkans came from a doctor, who at that moment was serving as the French Minister of Health. Still fewer of those people knew anything at all about the philosophers who had influenced the doctor. Finally, in an almost accidental twist of fate, Kouchner was called upon to implement his own theories: he was appointed by Kofi Annan as the UN Secretary-General's Special Representative for Kosovo, the war that Berman calls the '68ers' War.

Berman mentions in his account that I became a warm friend of Kouchner's. This is true. I visited Kouchner during his reign in Kosovo. I was the American ambassador to the UN in those days, and I thought he was doing a terrific job—despite endless second-guessing by mid-level bureaucrats back at UN headquarters in New York. He remains a dear friend, and continues to fight for his beliefs. In French opinion polls, he always ranks as one of the two or three most popular public figures. But because he refuses to be an orthodox figure—he is sometimes called a French member of the "American left"—his own Socialist Party still sees him as a maverick.

Ideas have consequences—even in the post-ideological age in which we are said to live. Political leaders and high appointed officials are driven by intellectual forces that they can only dimly sense, but which shape their responses to specific events. The end of ideology, like the so-called "end of history" that Berman discussed in his earlier book, *A Tale of Two Utopias,* can be much overrated.

Berman is a passionate believer in liberal democracy and the power of ideas. For him, liberal democracy is a never-ending project that has always aroused opposition and must always be defended, must always be examined and questioned and strengthened. To the scorn that many suspicious Americans may feel for an approach to history that takes seriously the utterances of obscure French *philosophes,* Berman would reply: ideas do matter, although they may take years to attain acceptance. And to theorists and thinkers who live only in the world of academic debate or scholarly journals, Berman also says: events matter; they affect ideas just as much as ideas affect events. Events, in fact, can turn a good cause into a bad one, and leave intellectuals trapped on the wrong side of history. This happened, as Berman shows and as Edmund Wilson showed long before him, with the Old Left, which believed in Marxism and Communism long after events had destroyed any conceivable rationale they may have once had.

Has something similar happened to the new kind of liberal antitotalitarianism whose origins and development Berman has chronicled? Have good new ideas led to bad results—in Iraq, above all? One of the most intriguing aspects of *Power and the Idealists* is Berman's account of a debate about this very question among some of the European '68ers themselves—among precisely the people who had pioneered the new ideas. Iraq presented a quandary to the people whom Berman describes. Every one of those people detested the archtotalitarian Saddam Hussein. Every one of those people looked forward to Saddam's overthrow—at least someday, if not right away. None of those '68ers loved the George W. Bush administration, and most of them were revolted by it. The Bush administration, in the understated words of the Polish '68er Adam Michnik, was "not their cup of tea." Even so, some of the '68ers hoped that the American-led intervention in Iraq would turn out to be a good thing, and in 2003 they gave their support to the intervention, begrudgingly in most cases. These veterans of the New Left hoped that, in spite of the unattractive qualities of the Bush administration, intervention in Iraq would end up resembling the intervention in the Balkans—a humanitarian policy with humanitarian results. They hoped that more people in Europe, instead of fewer people, would come to the aid of the intervention and of the Iraqis themselves.

Then again, some of the other '68ers in Europe predicted dire consequences from the start. They opposed the intervention outright, in some cases because they instinctively feared the incompetence of the Bush administration, in some cases for additional reasons, as well. The European '68ers argued with one another in a friendly and respectful way about these questions, but, as Berman shows, they argued very earnestly, too. Today the dire predictions have turned out to be all-too-true. The horrible, incompetent execution of American policy in Iraq has proved once again a cardinal rule of any policy: a policy badly carried out becomes a bad policy. This time the bad policy ended up catastrophic. Might it have been possible to work out an alternative, superior policy, as Bernard Kouchner wanted to do—an entirely different approach to bringing Saddam's monstrous dictatorship to an end? As Berman's book ends, the veterans of the European New Left, having succeeded in changing the rules for intervention through their arguments over the decades and their efforts in the Balkans during the nineteen-nineties, found themselves, like everyone else, up against a terrible reality in Iraq—a reality so desperate that it threatened to discredit the noble ideas that had led some of those veterans of the New Left, though not all of them, to support the original intervention.

So the intellectual debate will go on, with events in Iraq and Afghanistan and many other places playing a major role. I hope Paul Berman will return to these issues, to carry forward the story yet again, and to show how, at the savage intersection of history, ideas and events meet to form a new reality. "I am a critic and not a philosopher," Berman wrote in *A Tale of Two Utopias*. But he is a bit too modest. Intellectual history of this caliber can help shape political philosophy. In the future we are going to face many new humanitarian and international crises, as we already see in Darfur and the Republic of Georgia and other places around the world. We are going to have to find the proper balance between prudence, on one hand, and effective, calibrated involvement in the international arena on the other. We are going to have to ask ourselves difficult questions about matters of principle and matters of practicality, and Paul Berman's illuminating history of people and of ideas will help us ask these questions and search for answers.

Richard Holbrooke
New York City
January 2007

FOREWORD

Chapter one of this book, "The Passion of Joschka Fischer," originally appeared as an essay in the *New Republic*, August 28–September 3, 2001, in the literary section that is edited by Leon Wieseltier. I have revised this essay in a number of ways.

The rest of the book recounts the aftermath of the story that is told in chapter one—or, at least, one of the several aftermaths.

I invite the readers to regard the entire book as a freestanding sequel to an an earlier book of mine, *A Tale of Two Utopias: The Political Journey of the Generation of 1968*, which came out in 1996.

I am grateful to Jeffrey Herf of the University of Maryland, Mariam Lau of *Die Welt*, Anson Rabinbach of Princeton University, and Paul Stoop of the American Academy in Berlin (where I completed my work on this project) for their remarks on one or another portion of the text—not that any of these people should be held accountable for my errors of fact or judgment. In the interest of accuracy and clarity, I have altered in this new paperback edition a handful of sentences from the original hardcover edition.

CHAPTER ONE:
THE PASSION OF JOSCHKA FISCHER

I.

In January 2001, *Stern* magazine in Germany published a set of five grainy photographs of Joschka Fischer, the German foreign minister and vice chancellor, as a young bully in a street battle in Frankfurt. It was April 1973. The photos showed: a figure in a black motorcycle helmet, labeled as Fischer, facing off against another figure in a white policeman's helmet, with a dented Volkswagen squatting in the background; the black-helmeted Fischer drawing near, and a skinny girl or maybe a long-haired boy (this was an androgynous era) running to join him; Fischer and other people on the attack, the white-helmeted cop going into a crouch; Fischer's black-gloved fist raised as if to punch the crouching cop on the back, Fischer's comrades crowding around; the cop huddled on the ground, Fischer and his comrades appearing to kick him, with two additional people watching. And no more dented Volkswagen. The photographer has evidently been circling around the skirmish, snapping his camera in what must have been a frenzy of adrenaline, each picture taken from a different angle.

Those were brutal photographs. One glance at them and you were back in the days of left-wing street fighting from the late nineteen-sixties and nineteen-seventies, when young militants in West Germany were always pouring into the streets, and Volkswagens were getting dented right and left. And the photographs, having conjured the past, provoked an outcry. The Joschka Fischer of 2001 was a member of the party called, in expressively anti-bureaucratic fashion, the Greens—a man of the left on its hipper, friskier side. He happened to be the very first Green to hold a ministry in Germany's federal government, let alone the foreign ministry. A powerful man, therefore a man with enemies. The photographs gazed blearily at the world from the semi-glossy pages of *Stern*, and flames of Christian Democratic wrath erupted at once from those many partisan enemies. Germany's foreign minister had disgraced himself in those photographs; had embarrassed his nation; had lost the ability to represent Germany to the world; ought to be investigated, to be indicted, to resign.

The street battles of 1973 took place long ago, and it could have been supposed that Fischer's enemies, having given vent to a thousand pent-up furies and Christian Democratic resentments, would eventually calm down, and the scandal of those ancient photographs would fade. The editors of *Stern* seem to have anticipated that sort of development. The magazine advertised its photographs on the cover with a quotation from Fischer ("Ja, ich war militant"), but the big story in that week's issue was Europe's meat crisis, illustrated by a giant sausage skewered on the tines of an oversized barbecue fork. Mad cow disease, now that was a lasting story.

The weeks went by, though, and the Fischer affair, instead of fading, grew ever more intense. Like the broken tape on the door at the Watergate, or the girlish confessions on Linda Tripp's treacherous tape recorder, the

2

photographs in *Stern* acted as a kind of pulley, and a curtain slowly opened, which revealed ever more distant peaks of unsuspected scandals (or non-scandals, depending on your interpretation). The controversy spread to France. In London, the *Observer*, playing the part of the yellow press, gave the polemic a slightly demented sexual twist. The Italian press weighed in. The Fischer affair achieved at last a large enough dimension and a sufficiently accusatory tone to be described rather grandly but not inaccurately as "the trial of the generation of 1968" by the editors of the Paris daily *Libération* (who knew something about the generation of 1968)—an unforeseeably rich and vivid scandal, fecund with implications for Europe and modern life and thirty or forty years of history.

The photographs were delivered to *Stern* by a woman named Bettina Röhl, thirty-eight years old at the time, who described herself as an "independent journalist" but whose notoriety was owed mostly to her family background, which could hardly have been more sensational. Bettina Röhl was the daughter of Ulrike Meinhof. In the heyday of the left-wing movement of the late nineteen-sixties and seventies, Ulrike Meinhof was more than well-known in West Germany. She was a militant and a political theorist on the left's leftmost wing—one of the crazies, you would have to say, except that craziness and sanity were very much under interrogation.

In 1970, Ulrike Meinhof staged an armed jailbreak to free an imprisoned comrade named Andreas Baader, who was serving three years for his own violent antics. (He had set fire to a Frankfurt department store.) Baader and

Meinhof, together with Horst Mahler and a few other desperadoes of the revolutionary left, organized what became casually known as the Baader-Meinhof Gang, but was more formally and correctly called the Red Army Fraction. In American English, the German word *Fraktion* is usually rendered as *faction*, which falls easily on the ear; but anyone who remembers the old Communist phrase book will recognize that *fraction*, in English, used to be a perfectly legitimate and precise term, connoting a disciplined party unit akin to a cell— the opposite of a faction, which is a party unit that has escaped the party's discipline. A Marxist-Leninist party does not have factions, unless the party is in disarray. But a Marxist-Leninist party does have fractions, or party units that go out into the world and militate as best they can, according to plan.

Baader and Meinhof's Red Army Fraction was tiny. But it went out into the world and proved to be extremely violent. Kidnappings, bank holdups, murders: the group refrained from nothing. Bombings in 1972 killed four American soldiers. A few years later someone machine-gunned to death the prosecutor who wanted to try the group for killing the soldiers. Reprisals were a specialty. The Red Army Fraction was hardy, too. The West German authorities did their repressive best, but the guerrilla organization managed to keep itself alive, recruiting new members from ever younger generations to replace the fallen, and persisting in its killings and kidnappings from decade to decade into the mid-nineteen-nineties—a long run in a well-ordered place such as Germany.

4

Even today, a political legacy from the old Baader-Meinhof tendency has managed to linger on, though without a clandestine wing, or so it is said. The Red Army Fraction remained strong during those many years because its leaders were clever and its militants fanatical, but also because it enjoyed the secret backing of the government of East Germany, meaning the Soviet bloc, for as long as there was a Soviet bloc, which gave the group a real institutional power. (The Red Army Fraction was tiny, but the Red Army was not.) Yet the organization clung to life mainly for another reason, which lay at the heart of the several scandals that flooded outward from the grainy photographs in *Stern*.

The radical student movement during the years around 1968—I will call this movement the New Left, using the American and English term—was never especially powerful in the Federal Republic of Germany as a whole, not compared to the big political parties and the industrial groups and the trade unions. But in the world of the university students and the young people's neighborhoods and the younger intellectuals, the New Left was a gigantic presence. The sturdy Red Army Fraction grew naturally from that soil. Ulrike Meinhof herself was by all accounts an intelligent and articulate leader, a woman already in her mid-thirties when she helped to organize her guerrilla army, which meant that, in matters of age, she towered over the New Left's rank and file, the student naïfs. She knew how to drape the grand ideals of German philosophy across her organization and its doings. To be sure, her guerrilla army was reviled by an

5

overwhelming majority of West Germans, the put-upon bystanders and potential victims and frightened citizens.

But in the universities and the countercultural districts in Frankfurt and Berlin and a few other places, her tiny organization drew on the active and even enthusiastic support of a not-so-small number of people, plus the passive support of far larger numbers, the leftists who would never have endorsed a program of violence and who wanted nothing to do with murders, but who would have said that, even so, the Red Army Fraction did have reason to despise bourgeois society, and Marxist revolution was an excellent idea, and state repression posed a greater threat to society than any guerrilla resistance from the left. And shouldn't we progressives and reasonable leftists worry chiefly about civil liberties? And so forth: the many arguments and apologetics that people offer in circumstances when, out of confusion and moral timidity, they are too frightened to applaud the murders and the kidnappings, and too frightened to condemn them.

The Red Army Fraction claimed a fraternity with the new breed of revolutionary groups around the world. "We must learn," Meinhof said in her original manifesto back in 1970, "from the revolutionary movements of the world—the Vietcong, the Palestine Liberation Organization, the Tupamaros [of Uruguay], the Black Panthers." But mostly her organization resembled several other guerrilla currents that got their start in the New Left upsurges of Western Europe in those same years: the Red Brigades in Italy; the Irish Republican Army in its modern, Marxist version (which revived a defunct military organization from many years before); the Corsican

6

nationalist guerrillas; and the Basque ETA—small groups each and every one, but tough, and with a degree of popular support that made each of those groups nearly indestructible during the next decades.

The Red Army Fraction was not exactly invulnerable. In 1972, the West German police did manage to arrest a number of key warriors. They arrested Meinhof herself. But arrests only rendered the group fashionable. Jean-Paul Sartre expressed an admiring appreciation—a cagey admiration, designed to leave him unstained by any crimes that the guerrillas might commit. Meinhof wrote the famous philosopher a letter, inviting him to visit Baader in jail, "to give us the protection of your name and your gifts as a Marxist, philosopher, journalist and moralist." Sartre came. But the martyrdom only deepened. One of the imprisoned warriors had already committed suicide by the time of Sartre's visit, and in 1976 Meinhof likewise committed suicide in her maximum-security cell—though some people suspected an official murder.

Her death was followed the next year by the suicides of Baader and two others in the same jail, which even more people suspected were official murders. And the deaths, as they piled up, radiated a morbid glamour. It was a highbrow glamour—the kind of glamour that by 1995 led New York's Museum of Modern Art to devote an exhibition to Gerhard Richter's paintings of the dead militants, a sacralization in high art. But it was also a street glamour. The death of Meinhof alone, back in 1976, was enough to send crowds of young people swarming into the West German streets, enraged at the jails and at the revolutionary defeats and at a thousand injustices of modern life.

Joschka Fischer was among those angry crowds. He was a young firebrand in Frankfurt. At one of the Meinhof demonstrations, somebody tossed a Molotov cocktail at a policeman and burned him nearly to death. Fischer and a dozen other radicals were arrested and jailed for two days, though no charges were ever lodged against them. Fischer was not especially famous at the time, outside of the radical left, and in later years, as he rose in national politics, not many people remembered that he had spent those days in jail or had been under any suspicion at all. Still, some people, the left-wing insiders, not to mention the policeman and his friends, did retain the memory. And in those first days of 2001, when *Stern* published the photographs from 1973, Meinhof's daughter, Röhl, revived the accusation against him. She insisted that Fischer did, in fact, bear a responsibility for the Molotov cocktail and the policeman's injuries.

A couple of participants in the radical movement from those days backed her up, too. These people said that, in planning the particular demonstration in which the policeman was attacked, Fischer had never ruled out the use of Molotovs and may even have favored it. A retired colleague of the injured policeman was adamant about Fischer's responsibility. No one came up with any sort of indisputable confirmation. But Fischer was obliged to rise from his seat once again and, in his dignity as foreign minister, deny all connection to a very ugly event from long ago ("Definitiv nein!" he told *Stern*)—which would have been unpleasant under any circumstances but must have been doubly so in the light of the photographs, the five atrocious photographs that made him seem all too capable in his younger years of having organized a Molotov cocktail attack.

There was another accusation. Fischer was said to have tossed stones and Molotov cocktails during yet a different raucous demonstration, this one in 1975 at the Spanish embassy—an angry protest against Generalissimo Franco and Spanish fascism. Fischer denied that accusation, too, though he did acknowledge through his spokesman at the Foreign Ministry that he had participated in the event, which had never been a secret, anyway. The spokesman reminded the German public that demonstrating against Franco and fascism was nothing to be ashamed of. A good point: something to be proud of, at last!

Then another accusation: Fischer was said to have attended a meeting of the Palestine Liberation Organization in Algiers back in 1969, at which the PLO adopted a resolution to achieve final victory, meaning, the destruction of Israel. That was not so good, and seemed triply bad for a future foreign minister of Germany, even if no one threw rocks or bombs. The ministry spokesman conceded that Fischer did attend the conference; but, doing his best to cope with one more embarrassing revelation, the spokesman made the mistake of adding that Fischer had spent only an hour there, which was like admitting to using marijuana but not to inhaling it. And, of course, the part about spending only an hour turned out to be untrue, and the spokesman, backtracking, had to acknowledge that, yes, Fischer had participated throughout. (Which no one should have doubted. The man is a born politician. He loves meetings.) And still more accusations from New Left days of yore came raining down on Joschka Fischer's respectable middle-aged head.

It was not instantly obvious what drove Bettina Röhl to deliver the photographs to *Stern* and to dredge up her several hair-raising accusations. I looked at different European papers during the course of the affair, and I found a certain amount of political speculation on this matter, as could have been expected. Fischer's enemies in the Bundestag and at *Stern* tended to be, as I say, worthies of the conservative cause, who must have taken a fine partisan pleasure in making life miserable for a Green foreign minister. Yet the complications of contemporary politics are such that, on the left, too, Fischer had his enemies, who may have regarded him with an even deeper loathing.

Fischer had entered the government in 1998 as part of what was called the Red-Green coalition—the alliance of the very big Social Democratic Party, the ancient Reds (whose organization was founded in 1875), and the much smaller Greens (whose organization was founded in 1980). To have forced the powerful and venerable Social Democrats into a coalition was, from the Green point of view, a great victory, and Fischer's arrival at the Foreign Ministry was bound to arouse jubilant expectations from the hardworking party activists. But here was the left-wing difficulty. The Greens had made their way in German politics by sticking to their twin principles of ecology and anti-militarism. The Greens were the enemies of the military policies of the United States, beginning in the days of President Reagan and advancing through the Gulf War of 1991 and onward to the present. Yet their year of political triumph, 1998, was not a happy one for the anti-militarist cause. The wars of Serbian nationalism had been getting ever grimmer, and in 1998 the massacres took still another bad turn in Kosovo. NATO's involvement grew deeper and, from an anti-militarist perspective, more ominous. Many a Green looked to Fischer, as foreign minister, to oppose the NATO campaign, or at least to keep Germany, with its peaceful traditions in modern times, from taking part. But on matters of anti-militarism and NATO, Fischer was out of step with his own party. In his reasoning, the Serbian atrocities gnawed away at pacifism's logic. He looked at the ethnic persecutions and came away thinking that military action was not such a bad idea, after all.

Fischer was filled with conviction on this theme. When he got into office he took the fundamental Green commitment to antiwar principles, deftly heaved it overboard, and gave his official endorsement to Germany's participation in the NATO effort. A large number of Greens could only look at those ministerial actions and feel horribly betrayed. To have spent nearly twenty years building a new party devoted to antimilitarism, only to see its first foreign minister endorse military action by NATO, the imperialist alliance! That was galling.

At the Green convention in 1999, someone threw a bag of red ink at Fischer and broke his eardrum. Four hundred police officers had to stand guard when he got up to address the convention. His own party, the eco-pacifist assemblage, was a howling mob. The man did not

11

lack for political skill, and he managed to hang onto the convention's support. But there was no placating a good percentage of his opponents. What was to be done about that? Nothing, nothing. And so, when the accusations against Fischer came rolling down upon him in the early months of 2001, it was easy to imagine that motives from the left, antimilitarist and anti-NATO, and not just the traditional hostility of his enemies on the right, might have been at work.

Then again, the fury against Fischer might have wended its way into the press from the remote margins of German political life, from the very far left, well beyond the respectable democratic radicalism of the Greens—the fury of ultramilitants who had remained in some way faithful to the legacy of Meinhof and her martyred guerrillas. Or perhaps the fury had its origin on the extreme right, from well beyond the respectable zones of Christian Democratic conservatism.

But what did these terms mean in 2001, *extreme right* and *extreme left*? The political categories of right and left have gotten terribly bollixed up in modern times, and not just in Germany. In poking around the Internet, I found my way to the electronic discussion center of the fans of the Baader-Meinhof Gang—they have their own website, naturally—and I was interested to read about the curious case of Horst Mahler, one of the founders of the group back in 1970. Over the years, Mahler had slid down the corridor of extremist politics from left-wing terrorism into the circles of German neo-Nazism, where he set about promoting mad theories on Jewish themes.

Such things did happen. Mahler, I discovered, entertained his own opinions about the Fischer affair. He made the argument that Ulrike Meinhof, had she lived, would have likewise slid over to the extreme right.

But, in his view, as reported on the website, right-wing and left-wing counted for nothing in regard to the behavior of Meinhof's daughter. The real animus against Fischer bubbled up instead from a daughter's anger at her inadequate mother, the prison martyr. Or else, as was more widely said, Röhl's anger at Fischer derived from a still vaguer resentment against the entire era of 1968— from the resentment that, on an earlier occasion, she had already described in the pages of *Der Spiegel*. For what was 1968 to Bettina Röhl?

It was the era that had deprived her of a childhood. Her mother, in the grip of the revolutionary manias of the time, had once tried to ship little Bettina and her sister to a Palestinian camp, which failed to happen only because the two girls were kidnapped en route and were returned to their father (a publisher of a left-wing and somewhat pornographic magazine) back in Germany—a horrible childhood event. Then the mother had gotten herself jailed, and had ended up dead—she suffered every tragedy of the era. As had the children, in their fashion.

And who was Joschka Fischer? Someone who had participated in the radical cause and gotten away scot-free; someone who managed to profit from every horrible thing that had taken place. This was the cause of Röhl's holy rancor, or so it was said. A victim's fury at a survivor. In any case, everyone could agree that, whatever her deepest motives might have been, Röhl had put a lot of vim and energy into

13

her campaign. No one could doubt that she had displayed a canny skill at inflicting the maximum personal damage, too—as if to prove that, with or without her famous mother, she was a proper journalist in her own right.

One of Röhl's accusations pointed not at Fischer himself but slightly to his side, at an old roommate of his from the nineteen-seventies—another radical survivor, someone who had participated in nearly every phase of the movement, and had only managed to rise higher and higher in European life, and had suffered not one whit. This person was Daniel Cohn-Bendit, a well-known figure in Germany and all over Europe and beyond, even if, as a politician, he never achieved as lofty a post as Fischer. Cohn-Bendit was a man with an interesting childhood of his own. He was the son of German Jews, and he had spent his youth shuttling between West Germany and France. He attended university at Nanterre, outside Paris. And there, in the spring of 1968, he helped spark a series of student demonstrations, which sparked other demonstrations in Paris, which resulted, in May of that year, in a gigantic student uprising in Paris and all over France, which led in turn to a general strike by labor, which pretty much shut down the country for a while.

His hair was flaming red in those days, and he was witty and impish, and he became known as Danny the Red. He was the single best-known leader of the 1968 uprising in France, famous not just in that country but everywhere in some degree, if only because the May uprising in Paris was the largest of the student uprisings anywhere in the world in that year, and because Paris was

14

the capital of world revolution. Cohn-Bendit consequently had the experience of seeing himself elevated in a matter of weeks into the only person in any country who could claim to represent the generation of 1968 internationally, the human symbol of a worldwide seismic youth event—an odd personal fate for anyone to endure, an instant deification.

His legal citizenship, as it happened, was not French, but West German. And as soon as he made the mistake of stepping across the German border in 1968—he tried to do this secretly, his hair dyed brown, in an automobile borrowed from a young doctor in the left-wing movement, Bernard Kouchner—the French authorities banished him from France. One of the leaders of the French Communist Party, always a big enemy of the New Left, denounced Cohn-Bendit as a "German anarchist," which infuriated his admirers, who were many. Indignant crowds marched through the streets of Paris convinced that, within the Communist insult, they had heard a still nastier sneer, and they responded by chanting, "We are all German Jews!"—a touching slogan, and a fine display of loyalty to Danny the Red. (Nor were those chanting marchers wrong to have detected a nastier sneer. At a Gaullist rally at the end of May, a portion of the crowd began to cry, "Cohn-Bendit—to Dachau!") But there was no bringing him back to France, not for many years. He moved to Frankfurt.

He also roamed around a bit, stirring up trouble here and there. I ran into him in Britain in 1970. He sat on a hilltop and directed a small regiment of young French leftists, plus myself as interpreter, who invaded an Isle of

Wight rock festival in the name of anti-capitalism, free rock music, and anti-clericalism. (The anti-clericalism struck me as odd, but those were our reasons.) Cohn-Bendit, our leader, was a mischievous guy. Mostly he stayed in Frankfurt, though. He set up house with Fischer. And, ever militant, Cohn-Bendit and Fischer organized a group called *Revolutioner Kampf*, or Revolutionary Struggle, which was left-wing and counter-cultural both, a fixture of nineteen-seventies life in the happening districts of Frankfurt.

Fischer was the main leader of Revolutionary Struggle's militant political activities, and Cohn-Bendit of its countercultural side. Fischer led the revolutionary mob in the streets, and Cohn-Bendit directed the revolution in daily life. He ran a kindergarten, and did this for two years. Running a kindergarten might sound like an oddly modest thing for a famous revolutionary to do. But kindergartens were a big project for the German New Left. The goal was nothing less than to perform radical surgery on the German national character. The traditional educational system in West Germany had followed the standard old-fashioned authoritarian model. And, in the New Left analysis, the standard model had succeeded all too well in times past at producing standard personalities—people who responded well to authority and knew how to give orders and how to take them, the kind of people who might grow up to be Nazis or to accept a government of Nazis without protesting. Good Germans, in a phrase. Authoritarian personalities.

So the New Left set out to construct a new kind of education—an anti-authoritarian education, beginning at

16

the beginning, with the goal of creating anti-authoritarian personalities, people who would think for themselves and instinctively shrug off any attempt to impose a totalitarian domination. Sex education figured in the idea. The anti-authoritarian educators wanted to break down the sexual repression of earlier times—the sexual armor that, in their psychological figurings (with the help of Wilhelm Reich), had always surrounded the authoritarian personality. That was the idea behind the kindergarten campaign: the "anti-authoritarian kindergartens." The teachers wanted to encourage the healthy sexuality of little children.

The idea was more than German, to be sure. The notion of breaking down old-fashioned personality types, the idea that early education offers a fulcrum for moving mankind, the campaign to build new kindergartens and schools on radical new principles—this was a big impulse in the English left, too, on its anarchist side. It was a venerable notion: Rousseau, Godwin, Dewey. It was big in the United States. One of the national leaders of America's Students for a Democratic Society, Bill Ayers, began his radical career by organizing an alternative school for young children—after which he hurled himself into the guerrilla campaign of the Weather Underground, after which, correcting himself, he hurled himself back into early childhood education.

In Frankfurt, Cohn-Bendit not only ran his kindergarten, he also wrote about it in a book directed at the French public that had so amiably chanted about being German Jews. The book was called *Le Grand Bazar* and appeared in 1975. It was a loosely structured memoir of his life in the revolutionary movement, with chapters on the French student uprising, his own Jewish identity, his kindergarten, the objectionable nature of Communism, and several other topics. It was full of the inflammatory phrases of the day. Then *Le Grand Bazar* faded from memory.

In the early months of 2001, though, with the photographs of Fischer circulating in *Stern* and the many accusations of violent leftism surrounding him and a scent of scandal rising on every side, Bettina Röhl craftily plucked one of those inflammatory passages from Cohn-Bendit's book, declared the passage to be an undiscovered new outrage, and offered it for a fee (a tacky move) to the press. She approached *Libération* in Paris with her scoop. *Libération* declined to take her up on it, partly because the newspaper's policy forbade paying for news scoops, and partly because the book in question had been published long ago and could be freely quoted by anyone, but mostly because the paper's correspondent read the passage and, by interpreting it the way Cohn-Bendit had plainly intended, failed to see any scoop at all. The *Observer* in England did go for Röhl's item, and ran the excerpt. Then the item was picked up by *L'Express* in France, the *Bild Zeitung* in Germany, *La Repubblica* in Italy, and other papers.

The excerpt described Cohn-Bendit's kindergarten and was intended to illustrate the atmosphere of non-repression—the lengths to which the kindergarten teacher would go in order to prevent his little wards from looking on sex with fear. Cohn-Bendit had written: "It happened to me several times that certain kids opened my fly and began to tickle me. I reacted differently

18

according to circumstances, but their desire posed a problem to me. I asked them: 'Why don't you play together? Why have you chosen me, and not the other kids?' But if they insisted, I caressed them even so."

In the context of the sexual liberation ideas of the nineteen-seventies, his larger point in writing those words was clear enough, and not without sense. He did explain in the book that, even in the most anti-authoritarian of kindergartens, children need instruction and cannot be allowed to do just as they please. He considered that adults ought to ponder the sexual questions long and hard, with regard to children. But that one sentence did make it seem that he himself was not exactly pondering anything. If you lifted that one passage from its context, Cohn-Bendit could easily be made to look like a pedophile—like an adult having sex with children. And this horrendous insinuation, the suggestion that Joschka Fischer's roommate, Danny the Red, the spirit of 1968 itself, had been, in fact, a pedophilic creep of the first order, a child molester—this dreadful insinuation ascended into the scandal of the hour in the French newspapers and on television.

There was never any reason, none at all, to credit the accusation. A group of parents of the kindergartners in Frankfurt plus some of the children themselves, now grown up, made public statements in praise and in defense of the teacher Cohn-Bendit. Not one person stood up to denounce him or to lodge any personal complaint. Cohn-Bendit himself, the Cohn-Bendit of 2001, was apoplectic about the accusation. He acknowledged in his riposte that the passage in his book had been written carelessly, in the provocational mode of the day. It was, he said, a "literary exaggeration," stupid, foolish, and shocking. Everything about the New Left, even its descriptions of kindergarten life, had been meant to provoke the wrath of the bourgeoisie. But he stressed that, during the friskier days of New Left wildness, whenever someone did try to make a case for pedophilia, as occurred from time to time (in the form of "man-boy love"), he was one of the people who spoke up right away in disapproval—he and the feminists and just about nobody else.

Pedophilia, Cohn-Bendit pointed out, has always been a shameful reality of traditional family life—the traditional life that conceals abysmal behavior under a blanket of silence, ignorance, and patriarchal authority. Pedophilia is the kind of scandalous reality that the sexual liberation movements of the nineteen-sixties and seventies tried to eliminate by making sexuality into something to be discussed honestly, without shame—by creating an anti-authoritarian atmosphere in which crimes and abuses would no longer be covered up in the name of filial obedience. Those were not foolish arguments on his part.

Surely he was right in pointing out that sexual liberation in the nineteen-seventies has turned out to be—notwithstanding the excesses and even the crimes that were sometimes committed in its name—one of the grand social advances of modern times, for women especially. Nowadays people can talk openly about pedophilia and other sexual abuses and depredations, as was rarely, if ever, possible during the two million years before the sexual revolution. Knowledge advances, ignorance recedes. There might even have been something heroic about Cohn-Bendit's devotion to the kindergarten. What other leader of a mass European uprising has ever turned from leading a revolutionary crowd in the streets to running a kindergarten? The new kind of masculinity needed a living example of how to behave, and Cohn-Bendit offered himself—someone unafraid to take up a role that had always been assigned to women. Any proposed revolution of daily life was going to depend on the willingness of men like him.

As it turned out, this particular accusation in the course of the Fischer affair, the insinuated charge against Cohn-Bendit, got nowhere at all back in Germany. The kindergarten in Frankfurt and the parents who had sent their children there and the children themselves were too well known, and their refutations proved decisive. Besides, the experiment in anti-authoritarian education was conducted on a big scale in Germany in the nineteen-seventies and afterward, and large numbers of Germans had spent their infant years waddling through the hallways of that experiment, and had come away understanding its goals and methods as well as the sillier dogmas and fads—the essays of Adorno ornamenting every anti-authoritarian classroom, that sort of thing. Familiarity bred respect (and perhaps a tolerant smile). To hang Cohn-Bendit on the basis of a single bad-sounding sentence in a book that no one remembered anymore did seem a trifle opportunistic. Even some of the conservative politicians in Germany spoke up for Cohn-Bendit's probity.

In France, a number of people likewise rebutted the insinuation, and right away, too. The host of a book-chat show on French television recalled that Cohn-Bendit had appeared on a panel in 1977 to discuss his book, and none of the other guests, not even the Catholic conservative, had thought to raise such an issue. It was pointed out that *L'Express*, which made such a convenient fuss over the accusation in 2001, had reviewed Cohn-Bendit's book when it originally came out and had found nothing objectionable at the time. And yet in France—and in other countries, too—the accusation about pedophilia, once it crept into the press, turned out to be a big event. Nasty journalists in the newspapers and at the television studios felt they could attach any sort of horrendous story or fantasy to the famous face from 1968, and have a swell time doing it, and feel no shame at all. Among journalists, such are the joys. Besides, newspapers must be sold and viewers attracted.

But the main reason the smear about Cohn-Bendit spread in France and in a few other countries had to do with something more than yellow journalism. Serge July, the editor of *Libération* (and a Maoist from the good old days), put his finger on that reason right away. The insinuation lingered because, in France and in some other countries, it had lately become fashionable to hold up for inspection the radicalism of the period around 1968, and to search out the wildest episodes, some of which were wild enough, and to identify the radicalism as a whole with its most extreme moments. And it had become fashionable to take the social and cultural problems of our own time and to blame those problems on the radicalism of the earlier period, as exemplified in its extremes.

This particular fashion may sound familiar to American ears, but in Europe in the later nineteen-nineties it acquired a tonality all its own, without any American echo or equivalent. The European tonality consisted of—this was the strange part, to us Americans—youthfulness, instead of age. There was a stylish young people's pining for a long-ago era of order and hierarchy, when every person occupied his allotted place, and when rules were rules, and culture and language and relations between the sexes were properly fixed, and not, as they are today, so damnably fluid. The young people who indulged in that particular nostalgia yearned, in short, for the nineteen-fifties. (They could hardly yearn for the nineteen-forties.) And since nostalgic yearning always turns out to be, on its obverse, an indignant protest, the people who pined for the nineteen-fifties ended up raging against the nineteen-sixties, amusing themselves with indignant recitations of every scandalous outrage that was committed—and even a few that were not committed—by their own parents and older siblings.

You could describe their complaints as a right-wing reaction. That may overstate the case, though. Mostly the young reactionaries wanted to stamp their feet. As July pointed out, hardly anyone actually wanted to roll back the social and cultural achievements of the New Left era. To send women back to the kitchen, to resume the persecution of homosexuals, to return to the days of secrecy about child molesting, to resurrect the old superstitions about race, or to reconstruct the European imperialisms (to name a few of the antediluvian customs and social structures that had been swept away by the floods of nineteen-sixties radicalism)—no one seriously wanted to do any of that. To undo the reforms of an earlier age is always possible, if enough people feel suitably motivated; but the nostalgics of the nineteen-nineties merely wanted to reel with horror, and in that way to fend off the anxieties of the present age.

The writer Michel Houellebecq had a big success in 1998 in France, then in Germany and elsewhere, with a novel about the horrors of the nineteen-sixties called *The Elementary Particles* (which came out in the United States two years later). The blood-curdling portraits in his novel of the radical weirdness of yore, combined with a sentimental yearning for nineteen-fifties-style family life, combined with his ever-popular scenes of modern sex orgies, accounted for Houellebecq's success. Disgusting sexual cruelty in the name of liberation, cult manias, radical murders: *The Elementary Particles* hit every note of nineteen-sixties mayhem. The Fischer affair merely seemed to recapitulate in real life what Houellebecq had already imagined in his novel, down to the figure of Bettina Röhl, the distressed child of a New Left terrorist, who seemed to have stepped from his own pages. (If she had only read a bit further in Cohn-Bendit's *Le Grand Bazar*, she might have dug up a few sentences about group sex, too, and *The Elementary Particles* would have replayed itself in full.)

In the early months of 2001, then, it hardly mattered if any particular accusation against Fischer or Cohn-Bendit turned out to be unfounded. Either way, true or false, the accusations afforded a satisfying pleasure to anyone who felt a nostalgia for the excellent social order of long ago, and a resentment at the radicals who had so rudely overthrown the order in question. That was true in Germany just as in France. Feelings were expressed, even if truths were not told. The accusations constituted, as July put it, a "settling of accounts with the generation of 1968." And so the accusations and even the smears spread from Germany to France and outward to Britain and Italy and, in some degree, around the world, on the basis of a cultural anxiety that had nothing to do with the petty ideological and local concerns of Greens and Christian Democrats and other politicians in Germany who fretted over the career of the statesman Joschka Fischer.

And then, the Fischer affair, having floated upward into the airy zones of cultural anxiety, suddenly plunged into the concrete terrain of law. The legal issue came up at the trial of a New Left terrorist named Hans-Joachim Klein, who happened to be an old friend of Fischer's and Cohn-Bendit's in Frankfurt, from their days in Revolutionary Struggle in the early and middle nineteen-seventies.

The Fischer affair was a tale of people who had undergone life changes so vast as to be incomprehensible to outsiders. And among those many left-wing changelings, Klein was the king of kings. As a young man he had worked as an auto mechanic. He used to repair Cohn-Bendit's car. He followed Fischer to street demonstrations. He was one of the militants running to join Fischer in the grainy photographs from 1973—a tough character, not at all loath to mix it up with what we Americans used to call "the pigs." The terrorist wave rose in Germany, and Klein was carried aloft on the foam. When Sartre responded to Meinhof's letter by agreeing to visit Baader in the Stammheim prison, Klein served as his driver.

But he was no mere chauffeur. By then Klein was a secret soldier in a guerrilla organization called the Revolutionary Cells, which was allied loosely with the

Red Army Fraction and more tightly with the Popular Front for the Liberation of Palestine. One of the master achievements of the Revolutionary Cells was to help coordinate the Palestinian attack on Israeli athletes at the Munich Olympics in 1972. A New Leftist from Frankfurt made the arrangements. And, in 1975, Klein and the Revolutionary Cells joined with Carlos the Jackal, the Venezuelan terrorist, to attack, in the name of "the Arab revolution," a meeting of OPEC oil ministers in Vienna. Three people were killed. Klein was shot in the stomach and the shoulder, but he and Carlos and some of the others made their escape in a plane to Algeria.

As time went on, though, Klein reflected on what he had done. And, having reflected, he made the grave decision to desert his terrorist comrades. He renounced his own activities and denounced the terrorist doctrine. He fled underground from the underground, hiding equally from the police and the Revolutionary Cells and all the other terrorists, who would surely have killed him, given the chance. (There was an instance in West Germany of left-wing terrorists murdering one of their deserters.) Klein sought out his old friends who, unlike himself, had never taken the plunge into armed activity, and he pleaded his case, and they helped him. Cohn-Bendit was one of those people, together with André Glucksmann, the French "New Philosopher," who had been a well-known visitor at Fischer and Cohn-Bendit's Revolutionary Struggle house in Frankfurt. Cohn-Bendit and Glucksmann and the handful of other people who aided Klein rather admired him for having reconsidered his violence and for speaking out against his own comrades, the terrorists.

His friends helped him to settle in France. Sometimes they paid his rent. They tried to keep up his spirits. He lived in a little Norman village. He even wrote a book, and he granted a clandestine interview to Cohn-Bendit for a television documentary. In 1998, though, just three days before he was going to turn himself in, under an arrangement that Cohn-Bendit had helped to broker, Klein was tracked down by the French police, who delivered him to the German authorities. His trial in Germany took place, by unhappy coincidence, just as the Fischer affair got under way in January 2001. He was sentenced to nine years.

But before the trial reached its end, Fischer was called to testify, not in his capacity as foreign minister but as a private citizen. He was asked about his relationship to Hans-Joachim Klein back in New Left times. Fischer explained that in those days he tried to talk Klein out of joining the terrorists. And when Fischer had finished making his statement, he walked over to Klein in his defendant's chair and shook the man's hand. The handshake seemed innocent enough, given that, as Fischer had just testified, Klein was an old friend, and the old friend had long ago denounced his own crimes and was now about to expiate them. Even so, next day in the Bundestag, Fischer was asked to explain himself.

There was worse. In the course of his testimony, Fischer was accused of having harbored people from the Red Army Fraction in his house. The accusation infuriated him. He told the court, "Next we will hear that Daniel Cohn-Bendit and I organized World War III in that house!" He wanted to draw a thick line between his own

27

leftism and the terrorists'—to show that in those days you could have been a revolutionary militant and still not have had any truck with murderers and kidnappers. But Fischer's insistence on this point turned out to be misplaced. A woman named Margrit Schiller had spent some time in the Red Army Fraction—she had joined the group via the Socialist Patients Collective, a psychiatric patients' terrorist army in Heidelberg, led by their doctor. She had ended up in jail for a while. And, in 1999, she wrote an autobiography plainly stating that during the early nineteen-seventies, she spent a "few days" in the Revolutionary Struggle house. She visited the house out of curiosity. She wanted to see who these Revolutionary Struggle people were. She did see them, including Fischer himself. This awkward bit of information emerged in the aftermath of Fischer's testimony, and Fischer had to acknowledge that Margrit Schiller's assertion must have been correct.

The discrepancy did not seem especially damning. All kinds of visitors were always traipsing through the house in Frankfurt. Abbie Hoffman was there; Jerry Rubin came to visit. Who could remember every last person who had ever stopped by? But the news about a Red Army Fraction woman only managed to underline yet again how close Fischer, in his younger days, had been to the terrorists. And the revelation gave an opening to the prosecutor at the Klein trial. The prosecutor had already shown a nasty hostility to Fischer during his testimony; he had even been rebuked for it by the judge. Now the prosecutor charged Fischer with perjury. The Bundestag was put in the position of having to decide whether to lift

Fischer's ministerial immunity and allow him to be tried on the perjury charge.

So Fischer faced a legal problem, and not just a public relations challenge or a political problem, in the wake of those many accusations and scandals and insinuations. And with one scandal piling on another, the photographs, the resurrected accusations, the new accusations, the denials, the retractions, the outright smears, the undeniable acquaintance with more than one authentic bomb-thrower, and finally the perjury charge—with all of that, the general public was bound to gaze on Fischer with a nervous apprehension. What kind of man could this Joschka Fischer be? People did have to wonder.

Fischer's evolution was plainly a lot stranger and more extreme than might have seemed to be the case. He was not just a peacenik politician who in the fullness of time had metamorphosed into a NATO supporter—as had been widely believed, given his origins in the Greens. His political origins reached back to the era before there was any such thing as a Green. He was a street-fighting militant, someone on the fringe of terrorist New Leftism, a rough-and-ready revolutionary, who then became a Green, and then a NATO supporter, someone who had changed his colors not once but twice—or who knew how many times?—someone whose history was populated with tough and sinister characters from the left-wing underworld.

Didn't the several mysteries of his past political life suggest (as his political enemies insisted) that Fischer might, in fact, be a man without character? Didn't his political zigzags reveal a Machiavelli of the worst sort? A man desperate for power, someone who would adopt any position whatsoever, if only it would bring him what he wanted? That was how Fischer began to seem in other countries, including in our own faraway part of the world. Even before the scandal broke, the German journalist Josef Joffe presented Fischer in the *New York Times Magazine* as "a bit of a Forrest Gump," someone whose "business" is "self-reinvention"—which sounded friendly enough, until you stopped to think about it.

Then the waves of scandal rolled in, and Roger Cohen of the *Times* duly reported in the news section that Fischer was, in fact, "a man of startling changes, not least in his views on the use of force," which was certainly true. But the startling changes were bound to arouse a few worries about the man, especially if he was Forrest Gump. Some of those worries cropped up on the *Times* editorial page, whose editors felt sufficiently upset by the incriminating photographs and by some of the accusations to devote a small commentary to the affair. The editors concluded that Fischer, in their words, "should be allowed to continue serving his country"—which was not too surprising, given that his foreign policy had been controversial in Germany precisely in the degree to which it coincided with that of the United States. Not quite satisfied, however, the editors added the cautionary phrase "barring more damaging revelations"—as if one more telling photograph, or one persuasive proof that he did tell people to throw Molotov cocktails back in 1976, might have tipped the balance against him.

And who could blame the editors for having registered their careful reservation? For if Fischer were, in truth, a man without principles, a man whose history consisted of shadows and hidden crimes and whose business was self-reinvention, there would have been reason enough to fret over the power that he could wield from his desk at the Foreign Ministry in Berlin. But it was also obvious that, beneath the day-to-day politics, a deeper worry was all along trailing through this affair.

This was a nagging worry about the radicalism of the years around 1968 and its crazier episodes. Even some of us who went through a few of those episodes can hardly believe, looking back, that such things could have taken place. Might not a few dark after-effects from those days have lingered into the present? You could find yourself worrying that question even without pining for the arcadia of the nineteen-fifties. Out of the dark violence of the student left of three decades ago, might not a faintly criminal stain, a shiftiness, maybe a touch of ruthlessness, have crept across certain personalities and left an indelible mark?

The worry went well beyond poor old Fischer at the Foreign Ministry. In Germany under the Red-Green coalition, a greater number of veterans of the New Left had risen to power than in any other country among the big Western powers—risen through the Greens or else through the Social Democrats, where some of the New Left Marxists, having abandoned their revolutionary leftism, eventually found a home. Gerhard Schröder, the chancellor in 2001, used to be something of a radical socialist himself, before making his way into the safely popular regions of Social Democracy's "Third Way." Such was the long march through the institutions.

Fischer, in all his flashiness, proved to be a representative figure in these matters. That was why it was reasonable to think of the Fischer affair as the trial of the generation of 1968—to see in it a challenge to an enormous cohort of people who had fashioned their personal characters in the years of New Left rebellion. And it did seem, for a while, that the challenge was going to prevail, and that Fischer would sooner or later have to accept the price of his young man's wildness, hang his head in shame, and submit his resignation, just as his enemies were dearly hoping.

But not so fast. The letters pages of German newspapers began to fill with dispatches from middle-aged worthies from the business world and the learned professions, who confessed that they, too, had waged the revolution back in the years around 1968, and then had grown up and had sanded down the sharp edge of their views, just as Fischer had done, and Germany's foreign minister ought not to be persecuted for what happened long ago. The *Frankfurter Allgemeine Zeitung*, a conservative paper, published an essay by the American poet Charles Simic shaking his head over the hypocrisies of conservative indignation. If only Fischer had become a stockbroker or a college professor, Simic observed, nobody at all would have complained about his left-wing background. If only he had become, like so many ex-radicals from the nineteen-sixties, a right-wing newspaper columnist! The most amazing vote of support came from Fischer's own victim, the white-helmeted policeman in the photographs from 1973, whose name turned out to be Rainer Marx. Fischer telephoned Officer Marx to apologize for the gruesome beating in the Frankfurt parking lot, and Marx found admiring words to say about Fischer's conduct of foreign policy. Nor did Fischer seem to be collapsing in the polls.

But there was something about Fischer's ability to survive the scandal that aroused still other worries, nameless and deep, touching on matters well beyond the mayhem of the New Left. For what might it say about Germany if, faced with some hair-raising accusations and the dreadful photographs, the German people ended up supporting their foreign minister with more enthusiasm instead of less? What would it mean if the worse Fischer seemed, the more he was applauded? Americans have had some experience with that kind of question. The Clinton sex scandal hit its stride in the same year that Fischer became foreign minister, and week by week Clinton's personal behavior was revealed in ever more pornographic detail. Most Americans seemed to recognize intuitively that their president's sex life had followed a long-established if undistinguished tradition of husbandly wandering, and had no bearing on state policy or the fate of the nation, and was finally not the public's business—which was why Clinton's popular ratings remained high and rose even higher when his persecutors had their say.

Yet Clinton's conservative enemies, some of them, saw in his behavior something much more worrisome. They saw a shadow of the nineteen-sixties and its radical subversion of (as they imagined it) basic morality, a left-wing undermining of eternal principles of behavior, a menace to civilization. The right-wing accusation against the radicalism of the nineteen-sixties has always been a bit more shrill and intense in the United States than in Europe, and as the Clinton scandals unfolded, the conservatives in America grew ever more upset, not just at the sinning president but at the all-tolerant American public. What could it mean, the conservatives had to ask, that Clinton's legal situation was tottering and his public support was firming up? His popularity seemed to hint at something monstrous: that America had been corrupted in its ethics by the horrible radicals of the nineteen-sixties. The American public seemed to have sunk into a swamp of moral indifference, even depravity. Right and wrong had disappeared into a marshy haze. And the conservatives grew wide-eyed in astonishment and horror.

The deeper worry that ran through the Fischer affair had something in common with that conservative American fear, only in a German version that seemed infinitely more sinister. Some of the commentaries on the Fischer affair made the quiet suggestion that, if Germany's foreign minister were shown to be a man without character, and if the Germans ended up applauding him anyway, as did seem to be happening, it was because, in Germany, any number of people were living in the shadow of their own shameful political pasts, and the country was long ago shorn of its ability to make moral judgments, and nothing was to be done about it. Such was the implication, quietly hinted. Germany: a country incapable of looking things square in the face. Germany: a country unwilling to confront its own history. And, to be sure, in Germany's case, something in that suggestion did catch the eye.

34

Watching the Fischer affair unfold through the early months of 2001 was like studying a painting where your attention first focuses on the main subject at the center of the canvas, and then you begin to notice the background and how interesting it is, and then you notice, reflected in a piece of metal or seen through a window, a second background, which you can barely see. The main subject in the Fischer affair was a simple political scandal involving a well-regarded foreign minister. But the scandal was set against a background consisting of events from twenty-five or thirty years earlier, from the time of the New Left. The Fischer affair invited us, even required us, to make a few judgments about that background.

But the New Left background turned out, on closer inspection, to have a background of its own, barely visible, which was the Germany of long before. Not the generation of 1968, but the generation of 1938. Not the New Left, but the Nazis. The whole difficulty in making sense of the affair was to figure out what possible tale or narrative could account for all three of those elements: the foreign minister of 2001 in the foreground, the New Left behind him, and, half-hidden, the background of the background, yesterday's yesterday, bathed in darkest shadow.

II.

Everyone knows what was the Nazism of the nineteen-thirties and forties. But what was the New Left of the nineteen-sixties and seventies, in its motives, instincts, goals, and spirit? The decades come and go, and on that question no consensus has been achieved, none at all, not in Europe and not in America. That was why the Fischer affair went leaping from country to country, arousing different controversies in each new place. It was mad cow disease in the form of an argument about the past. It turned out to be a rather useful argument, too. Questions were raised; perhaps a few lessons were learned. And what were those lessons? I will give my faraway, transatlantic interpretation.

The New Left was a young people's movement motivated by fear. Naturally, not just by fear. New Leftists all over the world knew very well that, in the decades after World War II, European imperialism was steadily collapsing around the world, and certain kinds of social progress were advancing nicely in the Western countries, and might go on advancing, too, given a proper left-wing push. Utopian cheerfulness was a sunbeam that fell here and there. Yet fear swallowed all. It was a fear that, at least in the Western countries, social progress rested on a lie, a fear that prosperity was theft, and Western wealth was Third World exploitation, a fear that Western civilization comprised a system of manipulation designed to mislead its own people and everyone else—an iron cage cleverly designed to resemble the open air of freedom.

The social optimism of the New Left drew on visible realities of world history, and so, too, did the fear. New Leftists all over the world looked at the United States. They saw that America's ancient prejudices against blacks had come under challenge. But the spectacle of America trying to reform itself succeeded only in revealing how persistent were the ancient prejudices and therefore how limited and false must be America's claim on democratic virtue. New Leftists gazed at the Cuban Revolution and at America's attempt to overthrow it in the invasion of the Bay of Pigs. Che Guevara tried to stir up a social revolution in South America, and everyone knew that the CIA tracked him down in Bolivia and killed him. New Leftists gazed at Vietnam. The fighting there had the look of a colonial war in an extremely ugly version—a war no less racist under the Americans than under the French imperialists, except with a Madison Avenue smarminess ("defense of the free world") and a terrifying industrial face. American bomber planes overhead and cone-hatted rice farmers down below made an unbearable spectacle. And the smarmy slogans together with the old-fashioned race hatreds and the technological ghastliness—all of this aroused a dread, finally, that pointed to the terrors of the past.

It was a fear, in sum, that in World War II, fascism, and more specifically Nazism, had not been defeated after all—a fear that Nazism, by mutating, had continued to thrive into the nineteen-fifties and sixties and onward, always in new disguises. It was a fear that Nazism had grown into a modern system of industrial rationality geared to irrational goals—a Nazism of racial superstitions committing the same massacres as in the past, a Nazism declaiming a language of democracy and freedom that had no more human content than the old-fashioned rhetoric of *Lebensraum* and Aryan superiority. And so, the New Left in its youthful anxiety found its way to an old and mostly expired panic from its parents' generation, and bent over it, and fanned the dead embers, and breathed on them, and watched aghast as the dying flames leapt up anew.

In each country where the New Left happened to flourish, the revived panic over a newly discovered, cleverly disguised, still-flourishing Nazism seemed to be confirmed by strictly local circumstances. France in the early nineteen-sixties kept trembling on the brink of a right-wing coup d'état, and right-wing bombs exploded in central Paris, and French soldiers and police committed massacres and atrocities in Algeria and even in Paris, and a black cloud of those events hung over France throughout the decade. In Italy, the New Leftists looked at their own neighborhoods and schools and even at their own families and saw with perfect accuracy that the social structures and cultural habits and ways of thought from Mussolini's times had merely been covered over, as with a drop cloth. But no one gazed at the everyday vistas before their eyes with more pain and anger than the New Leftists of West Germany.

The New Leftists there could see all too clearly that Germany's conservative parties were comfortably maintaining quite a few continuities with right-wing customs of the past, and that big-time industrial figures from Nazi times were big-time industrial figures still, and that society had not entirely changed hands. Even the gas chambers retained a patriotic luster in the eyes of many a knuckleheaded West German curmudgeon, such that when the New Leftists marched in the streets, here and there an ornery old burgher could be counted on to mutter, "You should go to the gas chambers!"—more or less the way that in the United States some Neanderthal throwback to the McCarthy era would always be heckling, "Go back to Russia!" (And we Americans thought we had it bad.) In most countries, when the New Leftists described their enemies as Nazis, they knew that Nazism was a figure of speech. But West Germany was beyond metaphor.

The New Leftists there noticed that even the socialists had made their peace with German society, and that no one in the Social Democratic Party seemed to be trying too hard to root out the holdovers from Nazi times. Such were their observations. Maybe they were unjust. Sometimes they were on the mark. Of the many crimes committed by the Red Army Fraction, the most famous of all was the cold-blooded execution of Hans-Martin Schleyer, the president of the West German employers' federation, who turned out to have been a top SS officer in Prague during the Nazi occupation. And with a disguised Nazism apparently in command at home and across the Western world circa 1968, the need for an extremely radical resistance seemed to cry out from every stone. What was New Leftism, then? It was—it pictured itself as—Nazism's opposite and nemesis: the enemy of the *real* Nazism, the Nazism that had survived Nazism, the Nazism that was built into the foundations of Western life. And how did the New Left intend to act on that perception, with what tools and what ideas?

The commentators on Fischer and his photographs and his terrorist acquaintances, in looking back on those years, tended to shrink the New Left and its practical and philosophical quandaries into a straightforward argument about violence and nonviolence—about tactics, by and large. And, having divided the movement along tactical lines, the commentators wanted to know: was Fischer in his hotheaded youth a good New Leftist, meaning nonviolent, or (as the photographs and the accusations made seem likely) a bad New Leftist? But those questions, asked head-on, were never going to shed much light on the man himself or on the movement. This was because New Leftism in its fear and panic was always a super-emotional movement, and the charged sentiments undid any chance for lucid discussion, and the arguments for violence and nonviolence kept slipping illicitly into one another's arms, though you wouldn't think it possible.

In the United States, to cite a humbling example, some of the most notoriously violent street protests of the late nineteen-sixties and early seventies, during the mass mobilizations against the war in Vietnam, were led by the die-hard opponents of all violence whatsoever—by militants of absolute pacifism who, in their Christian zeal, chose to stand shoulder to shoulder with the helmeted warriors of sidewalk mayhem. And the helmeted warriors ran into the street and did what even the pacifists expected them to do. Were the pacifists good and the window-smashers bad? You may think so, but those people were arm-in-arm, and their differences shriveled at times to such tiny proportions as to seem mere variations in style, the pious and the polite over here, the blasphemous and the rude over there, each complicit with the other: good cop, bad cop.

The truly fundamental debates within the New Left, the arguments that really mattered about the crypto-Nazism of modern life and how to confront it, the arguments that finally did lead to violence or that led away—

40

those arguments broke down along lines that, in their origins, had very little to do with tactics. They were arguments about worldviews, about what it meant to be a leftist and what sort of world the left wanted to create—philosophical arguments, you could say. Those particular arguments tended to remain somewhat muted in the early years of the New Left, when tempers were relatively cool and the student movement was content to remain a student movement.

But the heat rose season by season, and by 1969 or thereabouts the New Left had lost any sense of balance that it might once have had—lost its balance because the Vietnam War had intensified and the anti-colonial movement seemed about to erupt in social and racial cataclysms here and there around the world, and because a good many New Leftists had by then undergone their own unhappy run-ins with the police, which led to dizzy spells of rage and tantrum. And the movement lost its old tranquility because many a simple-souled activist wanted to make the transition from student to grown-up and stop fiddling around—wanted to put together an adult force capable of wrestling the old society to the ground.

In each country around the world, some of the central figures from the student ranks, having grown older and more frustrated, set out to do just that, mostly by trying to organize a full-scale revolutionary movement, something that could no longer be described as a young person's merry carnival. Only what could that mean in the world of 1969 and the early nineteen-seventies? A revolutionary movement? In what fashion? In the

41

Western countries the New Left, stroking its chin, contemplated three main alternatives.

The crudest of those alternatives, the least imaginative, was simply to revert to the old-fashioned sectarian Marxism of the nineteen-thirties and to go about fighting Nazism in exactly the way that people had done in the past, by organizing disciplined, Leninist structures based on obedience, dedication, and self-sacrifice, the dream words of the Great Depression, and in this manner to sink into a sepia-toned memory of long ago. Leftism, too, can be a nostalgia cult. (Leftism may be the greatest nostalgia cult of all.) Resurrecting the nineteen-thirties turned into quite an enormous campaign around the world. Even in the United States, where the Marxist and Leninist traditions were venerable but never especially strong, some fifteen thousand New Leftists are estimated to have enlisted in the minuscule retro-Marxist sects, Trotskyist or Stalinist (though the Stalinists called themselves Maoists), which is no small number, if you consider that enlisting meant accepting the rigors of party discipline and not just sending in a dues payment or showing up at a meeting now and then.

In West Germany, the yearning for a heroic Marxist past—for the heroic past that had failed in Germany to be sufficiently heroic, that had failed to beat down the Nazi challenge—became irresistible to a much larger number of people. Rosa Luxemburg, the martyr, ascended into godhood. And the students were drawn to old-fashioned Marxism for another reason. The New Left in West Germany had originally taken shape in response to the Federal Republic's banning in 1956 of the West German Communist Party, a political event that allowed the students to feel that a heritage from the past had been denied them: the heritage that was flowering (they liked to imagine) in the part of Germany that never did stop struggling against the Nazi legacy, in the morally superior part, the egalitarian and civilized part. In the other part, that is: in East Germany.

The principal West German student movement happened to be called SDS (coincidentally like America's own SDS, or Students for a Democratic Society). In 1969, under the pressure of the revolutionary mood and the worldwide student uprising, the German SDS dissolved. The students from that organization, in their search for an adult politics, went about forming any number of brand-new Leninist parties—a new party in every city, it sometimes seemed. That became a big tendency in West Germany, bigger than in France and in the other countries of the West. As many as a hundred thousand people, perhaps even more, enlisted in the nineteen-seventies in these many parties—the so-called K-groups, for *Kommunistische*.

And yet retro-Marxism was never New Leftism's main impulse. A still larger number of people took up the second alternative, a Marxism that was distinctly of the nineteen-sixties and seventies: the Marxism of Ho, Mao, Che, and Fidel, mixed with a few doctrines of the Frankfurt School philosophers. This was a modern Marxism, free of retro touches. The people who took it up sometimes went about organizing militant parties of their own, but mostly they cultivated their radical aspirations in a cheerfully provisional mood, awaiting the arrival of the true, well-organized revolutionary party of

43

the future, and meanwhile biding their time in the agreeable fashion of the young. "Please, God, make me chaste, but not yet!" Modern Marxism was for this reason mostly a left-wing milieu without formal structures or central commands or any way of coordinating itself—a big milieu, though.

As for New Leftism's third alternative, it was fundamentally anarchist—a libertarian impulse that sometimes drew on the nineteenth-century pamphlets of Bakunin and Kropotkin, sometimes on the early-twentieth-century writings of Anton Pannekoek and the Dutch councilists, sometimes on the contemporary but equally obscure pamphlets of the autonomists in Italy and the Socialism or Barbarism group and the Situationists in France. But most often the anarchist alternative drew on nothing at all, on a breeze blowing through the university neighborhoods and on rumors from the California counterculture.

The libertarianism was typically less than libertarian. It was anarchist-leaning—or, as the French say, *anarchisant*—cultural more than political, oblivious to economics, a libertarianism under constant siege by the doctrines of the retro-Marxists and especially of the modern Marxists—a libertarianism that turned out to be, as a result, blithely inconsistent. The *anarchisants* of the New Left kept falling for the Third Worldist fantasies of the modern Marxists, kept wanting to celebrate Ho or some other tropical Communist as a hero of the libertarian cause—an odd thing to do. The *anarchisants* spoke about freedom and personal autonomy and, at the same time, nodded respectfully at Che's self-sacrifice, even though Che's unmentionable achievement was to

44

have established Soviet-style labor camps in Cuba. An anarchist salt and a Marxist pepper, sprinkled together.

Cohn-Bendit spoke for this third alternative. His own libertarianism was more sophisticated, and therefore more frankly anti-Communist, than that of almost everyone else in the New Left, outside of the tiny, old-school anarchist sects. Cohn-Bendit could draw on a solid acquaintance with the old-time anarchist groups and the revolutionary tradition that in France went back to Proudhon, a venerable heritage. And the venerable heritage did have its wisdom, which was available to him even as a child. Lenin's crimes were a revelation to everyone in the left-wing world, it sometimes seemed, but they were no revelation to the heirs of French anarchism.

Cohn-Bendit knew better than to sigh for the Popular Front. He was not a man for Mao buttons. He was a lot clearer than Fischer on these questions, back in their New Left days. (Cohn-Bendit has explained that, when he arrived in Frankfurt after his expulsion from France, he was surprised by how great the Stalinist influence on the German left was, by how little the German radicals knew about the true nature of Communism.) The phrase "visceral anti-Communism" would have sounded terrible, even fascistic, in the ears of many a person in the movement, but Cohn-Bendit was happy with that particular phrase and applied it to himself. He filled his writings with angry denunciations of the Soviet Union and Lenin and the Marxist-Leninist political tradition. *Le Grand Bazar*, the book that got him into so much trouble in the early months of 2001, was largely an anti-Communist tract.

Then again, in the spirit of inconsistency, even Cohn-Bendit made himself at home with all kinds of people who could never have postulated anti-Communism as a New Left principle. Those were his limitations. Or perhaps those were the limitations of the movement: Cohn-Bendit would have cut himself off from an enormous number of people if he had insisted on anti-Communist principles at every moment. He was a great fan of the freak scene in the United States, which he instinctively knew to be anarchist at heart, allergic to bureaucracies, allergic to anything like a Marxist-Leninist centralized organization—a scene devoted to individual expression and to the expansion of personal freedom in every possible dimension, plus a few other dimensions. The freak scene in America was surely the biggest of all the libertarian currents around the world in those years, and its size and friskiness excited his enthusiasm. America's freaks and Hollywood's westerns were a sort of ideal for him. He recommended their virtues in *Le Grand Bazar*. But then, America's freaks were just as inconsistent as everyone else among the New Left libertarians around the world. You could see the confusion in someone like Abbie Hoffman, the Yippie chieftan, whose level of education in matters of left-wing lore was fairly low, and who therefore tended to be rather gullible about Third World Communism. Hopelessly gullible, in fact.

No single phrase denoted the New Left's libertarian current around the world. The word that Fischer liked to use in West Germany (as I see from an interview that he gave to Cohn-Bendit back in the mid-nineteen-eighties) was the humorously clunky "anarcho-Mao-spontex"—an expressive phrase covering all bases. *Anarcho* meant the old tradition of the anarchist movements of the past. *Mao* meant an imaginary Mao—a Mao who, unlike the real Mao, was not a totalitarian. *Spontex* meant "spontaneist"—against formal organizations and against the bureaucratic and military discipline of the Marxist sects. Or, abbreviating, the doubly hyphenated phrase could be rendered as *sponti*, which was German for what we Americans meant by *freak*, more or less.

The "sponti scene" in Frankfurt meant the housing squatters whom Fischer used to lead around the streets, together with the "alternative" journals such as Cohn-Bendit's *Pflasterstrand*, or *Under the Pavement, the Beach!* The sponti scene meant the teachers at the "anti-authoritarian" schools, a wing of the brand-new women's movement, the street-corner layabouts, the politicized dope-smokers, and the avant-garde in the arts, except for the people who could more comfortably fit under a label of conventional Marxist—a big scene, block after block in Frankfurt and Berlin, the sponti capitals.

I do not mean to suggest that those three grand tendencies of the New Left, post-1968—retro-Marxists, modern Marxists, inconsistent libertarians—kept themselves in neatly separated columns. Events and fads came in torrents, and atop the waves people bobbed about from one tendency to another. Still, the debates that went on within the New Left, the crucial argument over violence and nonviolence, had to take place within categories of thought that were shaped by those fluid tendencies. The outside world sometimes had a little trouble in making sense of the New Left for that reason.

On the topic of violence—back to that now—it was a convention of the bourgeois press in the late nineteen-sixties and seventies to take the notorious old label of "anarchist" and paste it across every sort of left-wing scuffle, especially the acts of terror. This custom doubtless got its start with the police. The wanted posters in Germany proclaimed a hunt for *Anarchistische Gewalttäter—Baader/Meinhof Bande*. And the press adopted the usage. A volume of clips from the *New York Times* lies before me as I write, and I see the headlines and phrases: "Anarchist Leaders Seized in Frankfurt" (announcing the 1972 arrest of Andreas Baader and three other comrades of the Red Army Fraction). Or this, from the same year: "Miss Meinhof, thirty-seven years old, has been considered the leading ideologist of an anarchist group calling itself the Red Army Faction. . . ."

Yet the Red Army Fraction was not an anarchist group, nor was anarchism a main inspiration for New Left violence. A minor inspiration, yes. The June 2 Movement in West Germany (which kidnapped a Christian Democratic politician), the Angry Brigade in Britain, and the Direct Action group in France were armed groups that could plausibly claim an anarchist background. Some of the people in the Black Liberation Army in the United States (which came out of the Black Panthers) likewise invoked an anarchist origin. Anarchism's share of the violence of the New Left was, even so, strictly minimal. The police and the bourgeois press had it wrong. The true inspiration for the guerrilla or terrorist groups on the New Left was overwhelmingly Marxist—not in the retro-style of the traditional Marxist organizations (traditional Marxism, dating back to Marx, had always regarded terrorism with absolute disdain), but in the modern style.

The modern Marxists looked on life in the Western countries as hopelessly tainted and on Western society as inherently dreadful. The modern Marxists subscribed to the economic analyses of dependency theory, according to which the Western exploitation of everybody else around the world appeared to be unavoidable, owing simply to the laws of economic survival under capitalism, and not to some streak of cruelty or thoughtlessness that could be overcome. The modern Marxists, having studied their Frankfurt School texts, saw in Western culture an impermeable wall of total oppression. Hopelessly exploitative in economic matters, hopelessly mendacious and manipulative in cultural matters—that was Western society. What could anyone do but heave a bomb and hope for the best? A proper bomb might blow a hole in the Western web of total oppression.

Some people did manage not to draw those particular conclusions. Herbert Marcuse himself stood up against the Red Army Fraction, and did it in the *New York Times* to boot, just in case anyone might fail to notice what position he was taking. Still, the terrorist logic, such as it was, drew on a Marcusean social criticism: the criticism that saw no hope at all in Western society. There was another line of argument. The gap between the European student movement and Third World guerrilla insurgencies was not necessarily very large. The single most influential manifesto of the Latin American guerrilla movement, *Revolution in the*

49

Revolution?, was written by Régis Debray of France—a disciple of Louis Althusser's at the elite school in Paris, the Ecole Normale Supérieure. And if Régis Debray's guerrilla reasoning made sense for Latin America, why not for Europe, too—if only as a way of supporting the Third World guerrillas? "Be like Che," the Fidelista slogan, meant that you, too, should die a warrior; and this was a popular cry. Sartre, with an eye to the Algerian independence fighters, argued that violence was redemptive: "Violence, like Achilles' lance, can heal the wounds that it has inflicted." People believed this. Then again, in the case of the Irish and Basque terrorists and a few other people fighting miniature wars of national liberation, violence offered an encouraging sign that Ireland or the Basque country or some other benighted province of the West might be able to slip away into the Third World, where the sunny rays of a beautiful social revolution were deemed more likely to dawn.

Such were modern Marxism's guerrilla arguments. They had the curious effect of leading the guerrillas and the people who supported them to look sympathetically on the Soviet Union, even if without much enthusiasm. The armed Marxist organizations in the Western countries, if they intended to be at all serious, did need a helping hand—logistical support, military training, a place to which hard-pressed guerrillas could flee. And where to find that kind of help, if not from East Germany, or Czechoslovakia, or Cuba, or some other country of the Soviet bloc, or else from one of the Arab countries that enjoyed Soviet backing? And what is logistical support if not moral support?

That was definitely how the guerrilla argument ran in West Germany. Meinhof's defense of terrorism leaned on the Frankfurt School Marxists, who were not especially friendly to the Soviets and sometimes were quite hostile; but, on the Soviet question, Meinhof drew her own conclusions, which were positive. The Soviet Union: a progressive force in world history. Really, how could she think otherwise? And, sure enough, two years after her death, East Germany began offering secret military training and logistical support to the Red Army Fraction, and refuge for its fighters.

The gap between the New Left terrorists in their modern Marxist version and the New Left libertarians was, in a small word, big. The libertarians detested the Soviet Union, even if they deceived themselves about the un-Soviet nature of Communist regimes in tropical regions of the world, about which everyone felt free to fantasize. The libertarians never imagined that Western society was hopelessly oppressive. The libertarians went about building the freak neighborhoods and the sponti scene on the palpable assumption that Western society, in its accordion flexibility, could be stretched and squeezed to play melodic variations on "alternative" themes. The libertarians never expected to storm the Winter Palace. The hippie-dippies were much too culturally minded for that. The several modern Marxist reasonings that led to a New Left terrorism therefore tended to escape them.

Then again, like the Marxists, the libertarians did find themselves in a fury over local events and foreign wars and the state of modern life. They chucked rocks at the police, and the police clubbed them back, and then some. That was Fischer's experience: beaten by the police at a demonstration in 1968. And, from behind their overturned cars and makeshift barricades, the libertarians, nursing their bruises, had to wonder: why stop at rocks? Or at Molotov cocktails? They scratched their long-haired heads. They were not *entirely* resistant to the terrorist argument. So they dithered. That was a characteristic response. Meanwhile they labored at building their communes, kindergartens, food co-ops, new gender relations, and other elements of the New Left utopia in its countercultural version. Or else they followed the retro-Marxist example and colonized the factories in search of proletarian followers. They mooned nostalgically over the anarchosyndicalist vision of a revolutionary general strike. And they never did take the terrorist plunge. Or they dipped a toe in and out. This was the situation in the early and mid-nineteen-seventies. And at that moment the great black clouds of New Left moodiness and rage that had been gathering for a good ten years began to break up, all over the Western world.

The mood changed because the United States began pulling out of Vietnam, beginning in 1972, which tamped down the New Left hysteria, and because President Nixon, who managed to incite panic everywhere he went, soon enough began his long, slow fall from power. Watergate did wonders for democracy's prestige, and the refurbished prestige tamped down the hysteria still more. Maybe America was not unredeemably horrible, after all; maybe Hollywood's westerns and California's marvelous hippies were the true America, and Richard Nixon was part of a false America that was going down to defeat. And just as those encouraging American trends were getting under way, two very shocking developments took place, which quickly sobered up large numbers of people in the New Left all over the world, and perhaps the libertarians most of all.

The first of those developments involved the Palestinians and their struggle against Zionism, and it requires a little explanation. The war of Arab nationalism against Zionism had been going on since the turn of the twentieth century or even earlier, and, in ideological terms, had already flip-flopped several times in the eyes of the European left, such that left-wing had turned into right-wing, and vice versa, and back again. The early Zionist settlers, being solid European socialists and anarchists, basked in the sympathy of at least some portions of the European left. In the late nineteen-twenties and early thirties, however, the world Communist movement came out in favor of the Arab resisters. Then, in the nineteen-forties, both the Communists and the democratic left in Europe returned to, or re-affirmed, their original sympathy for Zionism—only to have things switch again in the nineteen-fifties, when Israel lined up as an ally of the British and French imperialists.

The 1967 war, in which the Israelis seized a lot of land, seemed to confirm Israel's imperialist nature. The Soviets became fierce enemies of Zionism. Palestinian Marxists stepped forward. Soviet resources poured in. And, under those circumstances, the New Left came up with one more interpretation of the Middle Eastern conflict, in which the New Left's vision of a lingering Nazism of modern life was suddenly reconfigured, with Israel in a leading role. Israel became the crypto-Nazi site par excellence, the purest of all examples of how Nazism had never been defeated but had instead lingered into the present in ever more cagey forms. What better disguise could Nazism assume than a Jewish state?

Israel thus advanced in the New Left imagination into the vanguard of imperialist aggressors, and the Palestinian resistance into the front rank of modern anti-Nazism. "We are all German Jews" came to mean "our sympathies lie with the Palestinians." In West Germany, the New Left's shift in attitude was probably more pronounced than in other countries. This may have reflected an East German influence. The East German Communists expressed a fiercer hatred for Israel than did any other ruling party in Europe, and the East Germans acted on their words, too, and secretly backed the anti-Zionist terrorist organizations of the Middle East, just as they did with the Red Army Fraction. The East Germans aided the Baath party in Iraq and Syria. The East Germans were ferocious. But the West German students had their own reasons for coming out against Israel. Israel's military triumph aroused a somewhat creepy excitement among German conservatives. The *Bild Zeitung* celebrated the Israeli general Moshe Dayan as a new Rommel, the "Desert Fox." Israel's tanks were greatly admired. An efficient army, at last! A Jewish Wehrmacht! And the student left recoiled. That was why a young adventurer such as Joschka Fischer would have traveled in 1969 to exotic Algiers to attend a convention of the PLO and might not have batted an eye when the convention solemnly voted to crush its enemy.

The whole outlook of anti-Zionism seemed to fit the left-wing worldview, not just in Germany. On the other hand, a theoretical sympathy for the Palestinian cause brought the European New Left into contact with actual Palestinian guerrillas, which, you might think, would have transformed the budding new sympathies into sentiments of love and brotherhood—an international fraternity of revolutionaries. But fraternity was hard to achieve. The Palestinian militants, once they had become known, ceased to be exotic. And as the European leftists got a closer look, the New Left's instinctive anti-Zionism—the interpretation that pictured heroic Palestinian resistance fighters combatting cleverly disguised Nazi Zionists—began to crumble.

This was the story behind the amazing evolution of Fischer's friend Hans-Joachim Klein, the penitent terrorist. Klein had joined the Revolutionary Cells in Germany and had united with Carlos the Jackal believing that he was going to put his mechanic's skills to good use in a left-wing military organization, fighting Nazism in its modern disguises. The Revolutionary Cells sent him for military training in an Arab country. In his interview on this theme with Cohn-Bendit in the mid-nineteen-eighties, Klein did not specify which country, but wherever it was, the place did not agree with him. He found himself in a military training ground where, in one part of the camp, European leftists singing left-wing songs received their anti-Zionist military training, and, in another part, European fascists singing fascist songs received their own anti-Zionist military training.

The Palestinian movement turned out not to be an anti-fascist or anti-Nazi cause at all. It turned out to be an anti-Jewish cause. Klein was horrified. His mother had been imprisoned for a while in Ravensbrück, the Nazi camp, and died later on from her sufferings there, when he was still a little child. In his adulthood, he began to imagine, or perhaps to fantasize, that she was Jewish— a not uncommon fantasy among modern Germans. That was why he abandoned the Revolutionary Cells and then went even further and accused his old comrades among the German guerrillas not just of having betrayed the revolutionary ideal but of being out-and-out anti-Semites. That was a shocking accusation. Klein was disturbed by something else at the Palestinian military camp, too, and this was a cult of suicide—a weird phenomenon that he was among the first to notice, back in the seventies.

A good many French New Leftists went through an identical turnabout, except without having killed anyone first. The French student movement never did generate a hard-line Marxist tendency of the sort that, in West Germany, produced the Red Army Fraction and, in Italy, the Red Brigades. I suppose that, in France, the libertarian currents in New Leftism were much too vigorous to allow such any such thing to take shape. The main revolutionary tendency to come out of the 1968 uprisings in France was, instead, a group called the Proletarian Left, which was usually described as Maoist (and its members as "Maos"), and which Cohn-Bendit liked to described as outright Stalinist, but was, more accurately, a Mao-spontex hodgepodge—an old-fashioned Marxist organization streaked with libertarian impulses. (The Proletarian Left kept having to expel people who, because of those impulses, insisted on smoking their unproletarian hashish and muttering about Stalinists. I spent a couple of weeks living in a commune with those people in Paris and felt their pain.)

So the Proletarian Left, in its spontex ambivalence, dithered on the road to terror. It was only in 1972, a late date by New Left standards, that France's Maos finally did their revolutionary duty and kidnapped an assistant personnel director of the Renault company. They did this under the rubric of the New People's Resistance, whose very name raised the honorable old banner of anti-Nazism. The kidnapping was halfhearted, though, and after a while the New People's Resistance let their victim go, without having received a single sou in ransom.

Half a year went by, and then the PLO's Black September group, with the Revolutionary Cells' helping hand, launched its attack at the Munich Olympic Games. A good many people on the radical left applauded. Ulrike Meinhof was thrilled. But the leaders of the Proletarian Left in France, having flinched at their own violence, flinched at the Palestinian violence, too. The obvious truth that terrorist action means the murder of random persons for political aims suddenly became, to them, obvious. And the French Maos, exactly like Klein, turned away in horror—not just at the killings in Munich and at the general strategy of Palestinian terror, but also at their own intentions of launching similar campaigns at home.

Joschka Fischer went through a version of that same shock. The recognition fell on him in July 1976, seven months after his friend Klein played his part in the assault at Vienna and shortly after the suicide (unless it was a murder) of Ulrike Meinhof. The Revolutionary Cells, acting on behalf of a number of jailed Palestinian terrorists, hijacked an Air France plane, took it to Entebbe in Uganda, and went about arranging a "selection" of passengers, Jews on one side, non-Jews on the other, with the Jews slated for execution. In that instance, an Israeli army unit, under the command of the young Ehud Barak, staged a spectacular raid and managed to rescue all but one of the hostages, though one Israeli soldier was killed. The soldier happened to be Jonathan Netanyahu, whose brother Benjamin was, like Barak, thereby propelled into a political career. A good deal of modern Israeli politics owes something to the events in Entebbe.

The same turns out to be true of German politics. The German terrorists were killed by the Israeli commandos, and only after their deaths did Germany's New Left discover who those people were. It was a revelation. The terrorist leader turned out to be a man named Wilfried Böse, who was well known and much admired on the Frankfurt left—a hammy thespian who used to play the evil capitalist in street theater events, a founder of various left-wing institutions, and a prominent member of Frankfurt's Black Panther solidarity committee. Fischer knew Böse. Now was his own moment to be astonished.

Suddenly the implications of anti-Zionism struck home to him. What did it mean that, back in Algiers in 1969, the PLO, with the young Fischer in attendance, had voted the Zionist entity into extinction? Now he knew what it meant. Fischer seems never to have gotten over the shock of Entebbe. Even in the early weeks of 2001, at the height of the scandal provoked by the photographs in *Stern*, the memory of the Air France hijacking haunted him. He spoke to a reporter from that same magazine and cited the hijacking and especially the "selection" of Jews as part of his *Desillusionierung* with the violent left. In his capacity as foreign minister of Germany, he happened to be in Israel a few months later, at the very moment when a terrorist blew up a Tel Aviv disco. He was close enough to hear the blast. And it was Fischer, more than any other foreign minister or religious leader or world figure of any sort, who took it upon himself to confront Arafat in person—Fischer who (so it was reported) berated Arafat ferociously and even forced him into declaring some sort of a cease-fire. The erstwhile militant for the PLO, now militant against Palestinian terror.

Entebbe had such an effect on quite a few of West Germany's New Leftists. A new suspicion was dawning on those people—a little tardily, you might complain (and, to be sure, some of Germany's New Leftists had been raising a point about left-wing anti-Semitism all along). It was a worried suspicion that New Left guerrilla activity, especially in its German version, was not the struggle against Nazism that everyone on the New Left had always intended. It was a suspicion that, out of some horrible dialectic of history, a substantial number of German leftists had ended up imitating instead of opposing the Nazis—had ended up intoxicating themselves with dreams of a better world to come, while doing nothing more than setting out to murder Jews on a random basis: an old story.

The terrorist actions at Munich in 1972 and at Entebbe in 1976 were not the only examples, either. Klein announced his turn against terrorism in 1977 by making the sensational gesture of sending to *Der Spiegel* a letter containing his own pistol from the Vienna attack and announcing that the terrorists were planning on murdering the leaders of the Jewish communities of Berlin and Frankfurt. Nor was that an idle threat. Carlos in person, gun in hand, rang the doorbell of the scion of Marks & Spencer in London and shot the man in cold blood, merely for the crime, as Klein reported, of being a Jew. (The bullet struck his teeth and was slightly deflected, which allowed him to survive.) There was an insane idea of murdering famous Jewish musicians such as Artur Rubinstein and Yehudi Menuhin. The discovery that some people in the terrorist brigades had actually descended into such thinking came as a pretty severe blow to the muddle-headed nonterrorists of the German New Left.

There was a further shock, and this resonated at still deeper levels, if only because many more people were involved. It was the news from Indochina. New Left movements all over the world had yearned for a Communist Indochina, had worked hard for it, had sacrificed, had struggled, and had done a lot of dreaming, too. The new utopian society was supposed to emerge there at last, in a bamboo-and-thatch version. That was a popular idea—an irresistible idea, really. Those cone-hatted rice farmers were actually defeating the B-52s, and if a Third World peasant insurgency could fend off imperial France and then the mighty United States, what couldn't be done around the world, given sufficient dedication and the rightness of a cause? Millions of hearts beat to that rhythm.

But when the Communists did triumph in Cambodia, and the new society turned out to be what it was, a new and unpredicted truth became clear, and not just in regard to the sorry turn of events in faraway Asia. For it was suddenly obvious to anyone with eyes that huge portions of the New Left had ended up supporting a cause that, in the case of the Palestinian guerrillas and their allies in Germany and other countries, was on a tiny scale resurrecting the old manias of the Nazis of the nineteen-thirties and forties, and, in the case of the Cambodian Communists, was engaged in slaughter by the millions. Anti-Semitism and genocide, a familiar twosome. And it became obvious that the New Left in its more radical or revolutionary version was not, as everyone had imagined, an anti-Nazi movement. On the contrary.

This was a vast, almost unimaginable shock—a shock that most people in the movement found much too horrifying to take in. For who had the emotional strength to see anything as unexpected, as undesired, as that? To have set out to fight Nazism in its sundry modern democratic disguises, only to have ended up, in a modern left-wing disguise, Nazi-like! That was absurd. To anyone gazing at the world through strictly Marxist glasses, the entire sequence of events and their implications in the early and middle nineteen-seventies lay outside the zone of recognizable reality. Marxism pointed to the workings of the capitalist economy and the manipulations of the

61

imperial powers and the crimes of the United States, and if you spoke about anti-Semitism and Communist mass murder, weren't you merely repeating the much-analyzed propaganda of the imperialist West?

Among the Marxists of the New Left—the retro-Marxists and the modern Marxists alike, the mass of non-terrorists together with the handful of terrorists—the response to those shocking discoveries could only be dismissive, or, at any rate, quietly baffled. A good many people on the Marxist side of the movement simply lumbered on as if nothing had happened. Some of those people lumber on still. The largest number of all drifted away, speechless and agog, until the years had passed and they could no longer remember having participated in the New Left and its several manias and fanaticisms—amnesiacs of a New Left radicalism that no one could recall anymore, the kind of people who, in their respectable middle age today, would indignantly deny having ever been anything but ardent liberals. Who, us?

On the New Left, serious responses to the events of the mid-nineteen-seventies tended to come instead from people with some sort of background on the libertarian side of the movement. Those people, the inconsistent anarchists and anarcho-Mao-spontaneists, could at least rummage through their bookcases and discover a useful trove of critical pamphlets. They could gaze at the terrible new developments and feel with some justification that anti-capitalism was a fine position to hold but had never been the main idea, not for the libertarian left. Those people could feel that authoritarianism, and not capitalism, had always been the real enemy. And having made that recognition, they had to imagine what might be a plausible libertarian response to the unexpected new events.

It was not that everyone with some sort of anarchist or libertarian background rushed to respond to the left-wing calamities with a sudden passion for thoughtful reflection. In the United States, the most influential of the anarchist-influenced writers was Noam Chomsky, who responded to the news from Cambodia exactly as any Third World–oriented Marxist would do: by wondering if the stories about genocide were not imperialist propaganda. Somehow Chomsky tilted in Marxist directions just when his anarchist background might have come in handy. Still, no great psychological obstacle prevented anyone who had done a bit of reading in the old anarchist pamphlets or in back issues of *Socialism or Barbarism* from interpreting the new events in a libertarian light. You needed only to be able to wriggle free of the Marxist influence and to give the world a fresh glance.

Here and there, a few people did respond in that way. The veterans of the old anarcho-Mao-spontex currents in France were the first to do so, and in the long run they had the biggest influence around the world. But there were people like that in every country. Joschka Fischer was one of them. It was just that, to shake free of Marxism's influence, to scoop up everything that was valuable about the New Left and abandon the rest, to come up with genuinely new responses—this was, intellectually speaking, extremely difficult. Several years of hard thinking and political experimentation were required. Some of the steps proved to be controversial, too. And the history of this new development, the move away from New Leftism toward something newer, a post-leftism, came up for public inspection and even a lot of jeering in the course of the widening Fischer scandal.

III.

Fischer's response to the crackup of the New Left entered into our American debates on one occasion to my knowledge; and a glance at that occasion may beam a light on how someone with an extremely radical New Left orientation could have ended up, in the fullness of time, a friend of NATO. The occasion was a discussion between Fischer and André Glucksmann, which originally ran in the pages of *Die Zeit* in 1986 and was soon translated into English and published in *Telos*, the philosophical journal of the American New Left.

Among the intellectuals of the American New Left, the *Zeit-Telos* item attracted a bit of attention partly because, to any of us in the United States who wanted to keep abreast of our comrades and peers in Europe, Glucksmann's name was already somewhat familiar. Glucksmann was a French '68er and a Mao who taught at the left-wing university at Vincennes—an old comrade there of Michel Foucault's. Woolly essays under Glucksmann's byline ran in the *New Left Review* in England. And he was known for having made a sensational about-face in the mid-nineteen-seventies to become one of the New Philosophers, much noted around the world and much mocked. Glucksmann was never the splashiest or most telegenic of the New

Philosophers. But that was good. He had a reputation for being the most solidly educated. He was a student of both Louis Althusser and Raymond Aron. So we were curious.

Fischer's name, by contrast, was not at all well known in the United States, except to the specialists in the German left and to any Americans who may have done a bit of hanging out in the Frankfurt sponti scene. Still, Fischer had become a leader of the West German Greens, and the Green connection counted for a lot in American eyes. The mass New Left in America had given way by the mid-nineteen-eighties to a panorama of single-issue movements—against nuclear energy and nuclear weapons, for identity politics, for solidarity with the Marxists of Central America. To anyone who participated in those movements, West Germany's Greens seemed rather attractive. They had evidently discovered the secret of how to convert an impractical, marginal, too-radical left-wing movement into a practical, democratic movement that nonetheless knew how to cling to its left-wing soul: a difficult thing to do, achieved by virtually no one else anywhere in the world. That was their reputation. So Fischer, too, as a leader of the Greens, aroused a curiosity in the United States.

There was a charm in his debate with Glucksmann. The New Left had always drawn on a warm internationalist spirit, an easy young people's camaraderie of Paris, Berlin, Frankfurt, Rome, Mexico City, New York, and Berkeley (not to mention Lawrence, Austin, Madison, Ann Arbor, Cambridge, Portland, and so forth around the country and the world). Something of that remembered spirit warmed the discussion in 1986. Glucksmann had spent a few weeks in Frankfurt back in the early nineteen-seventies with Revolutionary Struggle, and he had gotten to know Fischer and regarded him fondly, maybe a little patronizingly.

Fischer had never formally attended a university, though he did show up for some lectures, and at the time of Glucksmann's visit he was trying to give himself a proper education by reading the great philosophers in alphabetical order, starting with Aristotle. Glucksmann could only laugh. He and Fischer did seem to have enjoyed themselves, though. That was visible in the 1986 debate. But the debate seemed noteworthy mostly because, by the mid-nineteen-eighties, it had become obvious that, among the many responses around the world to the crack-up of the New Left, French New Philosophy, on one hand, and the West German Greens, on the other hand, seemed the most thorough and original, the deepest, the liveliest—the two responses most likely to blossom in the future, and not just in their own countries. They were opposite responses, of course. So there was drama in that debate.

Glucksmann's New Philosophy is easily enough defined, looking back on it. He went through the entire process of disillusionment of the New Left during the early and middle nineteen-seventies in a fairly radical French version—the shock at Palestinian terror doubled by the shock at Cambodia, the shock at the New Left's plans for its own terror campaign, the remorse, the self-reproach, the moral confusion. And then, having stopped at every station, he set about trying to construct a new set of political ideas. That was his project. He did this in three big steps between 1975 and the early nineteen-eighties.

His first step, in the mid-seventies, was to give up on his old-fashioned anti-capitalism and anti-imperialism, the fundamentals of the left, in favor of what he began to call antitotalitarianism—though by antitotalitarianism he meant something broad, an opposition to extreme oppression of every kind, whatever its shape or cause. Glucksmann belonged to the oldest contingent within the New Left, the people who were born before the outbreak of World War II—in his case, in 1937, three years after Ulrike Meinhof—which meant that he was pretty strongly marked by memories of the war. His parents were Jewish Communists and Resistance fighters. Even his older sister participated in the underground—she passed out leaflets in Nazi Germany. Glucksmann grew up thinking of pretty much everything he did as a struggle against Nazism. He came into the New Left from the Communist youth movement. But now, in the mid-seventies, he took his old anti-Nazism and extended it in novel directions. He read Solzhenitsyn. He became an enemy, and not just a critic, of the Soviet Union and of Communism in Cambodia and everywhere else. He became an enemy of every extreme dictatorship around the world, right-wing or left-wing. He declared himself the enemy of famines, too, wherever they might occur, as in Africa—the enemy of every extreme horror and catastrophe that leads to mass death and total oppression. And to all of those extreme dictatorships and catastrophes he attached a single name: Auschwitz.

He still thought of himself as a New Leftist when he adopted his new antitotalitarian position, and with good reason. He drew whole aspects of his new antitotalitarianism from his old colleague and fellow-rioter at

Vincennes, Foucault—the philosopher of institutional super-oppression. It may be that, like so many other intellectuals in the French New Left, Glucksmann picked up a few inspirations from the Socialism or Barbarism group in France, too. Those were his influences. They were impeccably left-wing. But he discovered that nothing was inherently or exclusively left-wing about counting himself an enemy of extreme suffering. The left-wing vocabulary was expressive, and he used it in the first of the books that explained his new position, *La Cuisinière et le mangeur d'hommes*, or *The Cook and the Cannibal*. He invoked the California Black Panthers.

But the left-wing vocabulary was not necessary; it could even be misleading. After a while he set it aside. Most of Glucksmann's comrades on the left despised his new analysis anyway, no matter what rhetoric he used. (They could not forgive his sympathy for Solzhenitsyn. They thought that he had gone overboard in his opposition to the Soviet Union.) Besides, he discovered that by dropping the left-wing vocabulary, he could free himself from an inhibiting political tradition. So he became an antitotalitarian with a vocabulary that was neither left-wing nor right-wing—his own vocabulary, hyperemotional (that was his heritage from the New Left), baroque, flowery, philosophical, but no longer ideological in any of the conventional versions.

His second big step was to answer Lenin's "What is to be done?" with a few thoughts that would have curled the lip of any self-respecting Bolshevik. Glucksmann's original notion of revolutionary action, back in New Left days, had been pretty much the same as everyone's—

among the super-radicals. He wanted to take the wartime French Resistance of his parents and his sister and update it with inspirations drawn from Mao and the Communist guerrilla fighters of the Third World. He wanted to rally the workers and to spark the revolution; and when the atmosphere hardened and violence was in the air, he wanted to fight the revolutionary war. Now he gave up on that kind of talk. He spoke, instead, about humanitarian action.

He adopted a new set of heroes, and the greatest of these was a man two years younger than himself, from a rather similar background in the French Communist student movement—a man who had already lived through several of the adventures of the modern left. This was Bernard Kouchner, the medical doctor in whose car Cohn-Bendit had sneaked into Germany, back in 1968. Dr. Kouchner organized emergency humanitarian rescue missions. In 1978, thousands of people were fleeing Vietnam in little boats to escape from the Communist victory in the Indochina War—the Boat People, as they were called, who were undergoing a thousand horrors. Kouchner proposed to rent a ship to go rescue those people. And Glucksmann was thrilled. He and a few other lively souls organized a network of supporters for Kouchner and his ship, the "Boat for Vietnam." Glucksmann began to see in Kouchner a new action-packed ideal: the fearless humanitarian doctor, instead of the Resistance partisan. The saver of lives, instead of the maker of a revolutionary new society. By the mid-nineteen-eighties, Glucksmann was already holding up Kouchner's humanitarian campaigns for comparison with the efforts and organizations of the orthodox political left. In Glucksmann's eyes, Bernard Kouchner was doing a world of good. And what were the leftist organizations doing? Not much.

Glucksmann's third big step followed more or less logically from his first two: his antitotalitarianism and his new ardor for humanitarian action. He wanted to oppose extreme oppression with something more than Kouchner's medical rescue missions—he wanted to put up a military resistance, too, whenever a military resistance might be needed. He came out for the military deterrence of the Soviet Union, and this meant coming out for NATO. The Soviets installed new missiles aimed at Western Europe, and President Reagan announced his intention to install new American missiles aimed at the Soviet Union. Glucksmann came out for Reagan's missiles. He even defended the logic of nuclear deterrence. This was a genuine shocker to his old comrades on the left, needless to say. Solzhenitsyn was bad enough, but NATO? In their debate in 1986, Fischer could not get over how far Glucksmann had strayed from their common origins. Fischer was irate. But to understand his indignation (and why his anger would slowly fade, until he himself had ended up following something like each of Glucksmann's steps)—to understand all of this, it is necessary to glance at his own reaction to the crack-up of the New Left.

Fischer's first important move, in the wake of the events at Entebbe, was fairly tentative. He gave a speech begging the German terrorists to put down their weapons. That was a useful thing to do, though it was not exactly a turn away from radical leftism. In 1976, Fischer was against bomb-throwing, but not against stone-throwing. Against guerrilla war, but not against street fighting. Against murderous violence, but not against unmurderous violence. Someone who looks back on those distinctions today might laugh. Punching a policeman in the back or kicking him when he is down can be pretty brutal, after all, even if not murderous; and besides, it can end up murderous. Still, those were distinctions with a difference.

The whole problem of civic life in West Germany was to find ways to shake people out of the old authoritarian habits of the German past, to get rid of the spirit of obedience, to encourage people to go out and protest, maybe with a bit of noise, too. That was the idea behind the left-wing street battles. The street fighters wanted to go too far, but not too, too far: to make protests that broke the code of obedience, but would not impose by violence a different code of obedience. The guerrillas, by contrast, wanted to establish their own system by force of arms: that was the whole point of founding even the tiniest of armies. The gap between rock-throwing and bomb-throwing was enormous, then, and in 1976 everyone could see this plainly—everyone on the left, that is.

Thinking back on Fischer's speech, Glucksmann has pointed out to me that Fischer showed a lot of bravery to say anything at all about the guerrillas. In Italy in those years, the Red Brigades adopted a grisly habit of "kneecapping" people who criticized them in public. There was every reason to worry that, in West Germany, the Red Army Fraction or the Revolutionary Cells or someone else might do the same, overcome by a feeling

71

of betrayal and rage or even something as pale as contempt at what Fischer had said. Those groups were growing stronger and more violent in 1976. And they did feel a contempt. Klein made this clear in an interview that ran in the American journal *Semiotext(e)* back in 1982. (Klein's mention of Fischer and his opposition to West German terrorism must be one of the earliest mentions of Fischer in the American press.)

So Fischer's speech in 1976 was a first step. There were others. Glucksmann came to Frankfurt, promoting his book about Solzhenitsyn and the Soviet prison camps and the necessity of being antitotalitarian. The militants of the left came out to jeer. Fischer stood by Glucksmann, though. Fischer and Cohn-Bendit presented Glucksmann at a public forum, quite as if Glucksmann's ideas were suitable for a left-wing discussion, which was something rare in those years of extreme dogmatism. Fischer was trying to get people to accept a principle of open debate—no small thing to do. Mostly, though, he dropped out of politics. He didn't have much choice about it. The guerrillas and the K-groups with their ridiculous doctrines were pretty much destroying the New Left. He drove a taxi. He worked in a bookstore. And when he returned to the political world, he signed up with the Greens, whose movement was strictly post–New Left.

The West German Greens resembled the French New Philosophers in a couple of respects. The Greens, too, wanted to escape the manias and delusions of the traditional left, wanted to make a sharp break with the left-wing past. The nineteenth-century proletariat, the war-to-the-death of economic classes, the cult of the factory, of Marx, and of the pioneers of socialism, the barricades and the street-fighting: the Greens wanted to be rid of every one of those archaic things. It was just that, where Glucksmann and the New Philosophers in France wanted to give up the habit of thinking in large philosophical systems and especially wanted to give up the exhilarating old habit of imagining future revolutions and perfect societies, the Greens in West Germany wanted to take the left-wing concepts from the past and, item by item, recycle them into notions suitable for the modern age. Instead of the old proletarian metaphysic with its catastrophic vision of capitalism and its dream of a future proletarian society, the Greens proposed a new ecological metaphysic with its own catastrophic vision of capitalism and a dream of a new ecological utopia. Instead of the cult of the factory, the cult of the forest. Instead of the class war, the ecological struggle. Instead of the socialist millennium, the ecological millennium. Instead of the color red, the color green.

The German Marxists of a hundred years ago split between the revolutionary "orthodox" and the moderate "revisionists," and in precisely this manner the Greens split between the revolutionary "fundis" (or fundamentalists) who wanted to resist political compromises, and the reformist "realos" (or realists), who were happy to push their program forward one modest inch at a time. Fischer, the new Fischer of the nineteen-eighties, was a realo. By the mid-eighties he was already needling his Green comrades for their hostility to NATO. The Greens voted a resolution calling on Germany to withdraw from

NATO. Fischer, by then a canny politician, declined to sign it. He remained a man of the left, even so. Nor did he lose his instinct for impudent gestures. One day in the Bundestag, in the course of a debate over political corruption, he shocked his colleagues by saying to the president of the Bundestag, "With all due respect, Mr. President, you are an asshole" (which got Fischer excluded formally from further debate, yet gave a boost to his national popularity, given that, on this particular matter of governmental corruption, Fischer and the Greens were right, and the powers that be were wrong). Nor did he line up with the United States in its struggle against the Soviet Union. He wanted to stay independent of both superpowers. The imperialist nature of the United States seemed to him a danger of the first order.

He said to Glucksmann, in their discussion in 1986, "I do not want to identify myself with either Communist or American imperialism." He wanted to move beyond power blocs and imperial confrontations, to arrive at a different sort of politics, still imbued with the radical values of the past and the insights of left-wing theory. Glucksmann's arguments could only seem, to Fischer's way of thinking, dismal in the extreme, like nothing more than a fancy French repetition of every bellicose cold war platitude of the American superpower, lacking a vision of the future, lacking ideals, lacking the red blood of a left-wing heart.

"What separates us," Fischer told Glucksmann, "is your return to a rigid anti-Communism as an ideological foundation." That was an icy phrase. Most people on the left in the nineteen-eighties, I think, would have seen that statement as the clincher in the argument—a devastating hit. Glucksmann had become a dogmatist of the right, a rigid instead of flexible thinker, an ideologue, every terrible thing. An apologist for the American superpower. A sad case!

But Glucksmann had more to say. From his own point of view, it was Fischer who had surrendered to the will of an imperialist superpower. The West German Greens pictured themselves as putting up a lively resistance to tyrannical impositions from the United States. Yet Glucksmann considered that, on the contrary, the Greens were merely lowering their submissive German necks in the face of totalitarian pressure—as Germans had done in times past. It was just that, in the nineteen-eighties, the totalitarian pressure was coming from the Soviet Union.

The Greens prided themselves on being a new type of German: rebels against authority. But Glucksmann saw in them Germans of the old type, the respecters of power and the enthusiasts of obedience. He knew very well that, in their own imaginings, the Greens were strictly independent of the Soviet Union, and contemptuous of the Soviet leaders. But he pointed out something to Fischer: the anti-missile demonstrators in West Germany had directed nearly all their indignation at the United States, and almost none at the Soviet Union. Which superpower was occupying half of Europe, though? "We are left with the scandal," Glucksmann said, "that five hundred thousand people demonstrated against Reagan, but only ten thousand against Brezhnev. This fact has a scandalous effect not only in Paris, but also in Prague and Warsaw, and on all those who struggle for freedom in Eastern Europe."

Fischer replied that Glucksmann seemed to expect some enormous turnabout in political life, some immense change. And no such thing was going to happen. "You are taking a perspective twenty years from now," Fischer said. "Gorbachev will not change. America will also not fundamentally change. Without a doubt, there is a huge monopoly of opinion in the Soviet Union. This is probably the case in two-thirds of the world, or even more. But Hollywood is essentially more effective as far as the monopoly of opinion is concerned."

From Glucksmann's perspective, Fischer had lost the argument right there. It was preposterous to suppose that Soviet censorship and America's Hollywood were in some way comparable, and crazier still to imagine that Hollywood was "essentially" worse. And Glucksmann responded with a terrible swift word: "No."

Back in 1986, it would have been easy to suppose that Fischer had merely blundered at that moment, and in the heat of argument had let loose a foolish volley of hyperbole, as anyone might do. But today we may look on that debate with a bit of accumulated knowledge and recognize that blunders such as Fischer's bubbled up naturally from the fundamentals of his anti-imperialist outlook—from a picture of the world that attributed the woes of mankind chiefly to capitalism, and therefore to the United States, the capital of capital.

Then again, maybe the foolishness in Fischer's remark was obvious even at the time, and not just to Glucksmann. What does seem plain, looking back today, is that Fischer's side of the argument—the popular side, many people would have said, judging from the mass demonstrations in West Germany and Britain and the United States and elsewhere—was not so powerful, after all. And Glucksmann's side—the unpopular one, judging from the malicious scorn that so many commentators heaped and still heap on the new intellectual generation in France, the non-geniuses, the less-than-Sartres—was gathering strength month by month.

This was certainly true in France. The shift in opinion from New Leftism or even Old Leftism to something like New Philosophy was already visible in Paris by the mid-nineteen-seventies. Foucault in his later years, as is sometimes forgotten, was rather a supporter of Glucksmann. Sartre himself, in 1979, the year before his death, stood with Foucault and even with Raymond Aron to endorse Glucksmann's campaign on behalf of Dr. Kouchner and humanitarian action—and, implicitly, to endorse as well Glucksmann's argument about burying the hatchet with the right wing. The new attitude was symbolized by a famous photograph of Sartre side by side with the conservative Aron and a Beatle-haired Glucksmann—three men, representing the old-fashioned left, the old-fashioned conservatives, and the new-fashioned younger generation, all of them united in solidarity with the victims of Vietnamese Communism. By the early nineteen-eighties it had already become obvious that, at least in France, a large group of the younger intellectuals was thinking along lines close to Glucksmann's—the '68ers, grown up now, "the former left," as they came to be called: Bernard-Henri Lévy (who worked with Glucksmann on the campaign for Kouchner and the Boat for Vietnam), Alain Finkielkraut, Pascal Bruckner, and quite a few other people, the veterans of the student insurrection.

The dissidents of the Eastern bloc went through a parallel evolution. Even as late as the early nineteen-eighties, a good number of the dissidents in the East, the radical intellectuals, '68ers by and large, might still have identified with Fischer more than with Glucksmann. Václav Havel has described how, in the intervals when he was out of jail, he would turn on his television and watch the mass demonstrations of the West German anti-nuclear protesters, and he would root for the people with long hair and pacifist principles. By the mid-nineteen-eighties, however, he and quite a few other intellectuals in the Communist countries were beginning to lose patience with the Western peace movements, at least on political grounds. (The cultural affinity remained—a complicating point.) Glucksmann was aware of this evolution in the East, too. That was why in his debate with Fischer he made a point of invoking the dissidents, which Fischer didn't think to do.

By the mid-nineteen-eighties, you could detect a few timid signs of an impending shift of opinion even within Fischer's circle of friends and comrades. Cohn-Bendit was the bellwether. In 1985 Cohn-Bendit was still living in a New Left–style commune, putting out *Pflasterstrand.* He, too, was a Green by then: Danny the Green. But he was keen on preserving a sense of continuity with the New Left past, and he went around the world that year with a television crew filming interviews with some of the heroes of the

1968-era uprisings in different countries, which he later turned into a book called *Nous l'avons tant aimée, la révolution*, or *We Loved the Revolution So Much*. His idea was to produce a series of interviews showing the international dimension of the New Left and the seriousness of the people who had been involved and the evolution in their thinking—to assemble a sort of '68ers' International by means of television and the book. He went to the United States and interviewed Abbie Hoffman, Jerry Rubin, Bobby Seale, Jane Alpert, and Susan Brownmiller—the American delegation to his '68ers' International.

He conducted an interview with Hans-Joachim Klein for this same purpose, though Klein was still on the lam. Klein and Fischer, together with the feminist Barbara Koster, were Cohn-Bendit's West German delegation. (The accompanying photo of Fischer showed him as a young politician in blue jeans and sport jacket, a great advance in visual imagery over the black-motorcycle-helmet look.) Glucksmann, by contrast, was definitely not on Cohn-Bendit's list, nor anyone else who had made the transition to something like New Philosophy. Those people, the New Philosophers, had wandered too far from the old left-wing habits of mind to make any sense to Cohn-Bendit. In the introduction to his book, he went so far as to complain about "defrocked Stalinists" who had made themselves virgins by turning into Reaganites. He meant the ex-Maos—people like Glucksmann.

Cohn-Bendit's '68ers' International was notable for one other large omission, at least in the television documentary and in the first edition of the book, which appeared in 1986. He had tried to arrange an interview with someone from the '68 generation in the Soviet bloc, namely Adam Michnik, a leader of the Polish student movement from those days. Only, the Communist government in Poland had crushed the Solidarity trade union, and Michnik was languishing in jail, where there was no interviewing him. Then he got out, and Cohn-Bendit was able to speak with him at last, if only for the mass-market paperback edition of the book. Michnik seemed eager to be interviewed. He very much thought of himself in generational terms—a '68er through and through. He insisted on this to Cohn-Bendit.

But Michnik's interview turned out to be unlike anyone else's. He and Cohn-Bendit argued about the Vietnam War. Michnik was not about to condemn the United States for having put up a fight against Communism. In this one passage of the book, the principles of antitotalitarianism, non-ideological solidarity, and respect for NATO—Glucksmann's principles, in a word—suddenly emerged as fairly reasonable, and deserving of their proper place in a survey of the heroes of '68: principles that could not be rejected out of hand just because the conservatives or the State Department might approve of them. Cohn-Bendit gave the impression of being a little astonished by Michnik's remarks, but he published the interview anyway and even advertised it on the jacket of the new edition. All of this was quite significant, seen in retrospect. Cohn-Bendit was the only person anywhere in the world who could claim to speak for the '68 generation as an international phenomenon, and this small alteration in his book, the addition of Adam Michnik, spoke volumes.

Those were the shifts in argument and mood through the nineteen-seventies and eighties. But the moment when large numbers of veterans of the New Left finally had to put aside matters of mere philosophy or attitude and adopt actual positions and accept the political consequences—that moment, the moment of truth, arrived only after the Soviet collapse had gotten under way. A first sign of it could be seen in the months after Saddam Hussein invaded Kuwait, in 1990. George Bush the Elder was president of the United States, and his arguments for a war to drive Saddam out of Kuwait veered sometimes into the cheesiest manipulations—a "war for jobs," as Bush's secretary of state said. This sort of thing guaranteed a pretty strong backlash against the war on the part of a lot of people on the left, all over the world. "No blood for oil!" Still, the poverty of Bush's arguments did not inhibit a number of other people from noticing a few additional aspects of Saddam's regime: the slaughter of hundreds of thousands of Kurds in northern Iraq, a danger of further atrocities to come, Saddam's threat to incinerate the Israelis. Questions of genocide: a twentieth-century predicament.

Among the old militants with New Left backgrounds, some people gave a lot of thought to this particular aspect of the crisis in the Persian Gulf, and that was especially so in France. The antiwar movement in France never got anywhere, as a result. In Germany the antiwar movement was infinitely stronger, as could have been expected, given the depth of pacifist emotion in Germany and the unusual vehemence of anti-Zionist sentiment in large parts of the left. Still, even in

Germany a handful of old-time heroes of the New Left—Wolf Biermann, Hans Magnus Enzensberger, and a few others—surprised their public by declaring themselves in favor of Bush's coalition and the war. Peter Schneider, who had come out of the anarchist half of the New Left, gave his endorsement. Cohn-Bendit did the same—an especially brave thing to do, given that he was a politician in the Greens by then, and the Greens were overwhelmingly and almost genetically antiwar. The '68ers from what used to be the Soviet bloc had no trouble at all supporting the war against Saddam. Havel was already the president of what was still Czechoslovakia, and he went so far as to send a small detachment of Czechoslovak soldiers, experts in gas warfare, into the Saudi desert to take their place in the grand anti-Saddam alliance. Even in the United States you could have seen a few small indications of a split on the left on this issue, at least in my own little world of *Dissent* magazine.

The big moment of left-wing evolution came the next year, though, when the ethnic massacres got underway in the Balkans. Then, at last, the old, profound question of Nazism and what to do about it rumbled up from the depths in a European setting, and not just in connection to a barbarous dictator in the Middle East. The veterans of the New Left had to ask themselves one more time about Europe and its past. They had to ask: why was it, how could it have been, that Germany, the center of civilization, had once upon a time gone Nazi? And how, why, did the rest of Europe, most of it, end up being conquered by the Nazis back in the nineteen-thirties and forties? Everyone knew the answer to those questions in a general way.

Germany had gone Nazi, and Europe had succumbed, because the Nazis were strong and well organized and powerfully motivated, but mostly because everyone else, the non-Nazis, had failed to resist.

And why the lack of resistance, in those days? A thousand reasons, of course. And here were mass graves once again in the early nineteen-nineties. And again a thousand reasons not to resist, and even a new reason—a thousand-and-first. The new reason was something never before imagined, a new mutation of an old argument, a novelty, almost a contribution to modern political thought. The Atlantic Alliance, having come out of World War II, did have to look on genocide as a fundamental enemy, at least in regard to Europe. When the massacres got going in the former Yugoslavia, the big Western democracies had to respond, if only to affirm what it meant in the nineteen-nineties to be a powerful democracy. So the big powers responded. They unfurled the bloodless blue flag of the United Nations. They came up with a principle of non-action through action: a resistance that was no resistance at all. A non-action that cannot be faulted because it calls itself action: that was the new mutation. And so, in 1995, when the Serbian nationalists made their insane "selection" of Bosnian Muslims to be killed en masse at Srebrenica, the Dutch troops and a French general and the other Western military forces in Bosnia—the foreign interveners—did what they had been sent to do, which was to not intervene.

How could the Western democracies have managed to come up with such an absurdity? It was because, by the nineteen-nineties, the vast public in the democratic world was definitively opposed to genocide in a general way; but somebody had to step forward to oppose genocide in a concrete and specific way. And who was that going to be? Who was going to argue for a genuine forcefulness and not just a morally pleasing display of high dudgeon? The champions of foreign policy "realism," by any chance? That was out of the question. Realism is never genocide's enemy. Genocide in modern times always takes place in the margins of what appear to be great events, never at the center; but "realism" is a calculation of power at the center—a calculation of Big History, in Finkielkraut's phrase, not of Little History. Genocide attacks the weak, but realism appraises the strong.

If genocide in World War II has come to seem central to the war against Nazism, that is only because, in later years, the kinsmen and friends of the slaughtered insisted on viewing the genocide as central, and the historians reconsidered the entire evolution of events and succeeded in changing public attitudes. The realists of the nineteen-thirties and forties had never looked on the war as a struggle against genocide at the time, and their heirs in the nineteen-nineties were not going to respond to genocide in their own time any differently. The realists were going to observe with perfect accuracy that massacres in the Balkans or anywhere else threatened the fundamental interests of not one of the great powers. Massacres were not going to knock over the giant chessboard of world power. What did worry the realist thinkers was that a NATO military intervention in the Balkans might upset Western relations with Russia. Intervention, not massacre, posed the danger, from the point of view of great power relations. Realism was non-interventionism in the nineteen-nineties.

The argument for intervention in the Balkans was going to have to come from some other zone of opinion, then—from the foreign policy "idealists," who put matters of conscience at the heart of their thinking. But who were these conscience-driven people going to be? The leaders of the Catholic Church? The Church turned out to have interests in the Balkans, and they were those of the Croatian Catholics. (Between the Yugoslav civil war and the massacres in Central Africa, the nineteen-nineties proved to be another less than splendid decade for Catholicism in the matter of genocide.) The political instinct of the Protestant churches leaned toward pacifism.

Would the idealist call for a Balkan intervention come from the political left, instead—from the parties and the movements that pictured themselves as the voice of the oppressed? But there were multiple lefts. There was an old-fashioned and even reactionary left (to call it that), which still felt a residual loyalty to the Soviet Union and therefore to Soviet Communism's child and heir, the Russian republic. Sympathy for Russia counted for quite a lot in portions of the Western European left—and leftism, from that perspective, meant a tender concern for Russia's national interests. This kind of thinking counted for something even in the United States, where the *Nation* published an amazing series of anguished editorials about the need not to upset the Russians and especially the nationalists among them, therefore the need to stay out of the Balkans.

Then again, there was also a realpolitik left, which was not in the slightest inclined to idealism in foreign policy. François Mitterrand, the president of France, realpolitik's master of masters, made an art of signaling his solidarity with the oppressed and the victimized while craftily defending a weirdly nineteenth-century vision of French national interests in the Balkans and in Central Africa alike. (It did mean something that Mitterrand, the Socialist, turned out to have been an old Vichy official in an earlier life.) The realpolitik left-wingers in Europe, just like the realpolitik liberals in the first years of the Clinton administration, were hardly going to press for forceful interventions in the name of something as vaporous as human rights.

In Europe, if any large group of people was going to make such an argument, these people would have to be the veterans of the student uprisings circa 1968—the people who, at age eighteen or twenty or twenty-five, had imagined that they were building a new civilization in Europe. Those people, in looking at the Balkans in the nineteen-nineties, were guaranteed to give at least a few thoughts to matters of genocide, to questions of resistance and non-resistance—the issues that, in their youth, had brought them to the left-wing barricades. A hatred of genocide was these people's oldest and deepest idea, together with the worried conviction that Nazism was capable of reappearing under new disguises.

But even if the old '68ers (and everyone among the younger generation who identified with the traditions of 1968) did give some thought to massacres in the Balkans, how were they possibly going to make a case for an intervention that would actually intervene? Here was a quandary. The '68ers were of two minds on military questions, divided into the warring attitudes that you could have seen in the *Die Zeit* and *Telos* debate back in 1986. In France the question of intervention was decided fairly quickly and easily among the intellectuals, and this was fairly predictable. The "former left" had long ago ascended into powerful positions in the French press and on radio, and throughout the later Mitterrand years those people pushed for the principles that had been laid out originally by the New Philosophers, years before: antitotalitarianism, humanitarian action, forceful means.

The "former left" had some French successes, too, in a painfully delayed version. Many phantoms haunted France's political imagination, all of which conspired against a powerful French intervention—the left-wing traditions of Mitterrand's cagey Socialists and the Russophile Communists; the sophisticated traditions of "realism" at the Quai d'Orsay; the historic reliance on a balance of power and on the Serbo-French alliance of ages past; the popular belief in an ancient Francophone mission to struggle against the historic enemy, the Anglophones. Yet once Mitterrand was out of office, and Jacques Chirac, the conservative, was president, the arguments of the "former left" and their fellow-thinkers began to exert a little more influence. The French government, for all its stammerings and duplicities, became the first of the Western powers to play any kind of forceful role in the Balkans. Quite a few French soldiers were killed, too (a fact that is always forgotten by Americans who love to sneer at the French). In this way the French opened the door to a more forceful involvement by the timorous Clinton administration.

But what could be expected of the '68ers and their heirs and followers in Germany? The Greens, above all—what could possibly be anticipated from them? Apart from Cohn-Bendit and a handful of other people, the Greens still insisted on interpreting anti-Nazism to mean anti-imperialism in the left-wing style. Didn't American hegemony pose a terrible danger to Europe and to the world, perhaps the greatest danger of all? A laughable question, you might observe, given the Balkan massacres. But the Greens had been asking that question all their lives, and repetition made it anything but laughable. The United States had committed crimes in the past. How could it not be doing the same in the present?

In their pacifist hearts, the Greens had to ask: what about the moral dangers of using any force at all? They wondered about the legacies of Hitler. In the nineteen-forties Hitler had sent German armies into the Balkans and had fought the Serbs. Now the advocates of war wanted to send German armies into the Balkans and fight the Serbs. Why would fighting the Serbs be, this time, anti-Hitlerian? Thus did ten thousand Lilliputian arguments swarm across the terrain, explaining why NATO was a monstrosity and nothing could be done about the Balkans, and life is tragic, and what about the dangers of nuclear energy?

The Greens needed to tear off their veil of ideology. And here was Joschka Fischer's achievement. Even as late as 1994, Fischer could never have imagined dispatching German soldiers to places where Hitler had dispatched German soldiers. But then, with the news from Srebrenica, he finally understood that anti-Nazism in its traditional Green version was going to end as no anti-Nazism at all. "I learned not only 'No more war' but also 'No more Auschwitz.'" For there, at Srebrenica (and at Omarska and other places), was Auschwitz, not just in the figurative sense that Glucksmann liked to bandy about but with greater and grisly exactitude, down to the "selection" by the master ethnic group of its victims. So Fischer made his choice, and Glucksmann's three principles—antitotalitarianism, humanitarian action, NATO—finally became Fischer's principles, too.

Only, how to bring along his fellow Greens? The governments of the United States, Britain, and France were not going to clarify the issue on behalf of Europe's pacifists. The Western powers seemed to have sunk comfortably enough into their swamp of make-believe action and their meaningless threats—their clever compromise between "idealist" antitotalitarianism and "realist" nonintervention. The Serbian nationalists alone could force the issue. And on that one point, the government of Slobodan Milosevic proved to be splendidly reliable.

In late 1998 and early 1999, Milosevic's military and paramilitary forces began to clear the ethnic Albanians from the whole of Kosovo. The new government in Germany was just then settling into power—the Red-Green coalition with its regiments of ex–New Leftists, now converted into Social Democratic and Green politicians. The emblem of those '68ers was Fischer himself, the new foreign minister, far more than Schröder—Fischer the notorious Frankfurt militant, the streetfighter outraged by Ulrike Meinhof's death, the Green anti-militarist in his anti-bourgeois blue jeans. And so, on top of the ten thousand Lilliputian arguments against taking any kind of forceful action in the Balkans came ten thousand further arguments, directed against anyone who had participated in the New Left of long ago—low, personal arguments, the arguments that invariably descend on anyone who displays the mental alertness to change his mind now and then.

Fischer and his advisers and co-thinkers among the Greens must have gritted their teeth when they contemplated those arguments. They had to have told themselves: if we do what seems to be necessary in order to prevent a giant catastrophe; if we endorse a NATO air campaign against the Serbian nationalists; if we, the Greens and '68ers and old-time New Leftists, come out for real intervention instead of fake intervention; if we approve a German participation in the NATO action—won't we be accused of inconsistency? Fischer surely had to tell himself: if I come out forcibly against Nazism in its current guise, which happens to be Serbian racism, won't I be accused of lack of character? If I stick to what have always been my principles, which are to oppose Nazism in all its forms, won't I be accused of betraying my principles?

And so it was. The foreign minister endorsed the intervention. Sundry institutions of the German government signalled their legal approval. Germany, which had failed to resist Nazism, resisted Nazism. Feebly, you may say. Even so, German soldiers departed German soil for the purpose of saving someone else's life. Something new under the sun! And Germany's foreign minister was, of course, accused of having been a brute and a man without principles, and the accusations spread around the world, until even the *New York Times* was fretting over the man's moral character. Fischer's friend and old-time roommate was accused of pedophilia, and those accusations, too, made their way around the yellow press of France and England and Italy. The world of Joschka Fischer was presented as a running scandal, and his enemies in the Bundestag congratulated themselves on their maturity and statesmanship in standing up to say of Germany's foreign minister, "This man can no longer represent us to the world." Fischer: A maneuverer without scruples. A thug, a cynic, a man with a dark past.

The Kosovo War has sometimes been called the Liberals' War, because it was the liberal idealists, more than the conservative realists, who were keen on intervention. But I am not the first to point out that NATO's intervention could just as easily be described as the '68ers' War. That was true of the European allies, anyway. The French participation was owed in large part to the circle of "former leftists," the intellectuals. The German participation could not have occurred without Fischer and his comrades. The first permanent UN administrator in Kosovo, after the Serbian military withdrew, turned out to be Dr. Kouchner, Glucksmann's hero. Kouchner's team in Pristina included a German '68er, Tom Koenigs, who had been Fischer's chief of staff for a while, and Dan Everts, a Dutch anarchist from the nineteen-sixties (or, to use the Dutch New Left terminology, a Provo), who, back in May 1968, had rushed in his

Citroën from the Netherlands to Paris to lend his support to the revolutionary students.

Those three men, Kouchner, Koenigs, and Everts, were, in Kouchner's phrase, the "hard core of veterans of May '68" in Kosovo. But they were scarcely the only such people. The UN official who preceded Kouchner in Kosovo in order to set up the UN headquarters was Sergio Vieira de Mello, a Brazilian diplomat who, back in 1968, was expelled from France for his radical activities. The Czech official who, in 1998, signed the treaty that brought the Czech Republic into NATO and therefore into the war was Jan Kavan—a man famous for his radicalism in the Prague Spring of 1968. The NATO diplomat in Kosovo for a while was Jiri Dienstbier, another Czech '68er. NATO's secretary-general during the war was Javier Solana, a '68er from the Socialist Workers Party of Spain. One of the NATO commanders who served under Dr. Kouchner's UN administration in Kosovo was a German general named Klaus Reinhardt, who had been a radical protester in 1968 before going on to pursue a military career. The '68ers' International that Cohn-Bendit had tried to assemble in an imaginary version back in the nineteen-eighties—here it was, in the flesh. It was the UN team. It was NATO. An irony, you might think. But this was not an irony.

At the height of the Fischer affair in 2001, Serge July, the editor of the Paris *Libération*, wrote an editorial called "On Your Knees!" accusing Fischer's and Cohn-Bendit's enemies of engaging in a reactionary campaign not just against two individuals but against something larger—against a vast range of reforms in society and in the social conscience that had come out of the uprisings of 1968. The attacks on Fischer and Cohn-Bendit, as July pictured them, were a prosecution by smear of whole portions of the population—against an enormous mass of people who, in their student days, had brought about those many reforms. That was why *Libération* settled on the inspired phrase "the trial of the Generation of 1968." But if the Fischer affair was, in some sense, a generational trial, you would have to conclude that, from *Libération*'s point of view, everything turned out well enough, after a few weeks. That was certainly the case in France. The charges against Cohn-Bendit were made, and were rebutted, and evaporated. In France, the animus against Fischer never congealed into anything worrisome or even politically awkward.

And in Germany? I followed an English-language Web edition of the *Frankfurter Allgemeine Zeitung* during the controversy, and I noticed that in Frankfurt, too, the affair was looked at precisely as Serge July had defined it in Paris—as an accusation against a generation. Naturally the scandal counted for more in Germany than in France, given Fischer's place in the government, and given those terrible photographs. Yet the polls never did tip against him. At one point Fischer was declared to have the support of 72 percent of the polling respondents, an astounding statistic for a man under daily assault in the press and in the Bundestag.

Even Fischer's keenest enemies eventually had to bow before that kind of public reaction. In April 2001, the prosecutor in the Klein trial, having allowed the foreign minister to twist slowly, slowly in the wind, at last dropped the perjury charge. This brought the Fischer affair to an end in a legal sense. But the affair had, by then, already dribbled to a close in the popular imagination. The true finale, in the judgment of the *Frankfurter Allgemeine*, came in late March, ten weeks after the affair had begun, when the results of one other poll came in, quite a fascinating poll precisely because its subject went beyond Fischer himself. The subject in this instance was the generation of 1968. The radicals of that period—were they mainly "interested in power"? Or were they "idealists"? Such was the question to the German public. The respondents stroked their chins. And a majority (whose exact size was left unreported) answered: "Idealists."

It is true that "interested in power" versus "idealism," taken as an either/or proposition, made for a pretty crude way of judging the motivating sentiment of vast crowds of people. You could have shrugged off such a poll easily enough. What did it mean, anyway, this word "idealism," outside of a specific setting such as foreign policy, where the word has a kind of technical meaning, connoting a particular group of values? Surely everyone understands by now that idealism has always been Satan's slogan, the father of fanaticism, the mother of self-righteousness, a license for crime. And is it always wrong to be interested in power? No one could have believed that Joschka Fischer had ever been indifferent to power. There had to be more to his politician's career than a love of meetings. The man was obviously a major conniver. And yet that naïve little poll in the *Frankfurter Allgemeine* surely offered an expressive commentary on modern life and its foreground from a few decades ago, not just in Germany.

We can be pretty confident that, thanks to the Fischer affair, no one among the respondents to that poll needed to be reminded of the realities of New Leftism and its history from a quarter of a century before. The movement's ugliest traits had been on public display for months. Nor did anyone need to be reminded of the politician's machinations that had brought Fischer to his lofty station, nor of the policies that he had adopted once in power. Shady associates and violent acts years ago, NATO bombings in 1999: everyone knew everything. Those were the givens in that poll. And given the givens, the real meaning lurking beneath that naïve-looking question was, I think, a little less naïve than might have seemed to be the case.

The real meaning, I propose, was this: knowing what everyone knew about the New Left of long ago, knowing the consequences of the New Left's many rebellions, knowing the characteristics and consequences of those alternative kindergartens and everything else, knowing the career that Fischer had followed, knowing the role that Fischer had played in 1998 and 1999 in the European crisis over the Balkans—knowing all that, did it make sense (Question One) to speak of a basically admirable quality in the New Left, a quality that could be branded with the approving honorific "idealism"? Did modern society seem (Question Two) better off in the wake of those many New Left rebellions? Did Nazism and its constituent traits and habits seem (Question Three) to have suffered a blow? Did a personal background in the New Left seem (Question Four) to indicate an attractive feature in someone's character today, lo these many years later?

Those were the real issues, the four questions, hiding beneath the pollsters' dopey-looking query about idealism and power. The answers, among a majority of the respondents, were plainly yes, yes, yes, and yes. In spite of everything, four yeses, and in a conservative newspaper, too: a sign of political wisdom in the heart of Europe, I think—though I grant that some people, the not-majority among those respondents, perhaps quite a hefty not-majority, answered those questions differently. And so *la lotta continua*, as we used to say.

CHAPTER TWO:
THE FISCHER AFFAIR CROSSES THE OCEAN

I.

The Fischer affair was strictly a Western European event from the moment that *Stern* magazine published the set of scandalous photographs in January 2001 until the controversy faded from German and French politics a few months later. The one *New York Times* editorial on the affair did raise the possibility that, with another twist of the screw—a new horrendous photograph or a dreadful confession by yet another of Fischer's wild-eyed comrades from long ago—the foreign minister's problems might arouse serious worries in the United States. But nothing of the sort came up, and the Fischer Affair failed to catch hold in the United States. That was before September 11, though—before the advent of a new sort of terrorist attack, something on a scale that had never even been imagined by the Red Army Fraction or the Revolutionary Cells in Germany, or by the Red Brigades and the other groups in Italy, or by anyone else among the guerrillas of the European ultraleft, not to mention the ultraright.

A reasonable person who followed the news from Europe in the first weeks after the September 11 attacks might have concluded that, in the field of transatlantic relations, all was well, and the friendships of ere had shown themselves to be strong and eternal. In Western Europe, the instant response to September 11 was an outpouring of sympathy and, if I don't exaggerate, even of love—a massive, spontaneous reaction, warm, emotional, and instinctive. Hundreds of thousands of people swarmed into the streets of Berlin to express their heartfelt support for the Americans in their moment of suffering. The city of Hamburg took out full-page ads in the *New York Times* conveying municipal condolences—Hamburg, where Muhammad Atta and his comrades had attended university and plotted the attacks, and where other people were aghast to learn what their own upstanding city had somehow helped to produce.

It is true that, in Western Europe, a number of writers and intellectuals rushed to their computers to compose essays accusing America of having brought these attacks upon herself: a commonplace of all modern political theory. (Massacres? Let us not be so naïve as to presume the innocence of the victims . . .) Parisian salons were full of babble. The *London Review of Books* outdid itself. And these responses did have a meaning. In huge swathes of the Muslim world, the September 11 attacks aroused instantly a wave of hatred for Israel and the Jews, in the belief, held by many millions of people, that Israel's Mossad, in close contact with the Jews of New York, had organized the assault. But many people also maintained that September 11 was a plot by the CIA, and this particular conspiracy theory came to be quite popular in Western Europe, too, after a while. Books about September 11 as a sinister American plot reached the bestseller lists in France and Germany alike. André Glucksmann, never shy to criticize the Germans, pointed out that, according to the polls, nearly a third of the

German population attributed the attack to the CIA—a sensational statistic. A great many Europeans eventually persuaded themselves that America under George W. Bush was no longer a democracy. The grumblings of Europe's anti-American intellectuals in the immediate wake of the attack were harbingers, then—early signs of what vast numbers of people would come to believe, all over the world.

Still, those grumblings aside, the principal reaction in Europe during the first days after the attack was unmistakably friendly and warm—a feeling of genuine solidarity with the United States. Only, what did this mean, solidarity, practically speaking? There was no obvious definition, at the time. The political leaders were going to have to thrash out a meaning of their own, in discussions among themselves. The president of the United States might have played a role here. But the president had no idea what to do. His administration was already contemptuous of the Western Europeans simply on ideological grounds, and seemed to feel no particular desire for European solidarity. Besides, even if the American president had wanted to address the many European publics and ask for their support, he wouldn't have known how to begin. Bush the Younger's ability to communicate with foreign populations was less impressive even than his father's, as was universally acknowledged—an embarrassment for America, yes, but nothing new or unexpected. The question of how to define Europe's solidarity with the United States was going to be left to the European leaders, then—to the members of NATO, above all. NATO's European members accepted the challenge. Right away they invoked Article Five of the NATO charter—a historic action, never undertaken in the past. Article Five is a sort of Three-Musketeer clause, mandating a policy of "All for one, and one for all" among the member states of NATO. This meant, under the circumstances, that NATO chose to look on the terrorist attack as an act of war and pledged to support or participate in America's military riposte. To be sure, something more than solidarity, a canny calculation, figured in this European response.

The Europeans did have their worries, the Western Europeans, especially—about terrorists, certainly, but also about the Bush administration. I think that, in the United States, not too many people understood these Western European worries or their origins or their depth (just as, by the way, a good many people in Western Europe never did appreciate how shocking were the September 11 attacks to most Americans). But nothing was mysterious, if you give the European situation any thought. During the previous dozen years, the Euro-peans had been through a full-scale revolution in their continent's eastern half—a somewhat unusual revolution, perhaps, as revolutions go: a "low-key" event, in Fischer's phrase (from a speech at Princeton University in the United States, a couple of years later), "with no gunsmoke or barricades," except in the Balkans, and "with no suppression or dictatorship." Still, the east bloc revolution was a gigantic affair. And, like all revolutions, it gave birth to gigantic dreams of a better society—utopian dreams really, though in harmony with the low key the utopian dreams denied being utopian dreams. And what sort of future did

Europe's post-1989 dreamers picture, in their revolutionary imaginings?

The utopian dreamers pictured themselves constructing, on the ruins of the cold war, a society different from every Europe of the past. They pictured a just and orderly new democracy, stripped of every stupid nationalism and prejudice of the past. They pictured a society without borders, resting on a compromise between capitalism and socialism—a society with socialism's security and modern capitalism's friskiness and novelty. They pictured a political structure loosely resembling the United States—a new society in which the name "Europe," like the name "America," was going to connote something more than a geographical zone: a set of large and universally accepted aspirations about peace, economics, justice, and the value of human life. Or maybe "Europe" was going to connote something grander yet, beyond anything that America had yet achieved or even contemplated—a society dedicated to cultural refinement and moral behavior on a global scale, a society dedicated to a notion of civilization as a project of high culture, dedicated to art, to cuisine, to the savoir faire of daily life, to generosity, sexiness, leisure, tolerance, and education.

Those were the utopian fancies, and the 1989 revolutions made those fancies seem viable, too, not just because the Soviet Union had begun to crumble away but because radical alternatives of several other kinds were likewise crumbling in plain view. A number of Trotskyists, anarchosyndicalists, councilists, and other people with far-left ideas in the antique style played honorable and distinguished roles in the 1989 revolutions.

But, once the Communists were overthrown, antique leftism failed to thrive, except in France—and, even in France, the Trotskyists never amounted to anything (except in their ability to divide the left-wing electorate and bring about conservative victories at the polls).

Radical alternatives on the far right, the fantasies of the ethnic populists and ethnic haters, fared a lot better in the years after 1989. In Serbia, the ethnic populists and haters ended up in power and scored wonderful successes, by their lights—which led, to be sure, to the Balkan Wars and the mass graves. It became easy to imagine that, in other parts of Europe, too, the radical populists and the ethnic haters might have their day, and the ideal of a modern, cosmopolitan Europe might come crashing down in defeat all over the continent, and Europe might erupt into ethnic warfare and stupid hatreds. An old story. And yet, outside of the Balkans, the old story did not renew itself. The future seemed to belong to liberal democracy, in one version or another. This was hard to believe, but the months passed, and the years, and it became easier to believe. And the liberal triumphs, combined with the failure of sundry radical alternatives on the extreme left and the extreme right, did seem to suggest that, for the first time in European history, the possibility of assembling a fairly broad and democratic political consensus might, in fact, exist—a low-key consensus of the not-too-radical.

The consensus duly assembled. It affirmed the dull-sounding principles of a "normal" society and "Europe." And a great many utopians-who-denied-being-utopians went to work to bring those low-key principles to life.

This was not entirely a new project. The conservatives of France and Germany and other countries had launched a campaign in the nineteen-fifties to build a common market in Western Europe, based on the most prosaic of industrial agreements about coal and steel, and with the most modest of goals—namely, to inhibit any further German impulse to conquer the world. The conservative project had thrived. The common market grew larger. After 1989, though, the project took on dimensions and energies that were no longer merely conservative. In 1992, at Maastricht in the Netherlands, serious negotiations got underway to endow the prosaic old agreements with new political institutions and many more economic aspects, and to spread those agreements to still more distant lands—an achievement that required everyone to leap deftly across the broadest of cultural chasms. The Spanish representatives at Maastricht were said to practice a "flamenco" approach to negotiation, which led them to enter the room, make their demands, stamp their heels, spin about, and leave. Dour technocrats from Northern Europe gaped in astonishment. And yet, the negotiations yielded results, and the project continued to thrive, and the new successes did set off a utopian jitter or two, here and there among the European political class.

The Europe that had committed suicide in its world wars, the Europe that had laid waste to vast portions of the globe, the Europe that had given rise to one demonic and sinister doctrine after another, the Europe that had clung to existence only thanks to military invasion and occupation by armies from the United States and its allies, the Europe that was genocidal and monstrous—

this Europe did not represent the only possible alternative for modern life. A better Europe was already visible, not just in a few corners of the continent. An admirable Europe. A magnificent Europe. A Europe that could claim to be the moral leader of the world. Those were the ideas. In the glow of those thrilling new aspirations, a thousand further negotiations got underway—always in the tranquil, dull style that had become de rigeur. And who were those dull and hard-working negotiators? The disciplined politicians, the bureaucrats and flamenco heel-stampers who moved on from Maastricht to Strasbourg and finally to Brussels to organize the new European Parliament—these people came in many varieties. And among them figured a number of stalwarts from the student left of many years before. These were people who had begun to see in the new institutions of the European Union the realization of some very old left-wing dreams. Nor was this a delusion.

The concepts of the new "Europe" took inspiration from Kant and the philosophers of the eighteenth-century Enlightenment, and from the American Founding Fathers. But these ideas traced back to left-wing origins, as well—to the nineteenth-century anarchists and socialists, who, in versions that were super-dreamy or merely hyper-imaginative, used to picture a workers' society without national borders, a society in which people and ideas and goods could flow about fluidly from place to place, according to natural needs and rational decisions: a society of social guarantees and democratic or libertarian political structures. The founding convention of the modern Socialist International, in Paris in 1889, already sketched out a few practical proposals that were intended to produce, in time, just such a cosmopolitan outcome. The anarchists of those times offered versions of their own. Most of the old-fashioned proletarian doctrines of the nineteenth-century revolutionary left may have evaporated during the course of the 1989 revolutions, but this one element in the classic left-wing imagination—the vision of a borderless, federal, peaceful, technocratic Europe—turned out to be solid and lasting. People with backgrounds in the revolutionary left could recognize some of their own principles in the European project. And the left-wing stalwarts duly threw themselves into the planning and negotiations, in the belief that now, finally, they had stumbled on a way to realize their own most fondly held ideas in a new and improved version, stripped of the grotesque errors of the left-wing past.

Cohn-Bendit had always known how to make himself the symbol of rebellion, and now he made himself a symbol of the new "Europe," as well. A provision in the electoral law of the European Union allowed politicians to run for a seat in the new European parliament from any district of their choosing. Cohn-Bendit, from his home in Frankfurt, chose to run for election as a Green from— why not?—France. He was elected, of course. Among French voters, the opportunity to cast a ballot for the spunky radical who had been shamefully barred from France on a legal technicality dating from 1968—this opportunity was irresistible. "Vengeance!—vote for Cohn-Bendit!" was the unspoken slogan. "We are all German Jews!" There are multinational corporations, but Cohn-Bendit was a multinational personality, and he took his place in parliament. Then he presented himself for a still higher office, this time as president of the parliament's pan-European Green caucus.

He won that election, too. A few years later he ran from Germany and was elected to the European Parliament yet again: a man with a continental constituency. Danny the Green was Mr. Europe, now. Bernard Kouchner, the humanitarian doctor, likewise presented his candidacy for the European Parliament. Kouchner ran in alliance with the faction in France that was called (by its enemies) the "American left," meaning, the anti-doctrinaire wing of the French Socialist Party, Michel Rocard's faction—the Socialists who were thought to resemble America's liberal Democrats. The anti-doctrinaire Socialists looked on Dr. Kouchner as a prestigious figure and happily inscribed his name on their parliamentary list. Kouchner, too, was elected. And the new parliament took on a very odd shape, politically speaking—a parliament containing a right and a left and national factions of every sort, assembling in a strangely cheerful mood.

Cohn-Bendit threw a fiftieth birthday party for himself at the parliament's seat in Brussels and managed to induce an amiable group of tolerant French conservatives to intone "The Internationale" in his honor. "No more tradition's chains shall bind us, / No more by custom be enthralled!" On the topic of intervention in the Balkans, Cohn-Bendit and the other left-wing interventionists found themselves collaborating in the parliament with Otto von Hapsburg, eighty-nine years old, the most reactionary of reactionaries (as befitted a Hapsburg)—who nonetheless favored the interventionist proposal.

Alliances of convenience or principle of this sort did begin to form in the corridors at Brussels. This was amazing. The socialists and anarchists of the nineteenth century had pictured many extravagant vistas in their futuristic utopias, but not in their wildest dreams did those revolutionaries of long ago ever imagine an anarchist comrade of theirs such as Cohn-Bendit huddling in parliamentary alliance with someone named Otto von Hapsburg. (The anarchists of long ago had other plans for the Hapsburgs.) (And the Hapsburgs had other plans for the anarchists.) Yes, the sun was smiling on a new Europe. So the delegates gathered, and caucused, and conspired. And, at those gatherings, the cosmopolitan reformed anarchists, the humbled pragmatic aristocrats, the humanitarian doctors, the anti-dogmatic socialists, the dogmatic socialists, the Christian Democrats, the Gaullists, the serenading conservatives, the unscrupulous opportunists and quite a few other people rolled up their sleeves and, in a hearty can-do spirit, went about trying to clear away the various obstacles that stood in the way of a unified Europe.

This was a task of unimaginable complexity. Simply on issues of health policy—Dr. Kouchner's area of expertise—the challenges facing the new union were nearly infinite, bureaucratically speaking. The healthcare system in Britain (to cite one example) had fallen on hard times over the years, largely because the British, under Margaret Thatcher and the Tories, had elected to pay not quite enough for their health system. The healthcare system in France, on the other hand, had gone into rosy bloom, largely because the French, under Mitterrand

and the Socialists, had elected to spend vast sums. French hospitals were greatly superior to their British counterparts as a result, and sickly Britons flocked across the Channel to check into the opulent French hospitals and give themselves a better chance for a longer life. The French, in their generosity, could hardly refuse treatment to the pathetic stricken refugees from an oppressed and impoverished land like Britain. Yet somebody did have to pay the bills. Who was that going to be?

Who, precisely, was going to reimburse the French? Through what transnational mechanism? How quickly? By what sort of agreement? And if this was the brain-bending challenge facing two such wealthy and comparable societies as France and Britain, with their history of friendship and military alliance lasting nearly a century, imagine the regulatory challenges facing all the other countries of Europe, each of which presided over its own ancient system of healthcare and its own accustomed way of paying the bills, not to mention its own medical schools and system of credentials, and its own level of national wealth, and its own history of bitter national resentment against each of its neighbors. Every last detail of health policy nonetheless had to be brought into alignment throughout the new Europe—and thus with every single practical aspect of modern society, every last policy and procedure, every method of billing, licensing, code-making, and contract enforcement, not just between the old and relatively equal industrial powerhouses but between all fifteen of the early members of the new European Union, together with the ten additional members that finally won admittance in 2004, together with another handful who were impatiently biding their time on the waiting list—the rich, the poor, the fallen, the risen, the old democracies, the new democracies, and the not-really-democracies.

In each of those European nations, a large portion of the political class was obliged to take up the complicated labor of untangling these issues. And, as the work continued, the many people laboring on this enormous collective project began to generate the kind of spirit that was required by their own efforts. This was a spirit of cooperation and sweet reasonableness. In Europe, the consensual mood became, after a while, all-engrossing—a mood to swallow up the universe. This was a good thing, and, in any case, an obligatory thing. Every bureaucratic challenge facing the new Europe was resolvable, but only if there was a will to resolve, and this depended on working up a mood of mutual respect, patience, and civility.

The violence in the Balkans during the nineties might easily have broken up the consensual atmosphere, but this particular disaster was avoided. The argument in favor of intervening militarily in Bosnia and Kosovo was, in its origins, a moral argument—the kind of argument that Kouchner, Glucksmann, and other people, the '68ers, had been making for many years by then. Yet, after a while, the argument for intervention took on a further dimension, which was "European" and not just humanitarian—the argument that insisted on Europe's responsibility for policing itself, for giving muscle to the utopian idea. This was the argument that proved decisive. For what kind of Europe was the European Union going to be, if the union could simply stand by, watching massacres take place in its own neighborhood? So the intervention was approved, and the meaning of that decision seemed, by implication, immense. The democratic left was in power almost everywhere in the big countries of Western Europe: Schröder and Fischer in Germany, Blair in Britain, Massimo d'Alema in Italy. Chirac was a conservative, but, because of the peculiarities of the political system in France, the Socialists, too, were in power, "co-habiting," as the French say, with the Gaullist president, which meant that France, too, tilted somewhat to the left. It was the golden age of the moderate left. And, in the gleam of that golden age, the decision to intervene militarily in the Balkans seemed like one more step in Europe's progress. The decision seemed to suggest that the European idea of the good society was now going to become bigger and more ambitious than before—was going to project itself outward beyond the official borders of the new European Union, even by force of arms. At least, some people pictured the decision to intervene in that fashion—as a vast, muscular, and admirable expansion of the utopian non-utopia that had begun to flourish in the wake of the 1989 revolution.

It was true that "Europe" still needed to rely on American military power in the Balkans, exactly as in the European past. The United States Air Force won the Kosovo War. This was chastening to some of the Europeans—not to mention irritating to some of the Americans, who had always hoped that Europe's big, rich countries would rise to the occasion. The Euro-strategists might have given a bit more reflection to these difficult realities. But, at the time, the reliance on the

United States seemed simple enough. The golden age of Europe's moderate left was the age of Clinton, too, and Clinton loomed, in European eyes, as one more representative of the new consensus: a man who had militated against the Vietnam War in his student days, and, as president, had done his best to institute universal healthcare in the United States; a man who fended off the persecutions of America's sexual Neanderthals and right-wing zealots. A progressive, then. One of "us." Besides, Clinton's foreign policy, in the later years of his administration, fell into the hands of people with activist and idealist inclinations in the new European mode. Madeleine Albright, the secretary of state, was herself a European. Richard Holbrooke, at the United Nations, was a militant for human rights, not to mention a warm friend of Bernard Kouchner's. These people, the foreign policy team in Clinton's second administration, were the living proof that European social democracy and the liberal or at least the Clintonian wing of America's Democratic party had pretty much converged, and the transatlantic gap was not much of a gap, after all. The "American left" was all-European, for the moment.

And so, the champions of the new European idea felt they had good reason to look on the United States as a comradely force—felt they could look on America's benign military strength and aid as a fact of nature, like the wind and the tide, reliable and eternal, which required no tending or attention. Some of the champions of the new European idea may have stirred uncomfortably in their seats at the spectacle of the Americans winning the war—conscious of their own weakness. But these people seemed to recover from their dismay, and, swept aloft on their own enthusiasm for creating new institutions, dreamed of spreading the new doctrine of universal regulation and law beyond their own borders. They agitated in favor of the International Criminal Court. They promoted a worldwide agreement on greenhouse gas emissions, the Kyoto Protocols. Perhaps they were giddy from their successes. In any case, they never quite took seriously the possibility of an unfriendly response from the United States, and they plunged forward.

This was a mistake. America had gone through nothing like Europe's political evolution during the nineteen-nineties. There was not much of a spirit of nonutopian utopianism in America during the Clinton years—not much zeal to create something like universal healthcare (hence the failure of Clinton's health-care proposal), not much temptation to see in the NAFTA agreement with Mexico and Canada a step toward new kinds of political and economic cooperation in the Americas. The Kyoto Protocols enjoyed some American support, and likewise the International Criminal Court, but hardly anyone in the United States looked on these things as stages in the construction of a new society; and the support was tepid. In the United States, nationalist demagogues painted the protocols and the court as dangerous threats to America's prosperity and sovereignty. This was nonsense. The negotiations behind the protocols and the court had produced a few cautious clauses to protect the United States, and, if the protections were insufficient, there was always an opportunity to elaborate additional clauses. But nobody on the American left or among the liberals was strong enough to shout those demagogues down. What could be done on behalf of the protocols and the court, under those circumstances?

The only possibility in the United States was to play for time—to keep the issues under discussion, in the hope that America's left-of-center might become a little stronger, and might fight a little harder to educate the public on these very complicated issues. Meanwhile, every effort had to be made to prevent anyone on the American right from delivering a fatal blow to the new ideas, and to prevent anyone in Europe from taking umbrage at the United States. This was Clinton's policy, then. He dithered. Clinton was good at dithering. He dithered with aplomb, creativity, ease, and charm. Dithering was perhaps his greatest political gift. He and his administration treated the international court and the gas-emissions agreement with utmost respect, yet without agreeing even for a moment to submit the United States either to the court or to the protocols. Clinton was genuinely well liked everywhere in Europe, outside of Serbia, and not just because his policies tended to please European opinion. He worked at being liked. And, having accumulated some good will, he brought his talent for dithering to Europe, too, and this seemed admirable. Dithering was civilized. Dithering was, above all, collegial, and this was the crux of the matter. Europe could survive without a gas-emissions pact (for a while, anyway), but Europe could not survive ten minutes without a spirit of collegiality.

Clinton dithered relentlessly, too, without a single gaffe, blunder, tantrum, personal insult, or embarrassing phrase caught by a hidden microphone during his eight years at the White House—an unbroken run of American affability. He was friendliness incarnate. He was energetic. After the U.S. Air Force had driven the Serbian army and militia out of Kosovo, Clinton's plane touched down in Pristina, and the American president greeted Dr. Kouchner and General Reinhardt, NATO's German '68er. And (as Kouchner has described) Clinton set about at once, with the very few hours at his disposal, to court the Kosovo Albanians and their worst enemies, the Kosovo Serbs—and, in the space of hours, he made progress even at this most intractable of problems. Clinton was a genius. Madeleine Albright conducted monthly telephone seminars with the foreign ministers of Europe—group discussions in which Secretary Albright always took the leadership role while managing to convince her colleagues that she was attending to everyone's needs and opinions. In these ways, the golden age of the European moderate left was the Atlantic Alliance's golden age, as well. But the Clinton administration did not last forever.

George W. Bush's instincts leaned in a different direction. Bush plainly felt no commitment at all to upholding the consensual spirit of the European Union. Even during his election campaign against Al Gore, in 2000, Bush suggested that, if he became president, he would bring the American troops home from the Balkans. He made clear that, given his druthers in the nineteen-nineties, American troops would never have gone there in the first place. Bush did not want to solve Europe's crises. This was not welcome news in Europe. If Bush were ever to pull the American troops out of the Balkans, the civil war was bound to start up anew, and a shadow was going to fall across the entire European project. Everyone knew this—must have known this—except maybe Bush, given the limits of his foreign policy experience. He stated his views—they tumbled from his lips during one of his campaign television debates with Gore—and the yelps from Europe were audible at once. Bush backed down and promised to keep the American troops in the Balkans, after all.

But, once he took office, his instincts reasserted themselves. Dithering seemed to Bush a sign of moral laxity. He boasted of speaking his mind, and he did speak his mind. (This was his error.) He made clear that, under his presidency, the United States was simply not going to submit to the International Criminal Court, nor was the United States going to sign the Kyoto Protocols, nor proceed with any of several other international accords. And, once again, an alarm went up in Europe—not so much because of the court itself or the gas-emissions agreement (though the Kyoto Protocol certainly mattered to the German Greens) but because Bush's outright rejection of these things seemed to threaten the European Union's founding principle, namely, the collegial spirit. Even in matters of personal style, Bush seemed out of step with Europe's new cosmopolitan civility. He appeared to be someone without education, without the ability to express himself, without a command of foreign languages (except for a few words of Spanish) or even his own language. He was unable to walk across a room in the natural and easy way of a cultivated person.

From a European viewpoint, Boris Yeltsin, back in the nineteen-nineties, used to look like a creature from

115

another planet, with his red-tippled nose and tottering alcoholic gait and his taste for shocking gestures; and George W. Bush, with his violently swinging arms and his habit of sneering, looked equally strange. Yeltsin and Bush: the two barbarians of the modern era, the strangers from the eastern and western extremes of the European world, the savages seated at the bourgeois table, one with too much liquor in front of him, the other with not enough. No, this was not a good impression for America's leader to make, and the bad impression touched on matters of deep importance. Vigorous displays of cosmopolitan sophistication had become the lingua franca of European politics. Cosmopolitan sophistication signified peaceful intentions, which each leader from each country expressed to each of his counterparts in the other countries and to each of the many European publics. Bush's violent shoulder motions and his habit of strutting emphasized, instead, his provincial singularities, and seemed to do so with an aggressive sense of purpose. Gotta problem with Texas? he appeared to be saying.

The European leaders did have a problem with Texas. The abolition of capital punishment was one of the great achievements of modern Europe, after a struggle lasting more than a century and a half, and the achievement symbolized the larger commitment to creating a continent of peace. Texas, on the other hand, was the death-penalty capital of the Western world. Worse, this barbaric custom in Texas, the cult of violence, was accompanied by a pious invocation of Christianity; and this, in a great many European eyes, was doubly alarming. The death penalty was scary, from a European point of view, but Christianity was terrifying. In the history of Europe, insistent Christianity had proved to be, over and again, a guarantor of violence. Christianity in politics meant the fascism of Franco. To be sure, in Spain, Franco's doctrines had pretty much disappeared. But who was Milosevic, in Serbia? Franco fought the Spanish Civil War of the nineteen-thirties in the name of the medieval Catholic Crusades, and Milosevic fought the Balkan Wars of the nineteen-nineties in the name of the medieval Orthodox Crusades. The past was not entirely past, in Europe. It was true that, in Poland and in other countries, Catholicism in politics had come to mean something much more liberal and democratic—the theme of one of the crucial documents of the east bloc dissident movement, Michnik's *The Church and the Left*, back in 1977. Lutheranism helped overthrow Communism in East Germany. And yet a lot of people in Europe continued to look on Christianity in politics with genuine fear, and these people, when they contemplated Bush's displays of Christian piety, were bound to have their worries. The particular style of his fervor was troubling all by itself. The Europeans had to wonder, wasn't there a touch of fundamentalism, which is to say, superstitious nonsense, in Bush's Christianity?

Did the president of the United States accept the theory of evolution? The Earth's rotation around the Sun? The theory of gravity? The answers to these questions were not entirely obvious. This was triply worrying. For what would happen if, in Europe, other political leaders began to imitate America's president and his folkloric habits, and the prime minister of this or that

117

country began to prance about in lederhosen, and the leader of some other country began to preach about national superiority, and provincial customs and ancient superstitions blossomed everywhere on the continent, and everyone took to snarling, the way Bush's face often seemed to do, and rational thought was cast to the winds? What would happen if, inspired by Milosevic and the Crusaders of the Balkans, still more Christian militants drew their swords and summoned the spirit of still more bloody and bigoted campaigns?

So the political class in Europe eyed Bush very carefully, wondering if he was merely a conservative nationalist like Chirac, except in a rustic, boorish, uneducated, and off-putting version; or, alternatively, was he a true right-wing populist like Jean-Marie Le Pen or Jörg Haider in Austria—a genuine menace to civilization. The Bush administration seemed unaware of these fears, therefore had no way to reassure people that, no, Bush was not a barbarian, nor a superstitious idiot, nor an enemy of civilization. Colin Powell, the new secretary of state, went on cultivating friendly relations with his European colleagues in a proper diplomatic tone, and this was wonderfully reassuring. Powell, the man from the Bronx, turned out to be a natural cosmopolitan. His every statement and gesture radiated civilization. But no one could be sure how much power or influence Secretary Powell exerted in the Bush administration. And the European leaders began to suspect that their beloved new creation, the European Union, this grand project to redeem Western civilization, might not be able to rely on America anymore—began to suspect that

Europe was generating one set of principles (sophisticated, cultivated, cosmopolitan, tolerant), and America was generating another (rude, ignorant, parochial, violent, and superstitious). America might turn out to be Europe's opponent instead of its guarantor. A fog of European anxiety rolled across the Atlantic during the first months of the Bush administration, and the fog consisted of these sundry fears, the reasonable and the utterly fantastical alike. And, through this fog, the European leaders gazed across the ocean at the attacks of September 11 and fell prey at once to their own worries—not about jihadi terrorists but about the European Union and its ability to survive the peremptory tone and cultural limitations of the Bush administration.

II.

In Berlin, the very first response to the attacks in the chancellery (as I have reliably heard) was to fret about Powell's standing in Washington—to fear that, if the White House crazies succeeded in elbowing Powell aside, the habit of taking European considerations into account might disappear entirely from American policy. The Germans were terrified of that possibility. They wanted to do everything they could to prevent anything of the sort from taking place. That was one reason to invoke NATO's Article Five—to pledge support to the United States in the hope of bolstering the political strength of the more worldly and sophisticated people within the Bush administration. Some of the Greens reasoned precisely along those lines. The Bush administration waited a few weeks before announcing the invasion of Afghanistan, and this delay was taken as a sign of coolheaded rationality—the very thing that so many Europeans were hoping to see, in Washington. A non-cowboy hesitation. Then the invasion was announced, and Schröder called for everyone in his Red-Green coalition to support NATO and the proposed action.

By that time the Greens held forty-seven seats in the Bundestag. A full thirty-nine of those Green representatives lined up at once with Schröder and his proposal. Schröder put the squeeze on the remaining eight, and four of them came around, which meant that, within the Bundestag's Green delegation, a mere four recalcitrants, out of forty-seven, finally voted against Germany's participation in the war. A minuscule number. The Greens assembled at a party convention in the town of Rostock a few days after the vote, and most of the delegates to the convention chose to adopt a slightly nuanced but unmistakably pro-war resolution—a party statement that allowed them not to endorse the war but, instead, to "accept" it. (An attractive nuance, in my view. For who in his right mind could ever truly endorse a war?) Such was the intellectual growth of the Greens since their pacifist days—a big step, really.

Fischer and his supporters were solidly in control of their own party by then. Nobody assaulted the foreign minister with a bag of red paint. And yet, there was less to these developments than met the eye. The crafty Green politicians, some of them, convinced themselves that, by voting to "accept" the war, they were going to win points in Washington, and were going to be able, in time, to use these points to revisit the question of the Kyoto Protocols. The Green politicians invoked this argument to convince themselves to accept the war. But this merely demonstrated that, in the wake of September 11, the Green politicians were still obsessing about their own customary issues: about gas emissions and about Europe. The reality in far-away Afghanistan, the nature of the Taliban regime, the meaning of revolutionary Islamism in Afghanistan and of Al Qaeda and its goals and methods— these were the central questions of the war. But the Greens did not address these questions, and neither did Schröder and the Social Democrats.

And so, the Bundestag voted in favor of German participation, but the vote did not express any large new German understanding of revolutionary Islamism, neither among the political elite nor among the ordinary public. A German TV network polled the rank-and-file Green voters and discovered that a full 42 percent of those people remained adamantly opposed to Germany's participation in the war—a big bloc of outright pacifists, indifferent to the pro-war views of their party's leading politicians and Bundestag representatives. An eagerness to take part in the Afghanistan War simply did not exist in Germany. The German participation ended up rather modest, as a result. Schröder offered to send medical units to Afghanistan, and some reconnaissance vehicles, and the appropriate backup personnel—but no more than a hundred or so combat soldiers.

Such was the meaning of NATO's Article Five, in Germany's interpretation. Once the invasion had turned out to be a success, the Germans sent more troops, and this proved to be helpful. Still, Germany's role was hardly comparable to Germany's share of the world's wealth. Nor were the Germans, in their reluctance to get involved, noticeably different from a lot of other people in Western Europe. The French voted to participate in the invasion, but sent no more than a few hundred combat soldiers to Afghanistan. In France's case, too, once the initial dangers had lessened, additional soldiers arrived, and the French took on more responsibilities. But France's effort was never huge. In these ways, the invasion of Afghanistan ended up being pretty much an English-speaking affair—American, British, Canadian, and Australian, in alliance with the Afghan rebels of the Northern Alliance and with some of Afghanistan's neighbors, and a smattering of help from other wealthy countries around the world. And this reality hinted at troubles to come.

Even during the debate over the Afghanistan War, some of the German Greens (and many other people in Europe and elsewhere) were already dreading that, once the United States had overthrown the Taliban, the question of invading Iraq and overthrowing the Baath was going to come up, and the invasion of Afghanistan was going to lead to a second invasion. This was not a foolish concern. Within a very few months of the Afghanistan War, the Bush administration made plain its thinking about Saddam and Iraq through a series of speeches, which went on escalating in vehemence. American military forces poured into the regions around Iraq. And, as these events unfolded, the transatlantic political tensions, already visible in the German and French hesitations over Afghanistan, broke into the open. In the case of Afghanistan, proponents of the war had a relatively easy time explaining their rationale. They described the war as a punitive expedition—a retaliation against the Taliban for having harbored Al Qaeda as official guests, and a frontal assault on Al Qaeda itself, in its Afghan camps. There was more to say about the war in Afghanistan, but these reasons seemed sufficient, in many people's eyes.

But why extend the war to Iraq? In the Western countries, people who paid attention to political matters did seem to understand that, in Iraq, Baathist rule was dictatorial in the extreme—though the awareness of the dire nature of this dictatorship seemed to vary widely from country to country. (Among the European countries, this awareness was probably largest in Britain, especially on the British left, owing to the activism of a good many Kurdish exiles over the years.) But the argument for war touched on many other issues, apart from Baathism's extreme oppression of the Iraqi people. The government in Baghdad was the most actively and violently anti-American government anywhere in the world. Baathist artillery had been shooting at American and British war planes in the "no-fly" zones of the Iraqi north and south for twelve years, ever since the 1991 war. The Baathists, in their official propaganda, had been inciting hatred against the United States among their own citizens and everyone else in the Arab world, with powerful consequences—or so it seemed. (Bin Laden himself cited Iraq's grievances against the United States as one of the justifications for his terrorist attack.) Saddam had made an ideological fetish of his weapons of mass destruction, which left open the possibility that he might use them someday—as he had already done against his own citizens, in his poison gas attacks on the Iraqi Kurds. Then, too, Saddam's government was the most rigid, anywhere in the Arab world, in maintaining the "rejectionist" front against Israel—the most rigid in plumping for a new outbreak of the eternal Arab-Israeli war.

Among the countries that clung to an extreme hostility to Israel, Iraq under the Baath was the only one to maintain an army large enough to worry the Israelis—an army sufficiently large to keep the Israelis on a war-footing of their own. Many people in the Arab world made a point of subsidizing the Palestinian suicide bomb campaign; but the Baathists of Iraq outdid themselves in generosity. The Iraqi Baathist support for the Palestinian terrorists did seem to suggest that Iraq's government was not above using third parties to wage its wars, and this, too, was worrisome. It seemed worth recalling that, after the first Gulf War, Baathist agents had attempted to assassinate George Bush the Elder when he was on a visit to Kuwait in his capacity as ex-president. Even before September 11, this sort of thing had begun to seem, from an American perspective, pretty alarming. Congress duly voted, back in 1998, in favor of an Iraq Liberation Act, which called for Saddam's overthrow, and Clinton signed the bill.

The efforts actually to overthrow Saddam seemed to be fairly desultory, but, after September 11, a good many people did begin to think that maybe the policy ought to be given a little more oomph. It was not just that Bin

Laden had invoked Iraq's sufferings at the hands of the Americans. The Baathist press in Iraq turned out to be the only official press in the Arab region actually to applaud the September 11 attacks. At least on the plane of anti-American propaganda, the Iraqi Baath and Al Qaeda were already allied. To be sure, many people argued that a theocratic movement like Al Qaeda could never strike up an alliance with an anti-theocratic movement like the Baath, simply on ideological grounds. But the Syrian Baath had been allied with the strictly theocratic Lebanese Hezbollah for two decades, just to show that such an alliance was entirely possible, under the right circumstances. All of this was worrisome, then. Some people even wondered if the Iraqi Baath might not have participated in the September 11 attacks and might not participate in some new such attack in the future. Those were the fears and suspicions. But did they justify going to war?

Everyone with a specialized knowledge of political affairs in the United States understood quite well that, in American foreign policy circles, some people looked on Iraq from a strategic overview, like generals on a high hill, and entertained large geopolitical ambitions, which rested on hopes as much as on fears and suspicions. The American strategists noticed that terrorism had begun to flourish across a wide swath of the Arab and Muslim world. And they argued that something had to be done about the political culture across the whole of that wide swath. The American strategists saw in Saddam's Iraq a main center of that political culture, yet also a place where the political culture could be redressed and transformed. There were liberal democrats among the Iraqi exiles, and liberal democrats within Iraq itself, who had been pleading for a Western intervention for decades.

In the Kurdish regions of the Iraqi north, Saddam's enemies had already succeeded in establishing a more or less autonomous zone under the protection of the American and British military, and the zone had taken on some of the qualities of a liberal society—the freest, most liberal zone in any of the Arab countries. The American strategists entertained the idea of spreading the Kurdish achievement southward into the rest of Iraq—where, it was presumed, liberal-minded Iraqi Arabs would turn out to be capable of following the Kurdish example. (This had certainly been Clinton's estimation of Iraqi capabilities, as he made clear when he signed the bill to overthrow Saddam.) Then, too, the strategists hoped that, by helping the Iraqi liberals stage a revolution in one of the central and most powerful of Arab countries, they could help set off a broader revolution for liberal values in the Arab world—the broader revolution that had already taken place in Eastern Europe and in nearly every region around the world, with greater or lesser success, yet for some reason had never caught hold in the Arab world.

The American strategists made one other argument, as if under their breaths, so as not to excite too much conspiracy-theorizing among their critics. This last argument touched on the matter of Iraq's oil reserves. The strategists did notice that, if Iraq's oil production could ever be restored, and if a liberal-minded government could be put in place in Baghdad to administer the oil industry, the oil reserves could be shrewdly deployed in the world market and might end up undermining the Saudi princelings. A liberal Iraq might be able to compete against the Saudi oil princes, and competition might put a damper on Saudi Arabia's Wahhabi missionaries—the Wahhabi proselytizers who had played such a pernicious role around the world in promoting an extreme Islamist radicalism. A vigorous Iraqi oil industry, in the hands of a liberal-minded Iraqi government, might, at the least, allow the United States to stand a little more firmly against the Saudi princes.

Such were the arguments among the foreign policy strategists—one set of arguments, anyway, which were quietly discussed, and duly reported in the press. None of this was a secret. Then again, the American strategists laid out another set of arguments, which was expressed in a somewhat louder voice and was more prominently reported. The strategists raised the idea that America ought to establish a military hegemony over the entire world. They made this argument quite openly, even officially, in the White House national security statement of 2002. The statement described "rogue states" as a great danger to modern civilization and called on the United States to build up the military strength to counter and overwhelm this particular danger.

Anyone who tried to fathom the White House thinking in the months after the invasion of Afghanistan was bound to be a little puzzled by these various arguments. Which of the several ideas were primary? Which were secondary? Which of those ideas were merely blather, uttered for propaganda purposes or to satisfy some faction or other within the administration, but without any intention of taking an appropriate action? The outside world could only scratch its head. Nor did the White House make any effort to untangle these matters. Bush delivered speeches extolling freedom for the Muslim world, and those speeches suggested that, in his mind, the triumph of liberal democracy was the central issue—the key to suppressing the terrorists. He spoke about totalitarianism. Then again, his national security statement flatly affirmed that totalitarianism no longer existed, and ideological disputes no longer played a central role in world affairs, and the antitotalitarian struggles of the past were no longer relevant to the present. The White House seemed oblivious to these contradictions.

In its most widely publicized presentations to the general public, the administration chose to emphasize, instead, a different set of arguments altogether, which were easier to explain in a popular fashion—tactical arguments without any strategic aspect at all and without much of an ideological content either. The administration suggested that Saddam might, in fact, have had a responsibility for the September 11 attacks—an argument that put Al Qaeda's relation to Saddam and the Baath in something of the same light as Al Qaeda's relation to Mullah Omar and the Taliban. This suggestion was not inconceivable. But the evidence for any such conspiracy was thin in the extreme—a record of meetings between sundry Baathists and followers of Al Qaeda during the nineteen-nineties, together with a rumor that Muhammad Atta, the Hamburg jihadi, had met in Prague with an agent of Saddam's government in the period before September 11. This last claim was said to be supported by the Czech secret police—though, after a while, Václav Havel himself, who was then in his last days as president of the Czech Republic, very courteously let it be known that nothing in the Czech police files offered any confirmation. The Bush administration pressed ahead with intimations of dark conspiracies, even so. A streak of conspiracy-theorizing did seem to run through the vice president's office—a hint of a simple-minded imagination at work, something worrisome to observe.

In any case, the administration rested its public case for war mostly on a fear of Saddam's specialized weapons, which he was thought to possess already, or was likely to possess in the future—his poison gases, anthrax, or nuclear bombs. Now, this fear was not preposterous, though it may seem that way in retrospect. The fact that Saddam had gassed Halabja was terrifying, but this was not the only terrifying fact. The regime had labored mightily, in the past, to produce nuclear weapons, and had made some progress, too—more progress than any of the outside observers had imagined, in the years before the Gulf War of 1991. After that war, as a part of the peace arrangement, Saddam agreed to allow arms inspectors from the United Nations to examine Iraq and guarantee that he had abandoned his unconventional weapons and wasn't trying to build any new ones. But, when the inspectors arrived, he gave them the runaround, quite as if he were trying to conceal a still-continuing weapons program. He may even have gotten away with quite a lot, for a while.

Even so—as the world eventually learned—Saddam's regime did get rid of its weapons and, at least temporarily, even its program to build new weapons. This happened over the course of the nineteen-nineties in some mysterious manner that has still not been described or explained. At least, this seems to have happened. But Saddam never wanted to acknowledge any of this. On the contrary, he had wanted to keep up his battle against the United Nations and the United States, if only to persuade his enemies and even his friends that he was still fully capable of massacring vast populations with some horrible new device; and the enemies and friends were persuaded. No one even dared to suggest that Saddam had destroyed his weapons. In 1998, the United Nations' confrontation with Saddam took a turn for the worse, and the inspectors withdrew. Clinton ordered missile attacks on weapons factories in Iraq. These attacks, as we later learned, turned out to have been pretty effective. And yet, with no UN inspectors in Iraq to examine the factories, no one could be sure. Almost everyone who speculated about these matters figured that, after 1998, Iraq's weapons production must certainly have resumed, in one fashion or another, and Saddam's arsenal must surely have contained unconventional arms. The evidence for this did seem impressive.

There was the uncomfortable fact that, as the likelihood of a new war with the United States and its allies increased, in the early weeks of 2003, Saddam's elite army units, the Republican Guard, moved out of their barracks to adopt positions of defense and brought along their chemical warfare suits. This suggested rather strongly that Saddam's army was expecting to wage a chemical war. (David Kay, the chief American arms inspector for a while, discovered later on, in the first months after the invasion, that Saddam's Republican Guard brought the chemical war suits to the front because, in the Guard's imagination, the Israeli army was going to invade Iraq and attack with chemical weapons— a mad thing to believe, except from the point of view of Baathist theory, which sustained a belief in a cosmic and sinister Jewish conspiracy as a matter of party doctrine.) Some of Saddam's top generals themselves believed that, somewhere or another, Saddam had kept hold of the terrible weapons—even if the generals did not happen to know exactly where. Then, too, some of the Iraqi exiles, in their eagerness to provoke an American attack on Saddam, spun a tale of frightening weapons in Iraq and whispered into the ears of the Defense Department and the American press, and these whisperings made their way into George Bush's speeches. The whisperings were confirmed, or were said to be confirmed, by the Egyptian government and other people in the Arab world. What were the odds, then, that Saddam did not possess the weapons that his worst enemies and his own generals and his Arab neighbors believed him to have?

And so, the Bush administration, contradicted by almost no one (except by a few skeptics within the CIA and other agencies, who could only raise an eyebrow at some of the unjustified claims and could never be certain of their own skepticism), concluded that Saddam's weapons and his program for more weapons were entirely real. Powell went to the United Nations in New York and delivered his unfortunate speech, replete with graphs and slide show illustrations, to show why the administration thought so—a fatefully distorted and wrongheaded presentation, which, at the time, very few people knew to be distorted and wrongheaded. And this contention—the belief that Saddam still retained his weapons and was hard at working constructing new ones—became, in the public presentations of the Bush administration, the principal justification for war. In some people's minds, the only justification.

Still, at the time, quite a few other people, and not just the experts within the CIA and other agencies, remained less than satisfied by these particular arguments. The American military build-up in the region apparently convinced Saddam that he had better re-admit the UN inspectors, and the inspectors arrived and renewed their searches. The searches did not go smoothly. The inspectors complained about Baathist officials, who were eager to keep the inspectors from poking their heads into this or that palace or building. Even so, the inspectors went darting around the Iraqi countryside in their convoys, popping up at one or another industrial site to examine what was going on. No one could doubt that, at minimum, the inspectors were making it difficult for the Baath to proceed with any weapons programs that might still have been underway. On one matter, the question of nuclear weapons, a big issue, the inspections pretty well established that Saddam's Baath was no longer in a position to achieve very much at all. Nuclear production requires elaborate bureaucracies, which are too big to be concealed. The inspectors discovered no such bureaucracies. That discovery should have been reassuring. Why, then, did the Bush administration keep insisting on going ahead with a full-scale invasion, and in such a hurried fashion, too? Why not let the inspections dawdle on and see what came of them?

It was Chirac and his foreign minister at the time, Dominique de Villepin, who most forcefully raised these points. Chirac and de Villepin did this during the later months of 2002 and the early period of 2003, and they convinced a lot of people of the wisdom of delay. On the other hand, these arguments, too, the French grounds for patience, had their peculiarities, and the peculiarities grew more pronounced as the months advanced. Everyone who paid attention to the crisis in Iraq seemed to recognize that, if Saddam had readmitted the UN inspectors, he had done so for a single reason: a fear that American and British forces in the region might go into action, and Iraq might be invaded. Some people hoped that Saddam might agree to leave Iraq peacefully, or that his own officers might overthrow him and offer to change the nature of the regime. But these hopes rested on continuing to convince Saddam and his generals that a hostile invasion was on its way, and war could not be avoided, and no one was going to step in at the last minute to rescue the Baathist dictatorship from its enemies—unless the Baathists did as the UN demanded. But the French government wanted nothing to do with this logic, nor with the military build-up. The months passed, and the French began to hint ever more clearly that, in the United Nations' Security Council, France's representative was going to veto any resolution that called for war.

The Bush administration pressed for support from countries around the world, and received quite a lot of it,

133

especially from Europe. Some eighteen countries in Europe eventually agreed to enlist in the American-led coalition—not just the British but the Italians, the Poles, and the Spanish. Chirac responded by sending de Villepin on tours of Africa, rallying opposition to any American call for invasion—which is to say, as time passed, the French showed ever more determination to undermine the very thing that made the inspectors effective, and this was the imminent threat of a full-scale invasion. The display tables in the French bookstores were by then filling with books proclaiming that America, and not the terrorists of the Muslim world and certainly not Saddam's Baath, posed the single greatest threat to civilization around the world; and French policy seemed in some degree to reflect the argument in those books—a policy designed not to disarm Saddam and certainly not to overthrow his regime but, instead, to inhibit America's ability to act against him.

Schröder spoke up about the impending invasion during these months—and he, too, sounded upset in the extreme, not at Saddam but at the Bush administration. Some people, observing the German political scene, figured that Schröder took a hard line against Bush in order to shore up his vote for the German election of 2002. And Schröder did shore up the vote. A cloud of anti-Americanism hovered over his electoral campaign, and the anti-Americanism did him a lot of good in fending off his conservative opponents. Large numbers of Germans voters plainly enjoyed seeing their chancellor sock it to the United States. Schröder kept to this policy after the election, too, even if he toned down his rhetoric. The man must have been sincere. He had always been less enthusiastic about the Kosovo War than Fischer, and, on the topic of the war in Iraq, he appeared to be truly indignant.

Eventually Schröder announced that Germany would not participate in such an invasion under any circumstances at all—not even if the French changed their position and the Security Council issued a formal endorsement. Schröder outdid even Chirac in this regard. Nor would Schröder dispatch troops to help sustain a military occupation, once the invasion was already completed. No troops at all, not from Germany, no matter what the United Nations might say—such was his position. He was adamant. And yet, during the fall of 2002 and the first weeks of 2003, as these debates went on, the American and British troops kept pouring into the regions around Iraq, and American planes began bombing targets in Iraq, though the bombings were unannounced, and fighting got underway in the Kurdish zones of the Iraqi north—all of which ought to have disabused everyone of the idea that a full scale war was going to be avoided.

In February 2003, Donald Rumsfeld, the secretary of defense, flew to Munich to participate in an annual event, the Conference on Security Policy, to shore up the European support that already existed and to make one last plea for still more support. Rumsfeld had his admirers, but, then again, in the judgment of his non-admirers, he gave off a manic and scary vibe. He had already sneered at the French and Germans as "Old Europe," which was not such a terrible insult, really. (The insult even contained an analysis of the Iraq crisis: "New

Europe," in Rumsfeld's phrase, meant the European countries that had recently shucked off a Communist or fascist dictatorship. These countries, in his view, were much more likely, because of the freshness of their experience, to wish to see Iraq liberated from the dictatorship of the Baath.) But then Rumsfeld went on to compare Germany, in its stance on Iraq, to Libya and Cuba—countries led by mad dictators—and this was fairly unforgivable, as insults go.

The Munich security conference took place at a grand nineteenth-century hotel, the Bayerischer Hof. In the conference room there, Rumsfeld invoked the Munich agreements of 1938—the moment when Neville Chamberlain did his best to avoid war by appeasing Hitler, which only strengthened Hitler for a war that was bound to come anyway. This was a pretty aggressive reference to make before a German audience. It was said that Rumsfeld tried to be nice in arguing his points—tried, at least, to avoid flinging any more outrageous insults. But, no use. In Germany, America's secretary of defense had already lost his public. Crowds marched in the wintry streets outside the hotel to denounce the American policy, led by the mayor of Munich himself. In the conference room, Rumsfeld, having had his say, took a seat in the audience, prominently in the front row. And, with his face set "in an almost theatrical glower" (Richard Bernstein's phrase in the *New York Times Magazine*), the secretary of defense turned his attention to the podium. It was Joschka Fischer's turn to speak.

Fischer's relation to the United States was not the same as Schröder's. Fischer, in the years since his political turnabout, was warmer toward America, genuinely warm—which was a sign, as I read it, of the sincerity of his new convictions. Schröder thundered against the Americans in the 2002 election, but Fischer did nothing of the sort. He was scrupulous on this point—and the Greens fared well enough in the election, even so. If anybody in the Red-Green government could have been expected to listen respectfully and sympathetically to the Bush administration's argument, Joschka Fischer was that person. So he listened. He offered practical objections to Rumsfeld's arguments. He warned against starting something that might have unintended consequences. He worried about bad results. And then, having expressed his reservations, Fischer switched from German into English for a few short sentences—a dramatic thing to do. Fischer's command of English turned out to be colloquial and fluent, marked with just enough imperfection to impart a smoky Teutonic spice to his outcry.

"You have to make the case," he said in English. His voice quivered. "And to make the case in a democracy you must convince by yourself. Excuse me, I'm not convinced. This is my problem. And I cannot go to the public and say, 'Oh, well, let's go to war because there are reasons,' and so on, and I don't believe in them."

Why did Fischer say this in English? To speak in English was a fairly odd thing to do for a German government minister at a conference in Munich. I think that no American official would ever dream of doing anything similar, for fear of offending the American public. (At a Paris news conference not long before, Bush had ridiculed an American reporter for having the effrontery to address a question in French to President Chirac.) But, in Fischer's case, the English words doubled the forcefulness, therefore the drama, of his remarks.

By speaking in English, Fischer appeared to be making a plain and eloquent statement to the German public. His English words said, in effect, that he had listened to Rumsfeld very carefully, and had done so in Rumsfeld's language, without risking any of the misunderstandings that creep into translated remarks. Fischer's English sentences demonstrated that he had bent over backwards in his effort to accept the American arguments; and, even so, he had remained unconvinced. Or perhaps Fischer switched into English because he was still speaking to Rumsfeld, man to man, and he wanted to be absolutely positive that Rumsfeld understood. He wanted to give Rumsfeld one more chance to look at the world through someone else's skeptical eyes.

Fischer was conducting his negotiation with Rumsfeld right there at the hotel, in front of all the world. And the tension in his voice? The quiver? This doubled the drama in those remarks yet again. Fischer's words did express a very sharp rebuke. To remind America's secretary of defense that imperial dictates are not enough, that in democracies the people rule, that government leaders cannot make decisions behind closed doors and impose their whimsical decisions on the obedient citizens—this was no small lecture to deliver to the United States. This was the statement of an offended man.

The English words suggested that, in his discussions with Rumsfeld or maybe with some other American officials, too, Fischer had felt that he and Germany were being pushed around—pressed to collaborate not because America had better arguments on its side but because America was strong. This was more than the complaint of an offended man, then—this was the complaint of an offended people. And so, the words tumbled out in a quivering tone. Or perhaps Fischer's voice trembled for reasons that were larger yet—perhaps he was filled with worry that the entire Atlantic Alliance was about to collapse, or that war was about to be unleashed across the world and not just across Iraq, that something dreadful and irrevocable was about to take place.

It should be noted that, during those months and weeks before the war, nearly every one of the principal leaders of the Atlantic Alliance ended up, at one moment or another, losing control of his voice or words or demeanor at a public event—a remarkable fact, suggesting that nearly every one of the leaders felt smaller than the events at hand, and there was reason for fear, even a touch of panic. Bush made a fool of himself at that press conference in Paris, when he ridiculed the American reporter (and this behavior of Bush's was viewed, by reporters who knew him, as a reflection of his exhaustion and upset, and not just of his provincialism and inexperience). Chirac, for all his wiliness, managed to do something much worse in Brussels. He upbraided the new European democracies of the east for having lined up with the United States, and he described those countries as "badly brought up"—a gratuitous insult, patronizing and haughty, which presaged a bumpy road for Europe in the future.

Schröder gave an interview to the *New York Times* in which the tone of his printed words sounded shrill, even a mite hysterical, on the topic of the upcoming war. Rumsfeld emitted puffs of lava every time he faced a camera. Powell was reported to have erupted in private, after a presentation at the United Nations by Chirac's foreign minister. Among the major leaders, only Tony Blair seemed to keep his cool at every point during those months. Fischer's trembling outcry in English, "Excuse me, I'm not convinced," and his brief scalding lecture about democracy, were hardly the most dramatic instance of a loss of composure during that period, and far from the worst. There was nothing embarrassing in Fischer's outburst, nothing foolish, nothing for Germans to cringe at, nothing that required an apology. This was not like saying, as Fischer had done in the Bundestag back in 1984, "With all due respect, Mr. President, you are an asshole." Not at all! In his confrontation with Rumsfeld, Fischer displayed an angry dignity. German newspapers ran his words, in English, in their headlines, with a feeling of satisfaction at how well the foreign minister had expressed himself. Still, his English-language remarks, in their sharpness, were anything but typical for a man in charge of his country's diplomacy.

And once Fischer's scathing "Excuse me" had escaped his lips at the Bayerischer Hof in Munich in February 2003, the Fischer affair from early 2001, which had long ago blossomed, shriveled, and scattered into dust in Europe, instantly sprouted up in the United States—as if a stray seed had wafted across the ocean and, after two years, had, at last, drifted to earth along the swampy banks of the Potomac and taken root.

III.

The renewed Fischer affair began to blossom at the *Washington Post*. One of the columnists there was Michael Kelly—though, in the world of American journalism, Kelly was more than a *Post* columnist, much more. During the first Persian Gulf War, in 1991, Kelly was just starting out in national journalism, and he went to Baghdad and Kuwait for the *New Republic* and the *Boston Globe*, and wrote battle-field dispatches that were lucid and passionate at the same time—a brilliant feat of journalism. These writings launched him into the upper orbits of the national press, where he made himself at home. In the next dozen years Kelly served variously as the editor of the *New Republic*, a Washington correspondent for the *New York Times*, a Washington correspondent for the *New Yorker*, and the editor of *National Journal*. Even while cranking out his column for the *Washington Post*, he took up the editorship of the *Atlantic Monthly* in Boston—the magazine with the grandest tradition of any journal in American letters, reaching back to the days of Ralph Waldo Emerson.

In one of his columns at the *Post*, Kelly took note of Clinton's ability to shift his rhetoric to fit the audience at hand—farmers, Westerners, auto unionists, or black college students, not the "language of the masses but of each diverse subset." Michael Kelly's ability to notice this kind of political skill showed something of his own talent, too. He was attentive to language and not just to politics—to the several ways that something could be said. I wouldn't wish to compare Kelly, as a journalist, to Clinton, as a politician. Kelly never did like or admire Clinton, and grew to despise him. Kelly felt that Clinton lacked a moral center. On the topic of the Monica Lewinsky scandal, Kelly grew positively vitriolic, not just at Clinton's efforts to conceal his private life but at the sexual relation itself.

In Kelly's eyes, Clinton was a repulsive predator, virtually a criminal, who had used Monica Lewinsky as a "sexual service station"—a particularly ugly phrase. Kelly shuddered with horror in his column over the pornographic details of the president's life. Oral sex seemed to infuriate him. Or maybe Kelly was not really horrified and infuriated—maybe he merely saw an irresistible opportunity to chuck rocks at the White House, and went about doing so with gusto. Maybe there was bit of the culture war in Kelly's reactions to Clinton, and cultural resentments drove him to write what he wrote. Kelly was eleven years old in 1968, which put him half a generation behind Clinton, and he did seem to harbor his grievances. Kelly glanced at Hillary Clinton—a student leader back at Wellesley College in the late nineteen-sixties— and wrote, "Can someone who helped lead the very generation that threw out the old ways of moral absolutes and societal standards now lead the charge back to the future?"

In short, here was, at the highest pinnacle of American journalism, a Clintonophobe, gifted at sneering, still seething in anger over the cultural revolutions of the nineteen-sixties. And yet, Kelly did resemble Bill Clinton in one respect, and this was his ability to come up with a different rhetoric for each diverse subset of the masses—the ability to shift smoothly from one silken presentation to the next, each in its own style. Setting himself down at his desk and booting up his computer, Michael Kelly must have hummed with pleasure at the marvelous range of prose styles available to him for his own journalistic purposes. He knew how to be crisply objective for the *Times*, suave and at ease for the *New Yorker*, judgmental and acerbic for the *New Republic*—by turns fierce, sentimental, and eloquent. Sometimes he wallowed happily in the rueful and congratulatory self-deprecations of bourgeois life, the lamentations of the flabby middle class with a bulging waist-line, the satisfactions of fatherhood at the family steering wheel. He was a master at political parody. His comic assaults could make you laugh out loud.

Then again, in his column at the *Washington Post*, he knew how to lead a howling mob through the streets with a flaming torch clutched in his manly hands. His column ran in the *New York Post*, as well, where rabble-rousing was the house style, and in other papers around the country, and this made Kelly a national journalist twice over—national because he cut a large figure in Washington, and because he spoke directly to the surly column-reading mob in different parts of the country. Sometimes in his column he played the part of a prosecuting attorney, hammering at recalcitrant witnesses. He was a police interrogator. He was a clinician of the third degree. He disapproved of one of Clinton's aides and called this man a "human ferret." The spirit of overkill made Kelly's columns wonderfully entertaining, unless you happened to be the human ferret.

I will quote in full Kelly's *Washington Post* column from February 14, 2003, because that particular column represented the principal moment in which the Fischer affair of 2001 finally blossomed in the United States. Kelly's column discussed the conference at the Bayerischer Hof in Munich—and incidentally cited my own report on the affair, "The Passion of Joschka Fischer," which had run in the *New Republic* in 2001 (and which, with a few revisions, constitutes the first chapter of this present book). Kelly's column bore the headline, "Who Is Joschka Fischer?" It began with a news flash:

"Excuse me. I am not convinced."—German Foreign Minister Joschka Fischer, lecturing to Secretary of Defense Donald Rumsfeld in Munich last week, following Rumsfeld's argument for war against Iraq."

Kelly wrote:

> Mr. Rumsfeld may have convinced the leaders of 18 European nations, but not you, Mr. Fischer. It's personal. This seems to me the right way to look at it. The question of failing to convince must be seen in the context of who we have failed to convince. Sometimes "who" explains "why."
>
> Mr. Fischer, who are you? You are the foreign minister of Germany. You have been that since 1998, when Germany's left-wing Greens Party, of which you are a leader, won enough in the polls to force the Social Democratic Party into the so-called Red-Greens coalition government. But for the formative years of your political life, you were no man in a blue government suit. You were a man in a black motorcycle helmet. That is what you were wearing on that day in April 1973

144

when you were photographed, to quote the New Left historian Paul Berman, "as a young bully in a street battle in Frankfurt."

In 2001, *Stern* magazine published five photographs of you in action that day. What these pictures depicted was described by Berman, in a deeply informed twenty-five-thousand-word article, "The Passion of Joschka Fischer" (*The New Republic*, Sept. 3, 2001). The photos showed you, Mr. Fischer, inflicting a "gruesome beating" on a young policeman named Rainer Marx: "Fischer and other people on the attack, the white-helmeted cop going into a crouch; Fischer's black-gloved fist raised as if to punch the crouching cop on the back; Fischer's comrades crowding around; the cop huddled on the ground, Fischer and his comrades appearing to kick him . . ."

As Berman reported, Mr. Fischer, you rose in public life as an important figure in the anti-American, anti-liberal, neo-Marxist, revolution-minded German radical left of the generation of 1968. This was the left that produced and supported the Baader-Meinhof Gang (or Red Army Faction), which, as Berman wrote, "refrained from nothing," including "kidnappings, bank holdups, murders."

You were not a terrorist yourself, but you were a good and active friend to terrorists, weren't you, Mr. Fischer?

In 1976, to protest the death in prison of Baader-Meinhof founder Ulrike Meinhof, you planned and participated in a Frankfurt demonstration in which, Berman wrote, "somebody tossed a Molotov cocktail at a policeman and burned him nearly to death." You were arrested, but not charged. In 2001, Meinhof's daughter, Bettina Röhl (who gave those damning photos to *Stern*) told the press that you were responsible for the throwing of that firebomb. Other contemporary witnesses, Berman reported, said that you "had never ruled out the use of Molotovs and may even have favored it." You denied it, for the record.

In 2001, the German government put on trial your old friend Hans-Joachim Klein, who had been an underground "soldier" in the Revolutionary Cells, an ally of the Red Army Faction and the Popular Front for the Liberation of Palestine. The Revolutionary Cells helped in the murder of the Israeli Olympic athletes in Munich in 1972, and Klein himself took part in a 1975 joint assassination operation with Carlos the Jackal in which three were killed.

During your testimony at Klein's trial, you were accused of having harbored Red Army Faction members in your Revolutionary Struggle house, the Frankfurt center for the group Revolutionary Struggle, which you co-founded with housemate Daniel "Danny the Red" Cohn-Bendit. You were forced to admit there was some truth in the accusation after it was revealed, as Berman reported, that Margrit Schiller, "who had served jail time for her connections to the Red Army Faction," had in her memoirs "plainly stated that she had spent a 'few days' in the early nineteen-seventies living in the Revolutionary Struggle house." (After your testimony, you shook hands with your old terrorist-friend Klein. Sweet.)

In 1969, you attended the meeting of the Palestinian Liberation Organization in which the PLO resolved that its ultimate aim was the extinction of Israel—that is to say, the extinction or expulsion of the Jews of Israel. Seven years later, Revolutionary Cells terrorists led by your Frankfurt colleague, Wilfried Böse, hijacked an Air France plane to Entebbe. The hijackers intended to murder all the Jewish passengers on that flight, but were killed by Israeli commandos.

"Suddenly," Berman wrote, "the implication of anti-Zionism struck home to (Fischer). What did it mean that, back in Algiers in 1969, the PLO, with the young Fischer in attendance, had voted the Zionist entity into extinction? Now he knew what it meant."

So, that's who you are, Mr. Fischer, the man we haven't convinced. You are the man for whom Munich wasn't enough, the man who needed Entebbe to convince him that Jew-murder was wrong. You ask to be excused. You have been excused.

Kelly's columns sometimes shaped the political conversation in zones far removed from the newspapers and

147

magazines. In the America of 2003, talk radio was king, and the king of talk was Rush Limbaugh, a master of high-dudgeon swagger, right-wing style. Limbaugh adapted Kelly's column for a harangue in early March, which was published on Limbaugh's website. The harangue went under the title, "Who Is This German Führer?," which, as titles go, was already horrendous.

Limbaugh said:

> On Monday, German Foreign Minister Joschka Fischer—leader (or "führer" in German) of the communist Green Party—piped up to slam Secretary of State Colin Powell. This guy claimed, in the face of all reality, "What we have learned here is Iraq is cooperating—not moving as quickly as we would like, but clearly there's no reason here to resort to military action." Fischer wants more appeasement of the sort that allowed his nation to roll across Europe in the forties.
>
> I've said before that the anti-Semitic force behind Europe's and the American left's behavior ought not be discounted, because Israel is the likely target of any Hussein nuclear weapon. No one examined the background of this man— except for Michael Kelly of the *Washington Post*. Kelly told us all about the anti-establishment supposedly antiwar Fischer who has now risen to foreign minister.
>
> Fischer was a member of the Stalinist Baader-Meinhof Gang (or Red Army Faction), which used kidnapping, bank holdups and mur-

148

ders to advance its agenda. In 1969, this cretin
attended a PLO meeting. . . .

And so forth, hot-air demagogic radio-style, with the
insults getting ever fatter; the facts, ever looser; and the
audiences, ever vaster.

My own response to these attacks on Fischer was a
little complicated—perplexed, indignant, but with some
ambivalence, too. I thought Michael Kelly was rather
courteous to have acknowledged my *New Republic* essay
so generously. He could simply have plundered a few of
the grisly facts, which were hardly my own property (the
interpretation, not the facts, was my property), and he
could have put those details to his own uses, without cita-
tion. He was too courteous by half, I would say, given my
interpretation, and his. Thus my perplexity. The insou-
ciant way that he worked up his accusations reminded
me of his columns about the Oval Office sex criminal and
the human ferret. There is more than one way to be a
bully. Thus my indignation. In response to Kelly, I wrote
a few comments in *Slate*, the online magazine, defending
Fischer's character and motives and the heritage of the
left. I blamed everything on Bush. The Bush administration had presented all the wrong arguments for war in
Iraq—had put too much emphasis on Saddam's weapons
of mass destruction and on purely speculative fears of a
conspiracy with bin Laden, and not nearly enough
emphasis on the kind of argument that might have
appealed to people like Fischer. In these circumstances,
I could understand why Fischer might have responded
to the administration with an exasperated "Excuse me."

And yet—here was my ambivalence—I wondered why Fischer didn't raise a set of arguments all his own: a position different from the arguments of the Bush administration, but different also from the simple Great Refusal of the antiwar attitude in Europe. The path that had led quite a few people from the left-wing movements of 1968 to a humanitarian intervention in Kosovo in 1999 did point in a certain direction, after all. I had hoped that, during the build-up to the Iraq War, Fischer might have spoken about this path, and about lessons learned, and the new realities suddenly visible after September 11. About a left-wing alternative. His own history seemed to me to require this. But, in order to explain my ambivalent response, I have to dive back one more time into the leftism of 1968 and its later evolution, in order to draw out a few additional observations. Only, this time, instead of looking at the left-wing militants of Western Europe from some decades ago, I want to glance at the Muslim world, and especially at a few corners of the Muslim world that have sometimes overlapped, neatly and effortlessly, with the student precincts of the American left.

CHAPTER THREE:
THE MUSLIM WORLD AND THE AMERICAN LEFT

I.

The student movements of circa 1968 flourished in many remote zones of the planet, not just in Western Europe and North America, and the movements in those distant zones were visibly related to one another—linked by fashions in clothes, iconography, slogans, habits, and doctrines, in plain demonstration that university leftism was a global event, and not just a random collection of local uprisings. And, in quite a few places around the world, the left-wing militants went through the identical phases of evolution—the path that led from radical protest to ultraradicalism, cultural creativity, super-ultraradicalism, overcreativity, delirium and, at last, self-obliteration. And then, in many countries and regions, not just among the French New Philosophers and the German Greens, the path took still another turn, and quite a few people wended their way to yet another phase, which turned out to be, in one style or another, a politics of liberalism and antitotalitarianism—something altogether different from the leftism of before. I could trace this evolution in several places around the world, in Mexico or Central America or Argentina, for instance—a simple thing to do, given how many books and memoirs have been written.

But what about the Muslim world? As it happens, a literature exists here, too, and the literature describes the classic trajectory: from the revolutionary leftism of the student movement in the late nineteen-sixties and seventies to a moral or philosophical crisis, to a new stage of antitotalitarian liberalism in adult life. Does this trajectory seem hard to imagine, in Muslim versions? Some readers are bound to think so. It has become fashionable to suppose—it has always, but always, been fashionable to suppose—that East is East, and never the twain, and so forth. Cohn-Bendit's imaginary '68ers' International—the worldwide movement that he assembled in the nineteen-eighties in his book *We Loved the Revolution So Much*—stretched from Poland to Brazil, yet managed to make room for not one person from a Muslim background, apart from the gruesome Palestinian terrorists with whom Hans-Joachim Klein got involved. And yet, even within the Western countries, any number of people from Muslim countries were in attendance at the big universities, as students or professors, and these people took part in the same left-wing uprisings as everyone else; and, afterward, some of these people, the leftists from Muslim backgrounds, went through the same evolution, too, in versions of their own. And they wrote their books. There is the example of Azar Nafisi, the author of *Reading Lolita in Tehran*, which should count as a classic in this particular genre—a book that seems to me doubly dramatic, not just because of the left-wing and revolutionary past that it recounts, but because of its date of publication, which was March 2003: the very moment when the invasion of Iraq was getting underway.

Nafisi is an Iranian, and she grew up in the gilded districts of Tehran under the shah during the nineteen-fifties and sixties—the daughter of Tehran's mayor (though he ended up in jail, a matter of pride for the family), with distinguished and cultured ancestors tracing back eight hundred years. Somebody might object that, with her glorious background, Nafisi can hardly be regarded as typical of her part of the world. But who is typical of anything? The medieval ancestry might suggest, at the least, that here is someone with a sharp eye for Iranian traditions. Nafisi went abroad to study—and this, surely, was a typical thing to do, for the educated elite in what used to be called the Third World. She studied in Switzerland and Britain until the serendipities of life and love brought her, in the nineteen-seventies, to the University of Oklahoma, at Norman. She explored American literature at Norman— the only foreign student in the department. The American New Left was at high tide, and Oklahoma did not escape its many currents. All over the American university system in the seventies, clever left-wing students were organizing study groups to pore over the texts of Marx, Lenin, Mao, Lukacs, Debray, and the Frankfurt School—the alternative syllabus of the world of Marxism. These groups formed at Norman, too, and Nafisi took her place among them.

All over the American universities, a good many students cultivated a nostalgia for the American Communist Party at its high tide, from the nineteen-twenties to the forties, in the rueful recognition that America's New Left was deplorably bourgeois and undisciplined, and needed to glean a few lessons from the American Bolsheviks of yore. The project of rediscovering and resurrecting the forgotten heroes of America's Communist Party (and a few other revolutionary organizations from long ago) became something of a fad in the graduate schools, and more than a fad—a serious project to rehabilitate, by means of academic study, a left-wing tradition that had been pretty much ruptured in the nineteen-fifties by McCarthyite persecutions. Quite a few students launched dissertations on these nostalgic and radical themes, and founded magazines, and dedicated their careers to researching the buried history of the left. (That was certainly my own project, for a while.) Azar Nafisi lent herself to this campaign, as well.

She set out to study Michael Gold, the forgotten king of the "proletarian" writers from the Communist Party during the Great Depression. Gold was famous in those years for having published a single novel, *Jews Without Money*, which came out in 1930. This was a classic text of the Old Left, an album of Jewish immigration and poverty on the Lower East Side at the turn of the twentieth century—a poetic novel, pungent with the odors of the New York sidewalks. Gold wrote literary essays, too, in a brash and obnoxious Marxist style, and some of those essays weren't bad. On the topic of Ernest Hemingway, Gold insisted on asking, how did these glamorous characters in Hemingway's novels afford to run around Europe the way they did? Where did their money come from?—which was a reasonable question to ask, even if, in asking, Gold pretty much missed whatever was valuable in Hemingway. Then again, Gold wrote a lot of brainless attacks on anyone who fell afoul of the Communist Party's Central Committee. If there was ever a journalist who deserved the label "Stalinist hack," this person was Mike Gold, the columnist for the *Daily Worker*. His career at the *Worker* was the principal rea-

154

son his reputation faded away in later years—this, and his failure to write another book. Those brainless attacks earned him the undying hatred of nearly everyone who might have kept alive the reputation of his one excellent novel. By the nineteen-seventies, hardly anybody in the literary world remembered Mike Gold anymore, the one-book wonder from long ago. Here was the young Nafisi, though, animated by the campus energies of the moment—the New Left radical from upper-crust Iran, bending over her study desk in red-earth Oklahoma to pore through the pages of the neglected Jewish writer from the New York slums of long ago.

Student leftism back home in Iran grew noisier and more militant over the course of the seventies, agitating against the shah. The shah's secret police, the Savak, cracked down, and students were killed in terrible massacres. And, as these grisly events took place far away in Iran, the Iranian students in America likewise grew noisier and more militant, and marched in picket lines that, as I remember well (from observing a demonstration in New York, not Oklahoma), were weirdly vehement, radiant with violence, and slightly mysterious, too, with the marchers' faces wrapped in scarves to conceal their identities from the agents of the Savak and the FBI. Iranian students were especially active at Norman. They were fervent for Maoism. They hung out in the Norman student union, sipping coffee and Coke, and declaiming in favor of Stalin and, as Nafisi remembers, "the need to destroy once and for all the Trotskyites, the White Guards, the termites and poisonous rats who were bent on destroying the revolution." This, too, expressed the spirit of the age.

Maoism did have its successes in the American universities, after all, even if not to the same degree as in France and Germany. The "New Communist" movement in the United States gathered around the Marxist newspaper the *Guardian* in the mid-seventies, in the hope of building an improved, new Communist Party—a party that was going to line up with the revolutionary Communists of China instead of with the reactionary "social-imperialists" of the Soviet Union. Several thousand people threw themselves into the New Communist campaign, and some of those people were well-known in the student movement, with admirers and political contacts around the country. A number of tiny splinter groups arose, and these, too, had their followers and the support of an occasional assistant professor or literary critic or philosopher. Two or three of those groupuscules sprung up from the wreckage of Students for a Democratic Society, after its split in 1969, and the liveliest of these proved to be the Bay Area Radical Union, which, in time, blossomed into the Revolutionary Union, which blossomed into the Revolutionary Communist Party, or RCP. The RCP was a California group mostly, but it was animated by an ambitious view of the proletarian revolution and a determination to cultivate fraternal ties with Maoist parties around the world. The RCP ran a curiously plush bookstore at Union Square in Manhattan, which stocked the most complete collection anywhere in New York of pamphlets from the Latin American left.

The RCP's comrades devoted unusual energies to celebrating Stalin, and this was not as odd as it may seem. Stalin had his charms, in some people's eyes. The mere invocation of the tyrant's name was guaranteed to drive liberals up the wall, which meant that, from a mischievous New Left point of view, Stalin-worship could seem appealingly impudent. But mostly the cult of Stalin reflected the influence of the Chinese Communists, who regarded Stalin as the heroic predecessor to Mao—the Soviet leader who, unlike Nikita Khrushchev and his heirs, did not betray the world proletariat. The RCP dutifully set about burnishing Stalin's reputation in the world of the American left.

The RCP took positions on cultural issues—on questions of feminism, gay rights, and the polymorphous perversities of the counterculture—and these positions tended to be fairly conservative. Or more than conservative: blatantly reactionary. This was not at all peculiar. An ultraconservatism on cultural matters dominated the retro-Marxist wing of the student movement and the sectarian left throughout the sixties and seventies—the world of the pullulating Maoist and Trotskyist groups, with each tiny organization upholding its own tiny position on who could sleep with whom, and whether it was okay to smoke marijuana or even cigarettes. Conservative attitudes proved to be popular, too, in some quarters of the student world—especially a short-haired cultural abstemiousness that, by describing itself as Bolshevik, could claim to be far more radical than anything proposed by the wildest of the long-haired dope-smoking hippies, and yet was, in the end, a lot less scary.

In this fashion, the RCP, with its posters of Stalin and its old-fashioned cultural postures, managed to attract members and followers, not only in the fervid zones of

Northern California; and one of those areas of success turned out to be Norman. The RCP took a genuine interest in Iran. In West Germany, a protest against the shah of Iran, back in 1967, helped launch the New Left. Nothing like that took place in the United States. Still, in 1973, the RCP, with its internationalist view of the world, began to agitate against the shah, and the Iranian students in America responded as might have been predicted. Nafisi tells us that, at Norman, it was the Iranians who transformed the RCP into a lively presence. Maoism did not make for an entirely pleasant political atmosphere. The Iranian students debated Chinese politics in preference even to Iranian politics—which is to say, the Oklahoma Iranians floated about in a Maoist dreamworld. They fretted over police informers and agents and the need to exterminate the poisonous rats and counterrevolutionary termites. The mood seems to have been delusionary and fearful at the same time. Nafisi played her part in this scene—she delivered passionate speeches at rallies, she chanted the chants, she listened to her left-wing professor warble a Wobbly ballad by Joe Hill—even if she also entertained, in her inmost hippie heart, some weighty reservations about the left-wing movement (as did a lot of people, to be sure, in their private ruminations) and a secret passion for the mandarins of English-language literature.

In 1979 the revolution broke out for real—not in Oklahoma but in Iran. Nafisi completed her dissertation on Mike Gold, and, two days later, with an edition of *Jews Without Money* packed in her luggage, set out for Tehran—she and a good many other Iranian radicals, full of enthusiasm for the revolution and for their own opportunity to play a role. The Tehran airport was bedecked with slogans written in black and red: DEATH TO AMERICA! DOWN WITH IMPERIALISM & ZIONISM. She took a position as a professor of literature at University of Tehran, where the Marxists were especially strong. And yet, in those early days after the shah's overthrow, to be alive was not necessarily bliss, nor was it Heaven to be young. The revolution came to power because Ayatollah Khomeini and his radical Islamists put together a broad front with the Iranian Communist Party (the Tudeh) and the Marxist Fedayin Organization, together with a couple of popular organizations that favored liberal democracy, and the mixture of mosques, Marxists, and liberals turned out to be powerful. The shah fled for his life. But Khomeini and his mullahs stood at the head of this absurdly wide United Front, and, once the mullahs had succeeded in establishing the United Front's revolutionary government, they and their Marxist allies turned against the liberals and crushed them. Then the Islamists turned against the Marxists. A battle for control of the university and of every institution of Iranian life got underway—mullahs against Marxists and everyone else. And the Islamist victory, as it crept across the landscape, turned out to be dreadful.

The Islamists took to arresting and executing people right and left. A hysteria got hold of the revolutionaries, and there was no stopping them: an old story. The principal of Nafisi's high school in Tehran had been, in the past, Iran's minister of education—one of the two women ever to hold a government ministry in Iran. Once the Islamists were comfortably in power, this person,

Nafisi tells us, "was put in a sack and stoned or shot to death." Some of Nafisi's comrades from the Iranian student movement in the United States, the leftists, were tortured and killed. Students from her own literature classes were arrested, jailed, and raped. One of her students was executed. The Islamists established the practice of suicide bombings as early as 1979, the year of their triumph. The Islamist students who captured the American embassy in Tehran and held the diplomats hostage composed slogans, which they scribbled across the embassy walls: THE MORE WE DIE, THE STRONGER WE WILL BECOME. And, with crowds chanting "*Marg bar Amrika!*"—"Death to America!"—and death-obsessed graffiti decorating the walls, people did, in fact, begin to die, and in large numbers.

Saddam Hussein came to power next door, in Iraq, in that same 1979—a year of paroxysm for the extremist political movements in the region. Saddam launched his own mad persecutions and his program of war, beginning with Iran. Young Iranian boys were soon enough marching into the Iraqi mine fields and poison gas, with keys dangling from their necks to symbolize the opening of the gates of heaven—boys marching deathward with the blessing of the fanatical clergy and to the cheers of their own mothers. In Nafisi's memoir, the violent atrocities take place off-stage, by and large—events that are mentioned but do not unfold before our eyes. Instead, she describes what might well seem, under other circumstances, scenes that are entirely benign, wholesome and even commendable— the vigorous intellectual life of her own classroom in those years, the formal discussions of her students, and the casual banter.

Iran is a land of literature, and the discussions in Nafisi's classroom, as she evokes them, exude a natural and easy fervor—the intensity of students who feel keenly about books and writers and the entanglements of literature and life. But there is something manic about this classroom intensity. Some of her students are Islamists, and they have their opinions. The Islamist students want to interrogate literature through the prism of their own ideology; want to draw moral lessons, or perhaps theological lessons; want to point fingers. They want to be ferocious; and they succeed. One of the students tells the class, "'All through this revolution we have talked about the fact that the West is our enemy, it is the Great Satan, not because of its military might, not because of its economic power, but because of, because of'—another pause—'because of its sinister assault on the very roots of our culture. What our Imam calls cultural aggression. This is what I would call a rape of our culture.'" And the student holds aloft a copy of *The Great Gatsby*.

This is a remarkable speech. But is anything in this speech bizarre or unintelligible, from the point of view of modern intellectual culture in the West? Does this speech sing a song we haven't heard before? The radical Islamists in the Iranian revolution declared themselves to be the champions of the seventh century, from the days of the earliest Muslim caliphate and the Companions of the Prophet Muhammad. All over the world, people took the Islamists at their word, and looked upon them, in an anthropological light, as specimens from the seventh century—autochthonous barbarians descending from the hills in their magnificent turbans to reignite the dormant embers of ancient Iran, or the true flame of Islam, in its Shiite denomination. But Nafisi's description of classroom debate suggests something else. The diatribe by this one student, holding up his copy of F. Scott Fitzgerald's criminal text, is not at all a seventh-century speech, nor a speech by a peasant from the hills, herding his goats.

This speech enunciates some of the principles established by the extreme right in Europe long ago—the notion of an authentic culture under insidious attack by evil cultural forces from abroad; the notion that modern freedom poses a danger to eternal values, and must be fearlessly opposed; the notion that culture is a field of struggle, and a novel is not merely a novel, but is, on the contrary, a weapon, to be wielded for good or for ill. These are not Koranic ideas. These are reflections of an entirely modern outlook, which has flourished at different moments all over the world—the outlook that came to dominate Europe and Japan during the fascist era, and quite a few other places. The *kulturkampf*.

Then again, these ideas have sometimes made themselves perfectly at home on the Marxist left, in a different version. Mike Gold was F. Scott Fitzgerald's contemporary and rival, and in the early nineteen-thirties Gold used to issue literary interdictions in precisely this condemnatory spirit on behalf of the American Communist Party— decrees of banishment and anathema that were intended to maintain the proletarian purity of the slum-dwellers and factory workers, and to rescue revolutionary ideas from bourgeois contamination. Even the sexual imagery in the Iranian student's classroom speech—"a rape of our culture"—strikes a familiar note. The American Stalinists in the nineteen-thirties used to complain about a homosexual danger to the masculine proletarian sense of virtue. Gold wrote a once-famous essay on this theme, denouncing the writer Thornton Wilder, whose prose and imagination seemed, in Gold's estimation, suspiciously prissy.

The similarities between the Islamists and the Stalinists of long ago could hardly have escaped Nafisi's notice, given her dissertation on Gold and American literature. "The revolution Gold desired was a Marxist one and ours was Islamic, but they had a great deal in common, in that they were both ideological and totalitarian." Then again, she might have noticed these similarities even without having written such a dissertation, simply by recalling the American student Marxism from New Left days, in its more emphatic versions. Radical leftists at the American universities did sometimes orate about literature and its nefarious influence—only, instead of citing "our Imam," as Nafisi's student did, the American New Leftists cited Mao Zedong's "Talks at the Yenan Forum on Literature and Art," a much-thumbed essay in its time. (This is the essay where Mao asks, "Literature and art for whom?" and ends by calling for the destruction of "feudal, bourgeois, petty-bourgeois, liberalistic, individualist, nihilist, art-for-art's sake, aristocratic, decadent or pessimistic, and every other creative mood that is alien to the masses of the people and the proletariat.") For that matter, some of America's English department radicals cited Stalin and not just Mao—a small fad, promoted by the RCP.

Nafisi remarks that, in her classroom in revolutionary Iran, the Islamist students "spoke from a script, playing characters from an Islamicized version of a Soviet novel"—the kind of novel in which heroic characters play noble revolutionary roles in the struggle for the radiant proletarian millennium. Only, in the Islamicized version, the heroic characters play noble roles in the sacred jihad to resurrect the ancient caliphate. Different mythology; similar spirit. I think that fantasy role-playing of this sort lies at the heart of a good deal of modern history, not just among Stalinists and Islamists. In their day, the Nazis went about conducting their German university battles in precisely this fashion, picturing themselves as heroic Aryans from a Wagner opera, cleansing away the Jewish impurities. Martin Heidegger, the university rector, presided over precisely this sort of thing at Freiburg in 1933.

Things were not really any different at the University of Salamanca in Spain in 1936, except with a slightly different mythology. A fascist crowd at Salamanca chanted "Long live death!" and the fascist general lectured the rector by adding the further cry, "Down with intelligence!"—and the crowd and the general pictured themselves, all the while, as the Warriors of Christ the King, smiting the atheist enemies of the Catholic faith, and lording it over the free-thinking intellectuals. Fantasy role-playing, it occurs to me, is the defining quality of all totalitarian movements and systems—role-playing by totalitarian militants who feel entirely justified in liquidating everyone who fails to have a proper role in the

164

grand tableau of the reigning mythology. Thus it was in Tehran. Professor Nafisi peered in wonder at her own students, the champions of the seventh century. Her thoughts flew back to the China-dreaming Iranian fantasists of Norman, Oklahoma. And, as she contemplated the Islamist students and their hatred of everything that fell outside the Islamist mythology, she found herself reflecting, "If the leftists had come to power, they would have done the same thing"—a heart-piercing comment.

Life at first one university and then another became harder to endure, not just because of the Islamist students but because the university administration was falling into Islamist hands. It became impossible for a woman to walk around the university grounds without wearing the veil of Islamist piety—this fearful political symbol of submission to theocratic authority. And, after many years, Nafisi withdrew from the university and began to run private classes of her own, from her home, in her field of English-language literature. Students came to her merely to savor the intelligent joys of literature and study. The students were women, plus one man, and their discussions are exhilarating to observe, in Nafisi's account—discussions proper to literature, discussions that wander back and forth from the pages of novels to the pages of life, now taking up public issues, now private issues, now veering into matters of sex and love, now back into literature.

Here, then, in Nafisi's _Reading Lolita in Tehran,_ is the story of someone who enlisted in the leftism of circa '68, and went on to discover moral and political failures in the left-wing movement, and came to adopt a different attitude altogether—an attitude of respect for the individual imagination. A liberal attitude. And it is the story of someone who, having set out in youth to fight against one kind of oppression, stumbles on the existence of a rather different kind—not capitalist exploitation, not imperialism, not the rule of neocolonialist elites such as the shah and his circle, but something newer, a modern phenomenon. Totalitarianism, in a word—the system of oppression that reaches into the coziest and most private corners of life, into questions of sexuality, conscience, and personal behavior, and sets out to squeeze each of these intimate and individual matters into the exact and peculiar shape that is required by the governing fantasy.

Or is it wrong to speak of totalitarianism? Maybe Khomeini's Islamist revolution represented something not at all like the totalitarian revolutions in other countries, except in a few unimportant and superficial ways—a development unique to Shiite Iran, or perhaps to Islam as a whole, but without any significant parallels to the European twentieth century. A good many political analysts do resist the totalitarian interpretation, and on the best of authority, too. They listen to the talk about Muslim or Iranian totalitarianism, and they respond by going to their own bookshelves and pulling down the many tomes written about the European experience, with their political-science checklists of totalitarianism's crucial traits. And the analysts pore over the checklists, looking for the parallels between Iran's history and Europe's. And, lo, Iran turns out not to be a European country, and no two things are exactly alike. Nafisi herself pauses over this question, if only by putting her finger on the single most unusual aspect of the Iranian revolution—its most striking peculiarity. "What differentiated this revolution from the other totalitarian revolutions of the twentieth century," she observes, "was that it came in the name of the past."

But here Nafisi has made a mistake. Over the course of the twentieth century, quite a few totalitarian movements have pushed their way into power precisely by invoking the past. It was Mussolini who coined the word *totalitarian*, and Mussolini's grandest dream was to resurrect the Roman Empire. When his followers staged their March on Rome in 1922, they did so as "centurions" of a Roman legion, preparing to plunge Italy back into the glories of ancient times. The crowd of Spanish fascists at Salamanca was dreaming precisely of the Middle Ages. As for the Nazis, their Wagnerian hoopla was meant to conjure a Germanic yesteryear of ancient forests and Norse gods. Then again, the Nazis also dreamed of resurrecting the Roman Empire, which they looked upon as the First Reich. And they dreamed of Ancient Greece. In the matter of fantastical reveries of an archaic past, the Nazis were prodigal.

Even the Stalinists of the Soviet Union celebrated a cult of the ancient communal virtues of the primitive Russian peasants. All in all, some sort of backward leap into the archaic past has figured in every one of the totalitarian mythologies in modern times. It's true that, in the matter of leaping backward, the Islamists (not just in Iran but in Afghanistan and Gaza and Algeria and other places) may have outleapt everyone else. A Koranic dream of ancient Medina and the early caliphs stood at the center, and not just at the margins, of Khomeini's revolution. But the mere fact of invoking the past was nothing special among modern totalitarians. Then, too, Khomeini's Islamists cultivated a number of futuristic hopes—a focus on social problems of the present day, and an expectation that modern technology, properly applied, would offer solutions. That was why, in the days of struggle against the shah, Khomeini spread his message by means of tape cassettes, which seemed the acme of technological advance in the nineteen-seventies; and why, after a few years, the Iranian Islamists began to make such a fetish of nuclear weapons; and why, in Iraq and other countries, the Islamist terrorists seized so fondly on cam videos and the Internet to advertise their beheadings and assassinations. These backward-gazing Islamists were forward-gazers, as well, eying with earnest hope and desire the perfect society of the technologically advanced future. The seventh century was the radiant future. And this, too, the forward-looking millenarianism that was also a backward-looking millenarianism, stood in the grand totalitarian tradition. "Reactionary modernism" is Jeffrey Herf's phrase to describe the German impulse that led to Nazism; and reactionary modernism was alive and well in the Iranian universities.

The Islamists in Iran cultivated a few additional peculiarities. The sexual zaniness among the Iranian Islamists does seem to have gone beyond anything you would have seen among, say, the Stalinists or Nazis of the mid-twentieth century—not just an extreme impulse to contain and control female sexuality but a number of bizarre and fantastical ideas that were expressed by Ayatollah

Khomeini in his opus, *The Political, Philosophical, Social and Religious Principles of Ayatollah Khomeini*. In this book, Nafisi tells us, Khomeini discusses sex with animals and even with chickens!—a bizarrerie that naturally accompanied the Islamist cult of the archaic. (The thrill in the radical Islamist movement derives precisely from the willingness to go ahead and enact the wildest customs of the seventh century—the amputations, the beheadings, the stonings, and so forth.) But, then, each of the totalitarian movements has boasted of its idiosyncrasies and has pioneered its own special taboo-breaking thrills, which always involve a shocking display of ruthlessness. This is not exactly a novel observation on my part.

In *The Origins of Totalitarianism*, back in 1951, Hannah Arendt analyzed with systematic zeal the Nazis and Stalinists, these erstwhile enemies and opposites of the nineteen-thirties and forties, whose mutual hatred and contradictory ideologies and rival Teutonic and Slavic brutalities led most people, at the time, to suppose that nothing could possibly link the movements together. Yet the whole point of Arendt's book was to sketch out the deep characteristics of each movement in order to notice the similarities, which turned out to be pretty substantial. Arendt wanted to identify these movements as examples of a larger, single thing, which might take different forms, Nazi or Stalinist or perhaps even something else, but whose correct name was, in any case, totalitarianism—the philosophical unity beneath the Hitler-Stalin Pact. Nafisi, in her own book, makes no effort to apply Arendt's philosophical analysis to the Iranian experience—which, by the way, would be a complicated thing to do, requiring all sorts of emendations and adaptations. *Reading Lolita in Tehran* is a memoir, not a work of philosophy.

Nafisi paints scenes, and this is not the same as making analyses. Most of her scenes are on an intimate scale—Persian miniatures, so to speak, sketched in hues that are oddly dark. The scenes may seem a little exotic at times, because Iran seems exotic to us non-Iranians. And yet, the sense of dread floating through these scenes ought to strike us as instantly recognizable—a dread that we have run across in other memoirs about Berlin and Leningrad, from many years ago. The political scientists, some of them, may go on waving their European checklists and objecting that Khomeini's Islamism cannot possibly be a modern totalitarianism. But I think that readers of literature, who judge by smell and feel, will sense at once that Nafisi is speaking of familiar experiences. Perhaps someone might argue that, in any common-sense definition, totalitarianism can only mean a "total" system of oppression, leaving room for not one square inch of autonomous thinking or activity—which is a kind of all-encompassing domination that, in Iran, has never existed. Yet this definition was not really Arendt's.

Totalitarianism, in her explanation, is a kind of ideal, an impossibility, toward which the totalitarian militants vigorously strive—a mythology, as I would put it, which the militants are never able to enact. That is why the totalitarians always end up slaughtering masses of people—out of frustration at the human race's stubborn refusal to be anything but the human race, and out of the lust for thrills, and out of a realization that only in death can the mythic universe be fully achieved. Arendt explains in a

170

crucial passage of her book that not even Hitler finally succeeded in creating a genuinely totalitarian state, for all his efforts. Arendt is subtler than some of her readers remember. But Nafisi remembers, and, in the course of her Persian memoirs, she duly nods in Arendt's direction, not out of doctrinaire adherence to a political theory but simply because a liberal-minded professor of literature in Iran under the Islamist tyranny would naturally find her thoughts drifting toward political philosophy, and certain philosophers turn out to be apropos. *Reading Arendt in Tehran* would make an entirely plausible title for an all-too-modern book.

Something else in Nafisi's memoir deserves comment, and this is her personal response to everything she encounters—a rebellious impatience, which is not exactly political, at least not in any straightforward way. She observes the revolutionary goings-on, and, recoiling, chooses to teach Jane Austen to her students—Austen, who, as Nafisi observes, may have been the earliest writer to offer a modern discussion of marriage and freedom. Nafisi teaches Scott Fitzgerald instead of Mike Gold because Fitzgerald wrote about individuals making personal choices, and not just about social classes and grand mythologies, as Gold did. She quotes Saul Bellow on the value of literature in the face of political oppression—on literature's ability to reach "the heart of politics." And what is the heart of politics? It is the precise spot where, in Bellow's phrase, "the human feelings, human experiences, the human form and face, recover their proper place—the foreground." That is the purpose of Nafisi's many scenes of literary discussion and university life and her hints about love and friendship. She wants to bring what is human into the foreground and to push aside the doctrines and ideologies. This is likewise Orwell's purpose in *1984*. It is Havel's purpose in his theater plays and prison letters, and Michnik's purpose in his own prison essays. And the purpose of how many Russian writers? And of what percentage of the twentieth century's most searing political analyses? At the very end of *Reading Lolita in Tehran*, Nafisi speaks at last about a feeling of "hatred"—her own hatred, and the hatred that she and her mother shared, back in Tehran. It is a hatred "of evil totalitarian systems which Nabokov denounced for holding their citizens hostage by their heartstrings"— a nod from an exiled Iranian to the exiled author of *Invitation to a Beheading*. Does hatred seem extreme? Nafisi doesn't mean by this word a wild rage. She means something more precise, a righteous anger, and this, too, ought to strike us as familiar. It is the hatred that totalitarian regimes have always aroused—the angry response that sooner or later flies up from the human soul to greet the tyrannical mythologizers.

I should add that Nafisi is hardly the only Iranian writer to speak about Islamism as a modern totalitarianism. But I don't want to linger over Iran or over the specific qualities of the Iranian revolution and Iran's liberal writers. I am trying, by citing examples, to describe the path followed by quite a few of people from the Muslim countries during the last few decades—the route traced by students who began on the radical left in the late nineteen-sixties and seventies, and, like Nafisi, ended up following a path to liberal antitotalitarianism. A generational trajectory. With

172

that idea in mind, I would like to leave the Iranians behind and wander across the border to Iraq in order to glance at Kanan Makiya, the political writer and architecture critic, who has described a very different set of experiences, which turn out not to be so different.

II.

Makiya grew up in Baghdad in the nineteen-fifties and sixties—he, too, a child of privilege. His father was an architect prominent in Iraq and throughout the Middle East. Frank Lloyd Wright, on his travels, once paid a visit to the Makiya home. The young Makiya studied at the Jesuit academy in Baghdad and then he, too, went on to study in the United States—in his case, at MIT, a proper school to immerse himself in the family business, which was architecture. He enrolled in 1967. The movement against the Vietnam War was just then beginning to swell into something massive, and went on swelling until the 1968-era uprisings had broken out, which, in Cambridge, took place in 1969. And so, like everyone else, Makiya found himself floating along in the floodtide of the New Left, participating in the antiwar agitations and the left-wing excitement. Afterward, he worked for his father at the architectural firm, in its London office. The father's status bobbed up and down among the Baath party leaders back in Baghdad, which led the elder Makiya, out of caution, to spend most of his time away from Iraq. Still, sometimes the father was summoned back home to engage in personal consultations with Saddam himself. Saddam bestowed commissions, and the father had not much choice but to accept, which meant that, for a while, young Makiya, as his father's employee, found himself toiling away on behalf of the tyrant. The young Makiya was never a Baathist, nor even a skeptical believer in the Baathist revolution, nor the slightest bit comfortable working on a Baathist commission. He remained under the influence of the student leftism he had seen at MIT and in the left-wing zones of London in the seventies. And so, even as he labored on his father's projects, he pursued his own career as a Marxist, in a retro version. Azar Nafisi was fascinated by Mike Gold, and Kanan Makiya, by Leon Trotsky.

Trotskyism proved to be exceptionally strong in the British New Left, much stronger than in Germany or even France, not to mention the United States, and this meant that young Makiya's Trotskyist affiliations seemed fairly conventional in London. Perhaps Trotskyism may have seemed a little idiosyncratic from a strictly Iraqi point of view—or so I can imagine. In Iraq, the main left-wing political tradition was Moscow-line Communism, which proved to be highly attractive for a while. The Iraqi Communist Party commanded an enormous following during the nineteen-fifties—though, in the course of the sixties, the party ended up getting out-maneuvered by the Baath, which began by stealing some Communist techniques, and concluded by crushing the Communists. By the late sixties, as the Baath solidified its dictatorship, the Iraqi Communists were getting decimated. One of the Communist factions (here was a Communist Party that did have factions) launched a guerrilla resistance in the Kurdish north. The guerrillas, too, were crushed. Still, the Iraqi Communist Party managed to cling to life in exile and underground in Iraq—an opposition party with traditions, heroes, international contacts, trade union connections, and the secret loyalties of various families around the country. A good many friends of the Makiya family in Baghdad sympathized with the party. Young Makiya in Massachusetts and London, with his enthusiasm for Leon Trotsky, must have felt a little estranged from his fellow Iraqis on this particular issue—a left-wing rebel against the left-wing rebels against Baathism. In London in the seventies, Makiya agitated on behalf of the Iraqi Kurds. But mostly he occupied himself with other regions of the Middle East, and didn't bother with his own country.

He looked for a workers' movement to arise all over the Middle East, in the Arab countries and even in Israel—a classic Marxist movement to overcome the sundry divisive nationalisms and, in a sweeping revolution, to right the wrongs of the region. Such was the Trotskyist program. Only, this idea failed to prosper, and Makiya took his old-fashioned Marxism and focused it, instead, on a livelier and more promising current of the revolutionary left. This was the movement for a Palestinian revolution. In the years after the 1967 war, the Palestinian movement aroused a vast and genuine enthusiasm everywhere in the Arab world and in the Arab diaspora, in the belief that Palestine's struggle against Zionism stood at the vanguard of the larger Pan-Arabist cause, or, alternatively, at the vanguard of the larger left-wing cause. Makiya lent his support to a small Palestinian faction called the Popular Democratic Front for the Liberation of Palestine, or PDFLP. The PDFLP should not be confused with the Popular Front for the Liberation of Palestine, or PFLP, from which the PDFLP derived— two distinct organizations with the same name, give or take the word *democratic*. The PFLP was the group that struck up an alliance with the German Revolutionary Cells in the early nineteen-seventies, during the period when Hans-Joachim Klein was a member—the group that participated in the attacks at Munich, Vienna, and the airplane hijacking to Entebbe.

The PDFLP, by contrast, considered itself far more sophisticated—a Marxist organization in a shrewd and up-to-date fashion. In the late nineteen-sixties, Edward Said was a young professor at Columbia University, already steeped in Marxism and French philosophy, and he, too, became a supporter of the PDFLP. I was Said's student in those days, studying literary criticism, and I used to stroll about the Columbia plaza at his side, listening to him celebrate the PDFLP as uniquely advanced among the Palestinian organizations—the group most likely to link the Palestinian struggle to the worldwide struggle for Third World liberation in its most progressive version. Said was already an accomplished intellectual, in the early stages of his career, and Makiya was a talented up-and-coming student; and with the backing of professors and students like these two men, the PDFLP seemed to be a promising group—a Palestinian organization capable of attracting the most brilliant intellects of the Arab diaspora, and capable, therefore, of influencing the political culture possibly everywhere in the Arab Middle East.

Only, the PDFLP, too, failed to prosper. The Lebanese civil war broke out, and the factions were

176

innumerable, and the Palestinian factions took their place among them. And, as the years passed and the war continued, the factions degenerated into bandit groups, each one battling against the others in a barbarous spirit and shouting the same old ideological slogans. A few years of this made the doctrines of the PDFLP look as pathetic and dishonest as everyone else's. Makiya in London was surrounded by Lebanese friends, his left-wing comrades, and the comrades had to accept the disappointing reality. (I suppose that Said came to the same conclusions about the PDFLP, given that he did seem to draw away.) Still, Makiya's Trotskyism could always find some new terrain in which to invest its marvelously cosmopolitan nineteenth-century dreams. In Cambridge, Makiya married an Iranian student from Harvard, and, because of his wife, he kept up an interest in Iran, where, as the shah began to totter on his throne, Marxism did seem to have a future. The Iranian revolution, when it broke out, excited waves of enthusiasm from the London Trotskyists. But Makiya had the misfortune of being well-informed on this particular topic. His wife went home to Iran to see how things were going, and she did see, and fled back to London right away, bearing her distressing news. Makiya had no alternative but to turn away from his still-enthusiastic and wholly deluded comrades in the Trotskyist movement. And now, at last, he began to rethink his political principles.

Many years later, he discussed this period of his life with the writer Lawrence Weschler, and, in 1992, Weschler published an account in the *New Yorker* (which you can find in his collection, *The Calamities of Exile*).

Weschler was an unusually well-qualified person to record Makiya's wonderings and thoughts, and this was because, instead of being a Middle East expert, Weschler was a Poland expert. He had reported on Poland's Solidarity for the *New Yorker* during the years of struggle against the Communist dictatorship, and his Polish experiences gave him a vivid sense of totalitarianism and the antitotalitarians—an unusual sphere of knowledge for someone writing about the ideological peregrinations of an Arab intellectual. Weschler questioned Makiya about his left-wing background, and Makiya recounted his serial disappointments with Trotskyism, with the Palestinian PDFLP, with the Lebanese civil war, and with the Iranian revolution. He recalled that, in London during the years of his disillusionment, he visited his neighborhood library in his search for new thoughts and ideas. He came across Arendt's *The Origins of Totalitarianism.* "It completely bowled me over," Makiya said. Weschler was astute enough to recognize that here was a crucial remark.

Makiya went on, "We in the Middle East had taken over certain themes from the West wholesale—Germanic nationalism, Marxism, the imperative toward industrialization—but we'd never experienced the Enlightenment, in which these themes needed to be grounded if they were going to make any real sense. Liberalism is a nasty word in the Middle East, but I came to feel that liberalism in the sense of the fight for individual rights, the claims of the part as against the whole—that was precisely what needed to be asserted in the face of the Baath." Makiya became a liberal. And, having taken this step, he began to think about his native Iraq, and not just about the Kurdish regions in the north. He wrote an account of the Baathist regime called *Republic of Fear*, which he originally intended for the publishing house affiliated with the *New Left Review* in London—a Marxist house, open to modern and retro-Marxism alike. But the publisher balked. Makiya sent his manuscript, instead, to the University of California Press, and the book came out in 1989 under a pseudonym, Samir al-Khalil, which Makiya was forced to adopt out of fear of Saddam's secret police. *Republic of Fear* appeared to be, at first glance, a study of Iraq under Saddam and the Baath dictatorship. But there was more to this book than a simple discussion of Iraq.

Saddam's Baathists exercised an influence all over the Middle East. The Baathists presented themselves as the most radical and intransigent champions of the Pan-Arabist cause anywhere in the region—a muscular party-state with a huge army (the fourth largest in the world, by 1991) and a gigantic oil wealth at its disposal. This was not a tiny groupuscule like the PDFLP. This was one of the fundamental political institutions of the Arab world, which seemed authentically capable of someday marching to Jerusalem and crushing the Zionist foe, as Saddam always promised to do. In writing about this organization, then, Makiya managed to achieve what Edward Said, in all his voluminous works, never did succeed in doing, and this was to examine in close detail, and at length, the nature and philosophy of a major Arab political tendency—to look at such a movement not just as a revolt against Western imperialism and the Zionists but as a movement with its own leaders, history, doctrines, and record of performance, which could be held up to the light and judged. And what did Makiya discover?

One of his achievements was to reveal in some detail several of the ways in which Western political and philosophical ideas had made their way from Europe into the Middle East. The Baath was founded in Damascus in 1943, during the period when Damascus was still under French colonial control, and when France, in turn, was governed by Marshal Pétain. Baathism's founders were intellectuals who had studied in Paris, and these people returned to the Arab world bearing with them a hodge-podge of German Romantic, Fascist, and Nazi inspirations, plus a few organizational ideas drawn from the Communists. The founders took these inspirations and grafted them rather cleverly onto themes from Arab political history and Islam. And, proceeding along this path, they managed to construct a grand mythology about the Arab world, something original, but, then again, not so original. For what was this mythology? The Baathists yearned for the ancient past, and, at the same time, for a high-tech perfect future—yearned in two directions at once.

The Baathists, as Makiya described them, wanted to resurrect the earliest days of Islam, from the time of Muhammad and the early caliphate—rather like the Islamists, in this respect. The very word *Baath* means rebirth. Only, instead of wanting to give new birth to the ancient code of shariah and the veiling of women and the rest of the Islamist dream, the Baathists wanted to give new birth to the glory days of Arab imperial power—to resurrect the early caliphate as a modernized Arab empire. Nor was this idea of theirs entirely secular. The Baathists wanted to infuse their revolutionary project with a spiritual or mystical zeal based on Islam, and yet also on something vaguer or perhaps more modern than Islam—a mystique of the irrational that went beyond Islam. Such was the mythology. And, having constructed their grand and slightly spooky narrative of Arab glory, the Baathist leaders succeeded in persuading their followers to take the mythology for reality. Nafisi, in *Reading Lolita in Tehran*, explains that Iran's addled Islamists managed to "inhabit a realm of pure myth"; and Makiya, in *Republic of Fear*, speaks about the Baathist "fabrication from above of an imagined/imaginary world," a world of "make-believe." Different mythologies; similar impulse. The Islamists in Iran generated a pious cult of suicide; the Baathists in Iraq, a nationalist cult of cruelty. Either way, the endpoint turned out to be the cemetery.

This was Makiya's discovery: the twentieth-century tone and color of Iraq's tyranny, visibly comparable to other experiences of totalitarianism. And, like Nafisi, Makiya found himself remarking, "No one has expressed it better than Arendt." He quoted Arendt on the topic of lies and their effectiveness in a society of total oppression. "The totalitarian mass leaders," Arendt wrote in *The Origins of Totalitarianism*, "based their propaganda on the correct psychological assumption that, under such conditions, one could make people believe the most fantastic statements one day, and trust that if the next day they were given irrefutable proof of their falsehood, they would take refuge in cynicism; instead of deserting the leaders who had lied to them, they would protest that they had known all along that the statement was a lie and would admire the leaders for their superior tactical cleverness." Arendt wrote this passage with Europe in mind—Germany, really, where she had seen the totalitarian system up close. But Makiya judged this to be a fair description of life in Baathist Iraq.

So here again, in Makiya's *Republic of Fear*, was a book by somebody who had enlisted in the left-wing student movements of circa 1968 in order to fight against imperialism and capitalism—only to stumble on the existence of another kind of oppression, which was even worse, and which he knew from his own experience and not merely from his readings. Makiya had discovered the existence of modern totalitarianism—a reality that was illuminated not by any of the philosophical giants of the nineteenth century, such as Marx, but by the giants of the twentieth century, such as Arendt. And, having discovered this reality, Makiya took a further step. He wrote his analysis with a genuine ardor. He adopted the scathing tone of the antitotalitarians—a recognizably modern tone. In this way, his book, too, was a contribution to the antitotalitarian literature of modern times—one more product of the '68 generation's turn from radical leftism to liberal antitotalitarianism.

Only, how was *Republic of Fear*, this well-elaborated revelation about life in the Arab world, received, on the part of enlightened people in other places? It is a little painful to pose this question. The age of totalitarianism got started in the years after World War I, and, as each new totalitarian movement arose and came to power and slaughtered its enemies, and the news began to spread, enlightened people in other countries tended to respond in a number of ways, and two of those responses remained strikingly consistent over the decades. There was the response of good-hearted people who refused to believe the news, and preferred to kill the messengers—to hurl abuse and insults at anyone who tried to explain the meaning and consequences of the totalitarian revolutions. This first response became something of an art over the course of the twentieth century, and Sartre was the greatest of its masters—disdainful in everything he wrote in this vein, dismissive, full of wild accusations, and yet, despite his ugliest traits, charismatic, therefore effective.

Sartre attacked the libertarian left of the nineteen-fifties as "dirty rats," referring to the Socialism or Barbarism comrades, who were busily trying to reveal Stalinism for what it was; and Sartre's reading public, which was vast, turned away from the dirty rats. Sartre responded to Glucksmann and Bernard-Henri Lévy and the New Philosophers in the nineteen-seventies in pretty much the same way. He called those people CIA agents. But it may be that, in the end, blatantly nasty attacks on the antitotalitarian writers never played as large a role in modern thinking as did a second response, which was not at all angry, nor vindictive nor dismissive, but was merely indifferent. Not an accusation—just a shrug. A refusal to pay attention. A lack of interest.

Makiya and his *Republic of Fear*—to stay with him for a moment longer—managed to arouse both of these responses, beginning in 1991, during the first Gulf War. Makiya's picture of Baathist Iraq was horrifying, and, naturally, having painted this picture, he called on the United States and its allies to force their way into Iraq and overthrow the dictatorship entirely—to march to Baghdad and not just push the Baathists out of Kuwait. Makiya went so far as to suggest that, by overthrowing the Iraqi Baath, the United States would set off a democratic transformation in the Middle East. He told Weschler, "I firmly believe that a democracy installed and encouraged in Iraq—previously the most totalitarian state in the Arab world—could have a catalytic effect throughout the region." It was Makiya and the Iraqi exiles who first proposed this idea, not the American neocons, as was widely believed later on. But this kind of outlook represented, of course, a major heresy to anyone who still believed that Western imperialism posed the greatest menace to the peace and prosperity of the rest of the world. And the insults descended, not just on Makiya's views, but on his character.

In 1993, to cite an example, the *Nation* published Eqbal Ahmad, one of the heroes of the Vietnam antiwar movement in the United States, and Ahmad pronounced his verdict on Makiya: "Cut off from traditional Muslim values and also having lost his acquired Marxist moorings, he is a man adrift, afflicted by a terminal case of self-love." This sort of thing became standard. Years later, Tariq Ali, the British '68er (of the unreconstructed school), writing in the *New Left Review*, listed Makiya under the rubric of "quislings—fraudsters and mountebanks." But the harshest of these assaults came from Edward Said, and never more ferociously than in December 2002—at the very moment when every serious reader of the press had come

184

to understand that Saddam's dictatorship was going to be, at last, overthrown by the American-led invasion, unless the peace movement was able to pull a rabbit from a hat. Said wrote about Makiya in the Egyptian newspaper *Al-Ahram*, a major journal in the Arab world. But it hardly mattered where the article originally appeared. By 2002, Edward Said was a titanic figure in the universities and on the intellectual left, all over the world—a Sartre, in his fashion, which meant that anything he wrote was bound to circulate, as well, on the Internet. In writing about Makiya in *Al-Ahram*, Said adopted Sartre's style of polemic, too, in its least attractive version—the disdainful air, the dismissiveness, the vindictive ferocity dealt out from on high, with the irritated air of an aristocrat shoving a peasant down the stairs.

Said in *Al-Ahram* recalled meeting the young Makiya in the days when both of them were supporting the PDFLP. But then Makiya disappeared from Said's view, and, when he reappeared, it was as Samir al-Khalil, the famous pseudonymous author of *Republic of Fear*, whom Said knew to be Makiya. The famous pseudonymous author seemed to Said to be an entirely shady figure: a man of dubious Arabness, feeble in his intellectual accomplishments, reeking of corruption and cowardice. "It seemed not to matter," Said wrote, "that Makiya himself had worked for Saddam or that he had never written anything about the Arab regimes until his *Republic of Fear*, until, that is, he was out of Iraq and done with his employment there." "Whatever meager writing he produced had been written behind a pseudonym and a prosperous, risk-free life in the West." "For someone who has lectured his peers about intellectual responsibility and independent judgment, he provides examples of neither one nor the other." "I find it incredible that Makiya allows himself such sanctimony and vanity, but then why shouldn't he? He has never engaged in a public debate with any of his fellow Iraqis, never written for an Arab audience, never put himself forward for an office or for any political role requiring personal courage and commitment." A dirty rat, in sum. "He is a man of vanity who has no compassion, no demonstrable awareness of human suffering"—and so forth, Edward Said's verdict on the writer who had done more than anyone else in the English language to reveal the principal sufferings of the Arab people in modern times, namely, the massacres and oppression inflicted by Saddam and the Iraqi Baath.

But the main response to Makiya's *Republic of Fear* over the years was not really hostile. The book came to be regarded chiefly as a monograph about Iraq—a study of a local despotism and not of anything larger. *Republic of Fear* appeared in print during the same year that Ayatollah Khomeini sentenced Salman Rushdie and his publishers and translators to death for the crime of having written and published *Satanic Verses*—a fatwa that expressed Khomeini's intention to spread his Islamist authority to every spot on earth. Islamist mobs rioted against Rushdie in Pakistan and in Turkey, and Islamist leaders denounced Rushdie virulently in Britain, and all of this was frightening to see. It was Rushdie who attracted the attention of liberals around the world in 1989, not Makiya, and for the obvious reason that Rushdie was the man who needed defense. Many people did rise to his defense, too—Makiya among them, and, for that matter, Edward Said, as well.

Still, it is striking in retrospect that, amidst the hubbub over Rushdie and the Islamist mobs, hardly anyone among the commentators, perhaps no one at all, paused to contemplate Makiya and Rushdie together—these two '68ers from Muslim backgrounds whose books came out at nearly the same moment. No one, or hardly anyone, remarked that Makiya in his political analyses of Iraq, and Rushdie in the portions of *The Satanic Verses* that touched on Iran (as well as on the Islamist radicals of "Londonistan"), appeared to have stumbled on a single theme, and this theme was the triumph of lunacy—the victory of murderous mythologies over any more realistic view of the world. The simultaneous arrival of these two books should have been a tip-off that a Muslim totalitarianism, in its different versions, did exist, and was creeping forward, and there was reason for worry. The year before Makiya's book came out, Saddam launched the bloodiest phase of his attack on the Kurds—his poison-gas assault on Halabja and a wave of massacres, one of the worst slaughters of modern times. Two years after *Republic of Fear* appeared, Saddam launched his repression of the Shiite rebellion, which turned out to be an even huger massacre. The age was raining blood.

There was a period around the 1991 war when Makiya enjoyed a fame and prestige, in spite of every terrible thing said about his character, Arabness, rootlessness, talent, principles, and intellect. The *New Yorker* published Weschler's skillful profile, which proved to be influential, and the *New York Review of Books* published Makiya himself. In those days it almost seemed that, in the United States and in the other liberal countries, the progressive intellectuals, some of them, were going to take up the cause of the dissidents from the Muslim world with the same eager enthusiasm that, during the nineteen-seventies and eighties, had animated their sympathy for the east bloc dissidents. But Makiya's fifteen minutes turned out to be fourteen minutes. The political and theoretical issues that he had so eloquently laid out in *Republic of Fear*, the questions of Baathism and its relation to European fascism, the question of modern totalitarian impulses in the Middle East—these issues, having come into focus for a brief moment, disappeared right away, at least from the intellectual debate in the United States. It may be that, in France and perhaps in other places, the intellectual atmosphere remained a little more welcoming to the Arab and Muslim dissidents during the next few years. The magazine *Esprit* never abandoned its commitment to the Arab scene. But I think that, on balance, the intellectuals of the Western countries, after their years of campaigning for the east bloc dissidents, grew a little blasé, quite as if everyone had come to believe in the "End of History," especially the people who denied believing any such thing—and no one wanted to think about totalitarian movements anymore or to pay attention to the enemies of totalitarian movements. Makiya's book never did get translated into German.

It took the September 11 attacks to reopen the public discussion of totalitarianism in the Muslim world—and, even then, the discussion got underway a little slowly. A genuinely broad and public debate broke out only in the later months of 2002 and early 2003—chiefly as a practical discussion, a pro-and-con argument about the impending American-led invasion of Iraq. Still, the practical discussion did take place, and touched on some big issues. This, finally, was the true meaning of that barbed exchange between Fischer and Rumsfeld at the Bayerischer Hof in Munich, back in February 2003. Rumsfeld was a bit provocative in invoking the Munich agreement of 1938 and the foolish errors of well-meaning people who, in the nineteen-thirties, had hoped they could calm Hitler down. It was easy to picture Rumsfeld's German audience listening uneasily to the American secretary of defense, and concluding that any hesitation at all on their part to snap their Germanic heels and obey the American diktat was going to get them tagged as Nazi sympathizers. A pretty offensive thing. And yet—this cries out to be said—Rumsfeld was not entirely wrong in trying to remind his audience of the Nazi past.

Makiya had already shown, after all, that Nazi ideas had exercised a genuine influence on Baathism's founders, back in the thirties and forties. It did mean something that, when the Baath was founded, a Nazi victory in the world war still seemed fairly likely. Nazi legacies remained all too visible in Baathism's later developments, too—the racism, the paranoia about Jews, the cult of the leader, the cruelty, the mystical aura. Michel Aflaq, the Baathist theoretician and Saddam's personal mentor, translated into Arabic the writings of Alfred Rosenberg, the Nazi theoretician. Nor were Nazi legacies confined merely to the Baath. By 2003, the whole of the Arab Middle East and much of the rest of the Muslim world was aboil in anti-Semitic literature and even cartoons that had wended their way into modern times from the European ultra-right, years ago. *The Protocols of the Learned Elders of Zion* was not an Arab document, nor an ancient manuscript from the Islamic sources; and yet the *Protocols* began to flourish in Arabic and other languages.

Surely this was something for Rumsfeld's German audience to puzzle over. Here surely were grounds for self-interrogation among the left-wingers who had devoted their lives to struggling against the legacies of Nazism! The path from 1968 surely ought to have led to a few discussions of these particular matters—a quick survey of totalitarianism in the Muslim world and the heritage of the European fascists and Stalinists. Nafisi, Makiya, Rushdie, and other people, too—the Muslim writers with left-wing roots—were thinking out loud about these questions (though, to be sure, each of these writers came up with different answers). Why not everyone else? In that same February 2003, Nafisi published an essay in the *New Republic* making a simple observation: "What we call Islamic fundamentalism, for lack of a better word, is a modern phenomenon, in the same way that fascism and Communism, both products of the West, are modern." But this was not the popular line. Apart from Rumsfeld's arrogant insult about Munich 1938, these kinds of issues figured hardly at all among the government-to-government debates and discussions over what was about to begin. Joschka Fischer, ordinarily so lucid on anti-Semitism and anti-Zionism, said nothing at all in those weeks about Germany's intellectual influences on Middle East extremism, nothing about the problem of totalitarian urges in the contemporary Muslim world—nothing that attracted public attention, anyway.

Still, during those days of heated debate, some of the people who, in Europe, had made the evolution from ultra-radicalism in 1968 to the liberal and antitotalitarian politics of a more modern age did take up these themes. Only, this time, if any one person dominated the discussion in the world of politics, it was no longer Fischer, nor anyone else with a high government position. The principal figure in this new discussion turned out to be, instead, Fischer's old roommate, Cohn-Bendit—Mr. Europe, who was free to say whatever he thought, without any of the inhibiting constrictions that come from wearing the three-piece suit of a proper foreign minister. Cohn-Bendit duly spoke up, and *con brio*, not just once but in three formal and very striking debates, each time facing a different opponent from a different country. These three debates laid out the issues with splendid clarity—the questions about left-wing lessons learned. About totalitarianism. About humanitarian intervention. About war, empire, solidarity, and prudence—the lessons of 1968 and its aftermath, applied to September 11 and its own aftermath. And what did those applied lessons turn out to be, exactly?

CHAPTER FOUR:
DR. KOUCHNER AND DR. GUEVARA

I.

The first of Cohn-Bendit's three debates about liberalism and war took place in Washington, D.C., in a room arranged by the German Greens. This was at the beginning of March 2003—a few days after Fischer's exchange with Rumsfeld at the Bayerischer Hof. Cohn-Bendit squared off against Richard Perle, the American neocon, on the topic of the coming invasion. Perle was one of the leading proponents of invading Iraq and had been so for many years. He was also a man of intellectual polish—a friend, oddly enough, of Régis Debray, the comrade of Che Guevara. Perle, as Debray has explained (not just once, but twice, to my knowledge, in his books), is the sort of person whose conversation veers from nuclear strategies to the verse-structures of Baroque poetry—which Debray took to be a sign of the friskiness of American culture, something admirable. Perle made a worthy sparring partner for Mr. Europe, then, in their Washington debate. Then, too, Perle held a semi-official position within the Bush administration, as an adviser on defense policy, which meant that when Richard Perle said "we," the United States government was speaking, or so you could reasonably infer.

Perle told Cohn-Bendit, "We are, in the first place, interested in disarming Saddam Hussein." There was also a second place. "Now, if we are going to remove

Saddam to get rid of his weapons of mass destruction, consider democracy as an added benefit. The Middle East is unstable, and, in many ways, it is becoming more unstable. Democracies do not wage aggressive wars. We want to bring real stability to the region. That's why we want to change the political system in Iraq." This "second place" was Kanan Makiya's argument—a point drawn from the Iraqi left-wing opposition, affirmed now by the neocon elite.

Cohn-Bendit listened, and doubted. He considered that, in Afghanistan, the American-led invasion had been left unfinished; that Iran, and not Iraq, was the key to the Middle East; that progress ought to be made between Israel and the Palestinians, in order to tamp down the Arab furies. These were strategic points. Cohn-Bendit worried about a bruised feeling of national pride among Iraqis, who might resent being occupied by the United States—a psychological point.

Perle was unfazed. He told Cohn-Bendit, "You are imagining a U.S. general riding roughshod over Iraqis and confirming the worst fears of Muslims around the world that we are an aggressive, imperialist power. I have another view. We have Ahmad Chalabi, chief of the opposition Iraqi National Congress, to enter Baghdad. Ending the current Iraqi regime will liberate the Iraqis. We will leave both governance and oil in their hands. We will hand over power quickly—not in years, maybe not even in months—to give Iraqis a chance to shape their own destiny. The whole world will see this. And I expect the Iraqis to be at least as thankful as French President Jacques Chirac was for France's liberation."

"Oh, come on," said Cohn-Bendit. Still, Cohn-Bendit was willing to acknowledge noble intentions in the American policy. He was too sophisticated to suppose that oil-industry greed and the avarice of the maleficent Halliburton corporation sufficed to explain the American's actions. Spreading democracy in the Middle East seemed to him entirely desirable. He never doubted America's achievements in the past. His own parents learned about D-Day while hiding from the Nazis in the Pyrenees, and, in the joy of the moment—or so Cohn-Bendit liked to say—he was conceived. Naturally he cringed at the Bush administration's line on the Kyoto Protocols and the International Criminal Court. But what truly worried him was Perle's sunny confidence in the radiant future. Cohn-Bendit worried that America had decided to revolutionize mankind. The grandiosity reminded him of the Bolsheviks in the Russian Revolution.

"You want to change the whole world!" he said. "Like them, you claim that history will show that truth is on your side. You want the world to follow the American dream, and you believe that you know what is best for Iraq, Syria, Saudi Arabia, North Korea, Africa, Liberia, Yemen, and all other countries." Here was arrogance. "Because you are Americans, you have the biggest army in the world—you can do anything you want. This is revolutionary hubris."

A few weeks later, with the invasion already underway, Cohn-Bendit went to Warsaw for *Le Monde* and took part in a new debate, this time with Adam Michnik, which meant a different sort of debate altogether. Cohn-Bendit must have found it easy and fun to argue against an

American neocon like Perle. Official Washington in those weeks before the war was in a state of giddy hysteria, and Perle radiated the mood, fanatical and naive: Pangloss on the Potomac. Cohn-Bendit must have enjoyed himself no end accusing Perle and the Bush administration of Bolshevism (though, when Cohn-Bendit repeated the same entertaining accusation to an interviewer from Michnik's newspaper in Warsaw, the *Gazeta Wyborcza*, the interviewer got a little frosty and pointed out that Cohn-Bendit had never lived under Bolshevism). But Adam Michnik was not a Washington neocon. To argue against Michnik, Cohn-Bendit's comrade and admired friend, the Warsaw hero of '68 who had suffered in the flesh and then, in his triumph, had played a central role in building Polish democracy, post-'89—this was something else. A weightier debate.

Cohn-Bendit was respectful, then. He didn't repeat his predictions of doom, if only because, in those first weeks of the war, the scale and gravity of America's blunders in Iraq had not yet become obvious. Still, Cohn-Bendit insisted on raising the issue of American domination. He wanted to know, who gets to decide these questions about invading another country? He acknowledged that, in the Kosovo War, NATO went ahead and intervened in Yugoslavia's affairs even without the approval of the Security Council. An awkward fact. Strictly speaking, the Kosovo War was thoroughly illegal. Cohn-Bendit pointed to a mitigating factor. Most of the countries in the Security Council did support the Kosovo intervention, even if, because of the Russians and the Chinese, the council couldn't get a resolution passed. From this angle, the Kosovo War may have been illegal, and yet a smidgen of international legitimacy attached to it, even so.

Such was his argument to Michnik—a political argument, a little flimsy on the juridical side. Cohn-Bendit stressed his nonpacifist credentials, and here he was perfectly in the right. Back in 1991, when Saddam invaded Kuwait, Cohn-Bendit endorsed the war against him, which was not a typical thing to do for a European leftist, and was super-untypical for a German Green. In '91 it would have been right and proper, Cohn-Bendit figured, to march to Baghdad and overthrow the dictatorship once and for all. "Papa Bush could have liberated us from Saddam Hussein." But Papa Bush did no such thing. By 2003, there were no longer grounds for doing what should have been done in 1991. Nor had the younger President Bush offered any convincing reasons for doing so. Bush the Younger had merely offered lies, and the United States had not done anything since September 11 on behalf of the liberation of peoples—or so Cohn-Bendit argued.

Michnik took a different view. Michnik, who understood Bolshevism all too well, was still afraid of the Russians. He was afraid of right-wing nationalists and populists, who might stage a comeback in Central Europe or even in Germany. He was New Europe in the flesh, which meant that he guarded his very old memories; and the old memories inclined him in American directions. What was going to happen if Poland were ever in danger again? Who was going to stand up for the Poles? It was not going to be France. But Michnik's main argument had nothing to do with advancing Poland's national interest and safety. He wanted to look at Iraq from the viewpoint of Saddam's victims. He wanted to keep in mind the totalitarian experience in all its vividness—wanted to remember what life in such a dictatorship is like, and how the ordinary people feel when they have been abandoned by the free and democratic countries of the world. The Bush administration was not what Michnik called his "cup of tea." The administration's rhetoric struck him as "conservative, demagogic, arrogant, populist." Still, he figured, "a bad government, with bad arguments, has prepared a very good intervention."

"The bad American government?" Cohn-Bendit asked.

"Yes, certainly," Michnik said.

He entertained his own strategic ideas. September 11 had opened a new chapter in world history. He compared the attacks to Kristallnacht in Nazi Germany—a violent atrocity that announced the arrival of new and terrible times. He gave a few thoughts to the American neocons. The neocons, he said, had begun to talk about World War IV (he may have been thinking of James Woolsey, Clinton's former CIA chief, or of Norman Podhoretz)—a phrase which suggested that World War III was the cold war against the Soviet Union. And now the new planetary battle had begun against the totalitarianism of the Muslim world. Michnik thought about the Nazis. He didn't need Donald Rumsfeld to focus his attention on the Munich spirit of 1938. Michnik thought about North Korea and its weapons. He worried that, if the world delayed any longer, Saddam, too, might acquire superweapons, and the time to overthrow him with relatively few risks might have come and gone.

Michnik thought about Iran. The mullahs reigned supreme, but there was also a democratic opposition in Iran, and those people, the democrats, could be supported from abroad. Someday the Iranian democrats might push aside the mullahs and establish a decent society, just as the east bloc dissidents had done. This was imaginable, and democrats in other parts of the world had every obligation to help the Iranians as best they could. But in Iraq, there was no sign of democratic opposition at all, not a single visible indication. Saddam's dictatorship was limitless. There was no prospect of overthrowing him, not now and not in the future, except by an invasion. Michnik thought about America's history of intervening in other countries. Some of those American interventions had turned out badly—and yet, the successes were pretty striking, all in all. Michnik proposed a theory about the sundry American failures and successes. American invasions of nontotalitarian countries, in his theory, ended as disasters. Such was the sorry history of Yankee intervention in Latin America. But when the United States invaded totalitarian countries, the results turned out pretty well, and democracy went into bloom, after a while. An interesting theory! American actions, Michnik thought, did have something to do with the liberation of peoples. He disagreed thoroughly with Cohn-Bendit on this, the most crucial of points. "The essential thing is this," he concluded. "Today the Americans are not bringing a dictatorship with them."

But there was no way for Cohn-Bendit and Michnik to square these two approaches. In Michnik's judgment, Cohn-Bendit had fallen into a groundless fear of

American domination, and at precisely the wrong moment, when people all over the world needed America to lead a resistance against the new totalitarianism of the Muslim world. Cohn-Bendit, for his part, figured that Michnik had projected his east-bloc experiences onto Iraq, which might have been personally understandable, but was bound to lead to misperceptions. And so, Cohn-Bendit turned to his third debate, this time not with an American neocon, and not with an east-bloc '68er, but with somebody rather more like himself. This person was Bernard Kouchner, and the debate, this time, displayed a different quality, deeper, personal, and soulful.

This third debate was entirely French, though with universal implications, at least for anyone with an interest in the '68 generation. The debate was luxuriously relaxed and lengthy, too. An old comrade of Kouchner's from the student movement of the early sixties, Michel-Antoine Burnier—famous in those days for his agitations on behalf of Algerian independence—taped the discussion. And, in 2004, Burnier brought out the results as a book under the droll title, *Quand tu seras président . . .*, or *When You Become President*—a droll title because Cohn-Bendit and Kouchner, both of them, were politicians, in their raffish fashion, and each of those men had surely entertained a midnight dream of ascending to the presidential palace; and neither man had the slightest chance of doing anything of the sort. Nor did either man act as if he gave a damn—not in this discussion, anyway. The two of them snickered at the pomp and rites of political power. Honor guards made them roll their eyes. They did seem to agree that holding a lofty office can help in seducing women.

Kouchner cheerfully proposed, "Office makes orgasm!" He confessed to savoring the luxury of being chauffeured around in an official car—though he worried about getting corrupted by this kind of privilege. He wondered about Cohn-Bendit's attitude toward official cars. Cohn-Bendit explained that, being a Green, the only vehicle at his disposal was an official bicycle.

Václav Havel has written about "the postmodern politician"—the politician who doesn't take his own power too seriously, who refuses to be seduced by the illusions of his own lofty position. "I am not the state" is the motto of a postmodern politician. Kouchner and Cohn-Bendit, by this standard, were ideal postmodernists. The cover of their book showed them already laughing—Cohn-Bendit with his cherubic face and still-red hair, Kouchner with his vigorous nose and sculpted chin, seated on cartoon-like overstuffed red-leather chairs incongruously set on a weedy lawn. But the dominant note in their discussion was not really merry or mocking.

The two of them went back a long time. Burnier, the book's editor, recalled in his preface their original meeting, in 1967 at a cafe around the corner from the Sorbonne and the French Communist student headquarters—a mythic setting for people of their generation. And, with the Left Bank and the student movement of long ago duly invoked, Cohn-Bendit and Kouchner launched their discussion and found themselves delving almost at once into a deep question about their own lives and identities. Those early times and the student left, the mass marches down the Boulevard St.-Michel and the building occupations, the leftist ideologies and debates, the crises, newer ideologies, disasters, and sufferings, the revolutionary commitment, the personal dedication to the militant cause—what was this all about, finally? What had drawn those two men into this kind of life, when they were young? What had been driving them ever since? Their fundamental motive—what was it, at bottom? They did wonder. And, in quizzing one another, they discovered, after a few minutes of conversation, that each of them was gazing back on childhood experiences, and these experiences turned out to be roughly the same.

Kouchner was born in 1939, and Cohn-Bendit, in 1945, which normally ought to have made for a huge difference, given that, in a student movement, two-year gaps are large, and six-year gaps, quasigenerational. Even so, Kouchner and Cohn-Bendit, the elder and the younger, grew up, both of them, under a shadow, and this turned out to be the same shadow. It was the swastika. Cohn-Bendit's parents were Jews from Frankfurt who, when Hitler rose to power, fled to France, and then, when the Wehrmacht invaded France, kept on fleeing from pillar to post southward to France's Spanish border, sometimes in the company of Hannah Arendt, their friend and fellow refugee. (A quotation from Arendt serves as one of the epigrams of *When You Become President*—a line about human rights as a modest ideal, which is also the grandest of ideals, and the most difficult to achieve). If little Danny grew up to become Mr. Europe half a century later, this was because his parents, having been knocked out of their original home by the Nazis, went on careening back and forth between Germany and France ever afterward—the family history that gave Danny his childhood in France, his adolescence in Germany, his university education in France (paid for by the Germans, as part of the reparation effort), and his citizenship in Germany: the mix-and-match of a postmodern personality.

Kouchner's parents were French, Protestant on his mother's side, Jewish on his father's—which led Kouchner, in later life, to declare that he was Jewish "when I want to be." The Kouchner family, too, fled southward to escape the Nazis. Only, they weren't able to find a place to stay, and wandered back to Paris. And, amid the confusion, his paternal grandparents—the Jewish side of the family—took refuge in a center for homeless Jews which had been established by the Rothschilds. This was the worst of all places for any Jew to be, and the Nazis rounded them up and shipped them to their deaths in Auschwitz. Little Bernard was four years old at the time. And so, Cohn-Bendit and Kouchner, both of them, grew up saturated in the fears and pathos and bravura of these terrible events, and, from these experiences, they absorbed some of the same ideas, too. The most important of these ideas had to do with moral character. The idea was extremely simple, really—the answer to a straightforward question, namely, how to judge someone's moral character? By what measure? Both of those boys grew up knowing exactly how to do this. The way to judge anyone's moral character, including your own, was to pose a hypothetical question about France and the Nazis. To wit, what would you have done, in France under the German occupation? In 1943, say—before it was obvious that D-Day was coming to the rescue. Would you have risked your neck and joined the Resistance? Or would you have kept your head down—perhaps even collaborated with the occupation? Would you have been a *résistant*? Or a *collabo*?

On this one matter, Bernard and Danny, for all the difference in age, grew up in total agreement. A good person was a *résistant*. This was an indisputable given. The rock of all wisdom. Then again, back in the nineteen-fifties, there was more than one way to remember the Resistance—and here was the difference between Kouchner and Cohn-Bendit. Kouchner's father was a doctor in Paris, whose sympathies lay with the Communist Party. Young Bernard was brought up to believe that a proper *résistant* esteemed and loved the party. The Communist Party boasted of having been the party of the *fusillés*, the ones who had been shot—the party of the Resistance heroes who had put up the toughest fight. The martyrs. In the years after the war, a sullen memory of the Nazi executions hovered over the Communist Party's every turn and maneuver, and this gave the party an unusual glamour, sulky, grim, and determined. At age fourteen, Bernard enlisted in the Communist youth organization. This was an entirely natural and normal thing to do, and, besides, an exciting thing to do. Young militants were expected to go into the streets on Sundays and hawk the party newspaper, *L'Humanité*, and this led to weekly battles with the *fachos*, in the jargon of the time—the fascists. Sometimes those battles ballooned out of control.

In 1956, the Communist leaders of Hungary declared their independence from the Soviet Union, and crowds of Hungarians poured into the streets in support of this idea. But the Soviet leaders were not about to accept Hungary's withdrawal from the Soviet bloc, and the Red Army went rolling into Budapest to put the insurrection down. In Paris, thirty thousand people gathered on the Champs-Elysées to express their outrage and demonstrate a solidarity with the rebellious Hungarians, and, after a while, some of those indignant demonstrators went marching across the whole of Paris in a fit of rage to lay siege to the Communist Party's headquarters. A mob tried to assault the offices of *L'Humanité*, and the Communists called on their own militants to rally around the newspaper building and defend it bravely. Young Bernard manfully rushed to *L'Humanité* to help fend off the angry crowd. *Résistant*? He was a teen-age *résistant*.

But Cohn-Bendit grew up with a different view of Communism and of Hungary and of everything else. The elder Cohn-Bendits, father and mother both, died while Danny was still a child, and he was brought up by his older brother, Gabriel, whose own instincts were libertarian, in a left-wing vein. Gabriel made his way into the ranks of France's anarchists, and this, in the nineteen-fifties, was not at all like joining the Communists. Once upon a time, the anarchists had played a big role in the French workers' movement and in the artistic avant-garde. But that was ancient history—a memory from the 1890s. By the nineteen-fifties, the anarchists survived in France mostly as a stubborn sect of blue-collar nostalgics, surrounded by a nimbus of intellectuals who amused themselves by flaunting the words *anarchism* or *anarchosyndicalism* as a kind of provocation—the free-thinkers of the anti-

Communist left, a pretty small group. But Gabriel Cohn-Bendit lined up with this tiny group, and he brought his little brother along.

Anarchists loathed Communism. They despised the Soviet Union. They detested the French Communist Party. Anarchists couldn't abide *L'Humanité*. In the anarchist movement, even the knee-high tykes knew that a Soviet invasion of Hungary was an outrage. Most of those thirty thousand people on the Champs-Elysées in 1956 were conservatives or right-wingers, but some of those people subscribed to the tenets of the anti-Communist left, and the anarchists were a current within the larger sea. The mob set out to attack the *Humanité* building, and the anarchists did not pass up the opportunity. From the upstairs windows, the Communists threw firebombs and printers' lead down to the street, like Charles Laughton's Quasimodo in *The Hunchback of Notre Dame*. Fires broke out inside the building. People were wounded. Some people were killed. This was not a minor fracas in the history of the French left. And among the anarchists rioting down below was little Danny—which is why, many years later, when he had become the symbolic leader of the worldwide New Left, he had every right to claim for himself the shocking label, "visceral anti-Communist," a perfectly legitimate honorific to bestow on anyone who, at age eleven, had done what he could, if only by lurking among the enraged mob, to burn down the French Communist Party's newspaper building.

On the topic of antifascist memories, the anarchists cultivated their own magisterial pride and feelings of accomplishment, and their own surly resentments. The anarchists sighed over the Spanish Civil War, their finest hour. The Durruti column from 1936 was a living memory. The anarchists recalled their own militant role in the French Resistance. Young Communists were brought up to revere their antifascist elders, and young anarchists, the same. It was too bad about the fighting between anarchists and Communists at *L'Humanité* in 1956, and too bad that, in the matter of utopian dreams, anarchists and Communists stood for opposite principles, and too bad that Communists, in Cohn-Bendit's phrase, were *crapules de Stal'*—crapulous Stalinists, odious in the extreme. And yet, from a strictly generational point of view, if you were a left-wing kid in France in the nineteen-fifties, it hardly mattered which of these tendencies you ended up joining—the gigantic, centralized Communist Party in one of its affiliated youth organizations, or the scattered lackadaisical circles of nostalgic anarchism, or, for that matter, some other left-wing youth movement entirely, perhaps a youth group affiliated with the Socialists, or the Trotskyists, or the Zionists (a remarkable number of French student leaders in 1968 came out of Hashomer Hatzair, the socialist-Zionist youth movement), or some tiny faction of the Christian left. You joined one or another of those groups in the knowledge that giants had trod the Earth, not very long ago, during the war against fascism; and you were marching in their over-sized footsteps; and someday you hoped to become a giant yourself and wield mighty blows on behalf of the working class. And you sang the militant songs of the nineteen-thirties and forties, and your heart swelled with antifascist zeal.

II.

And yet, in lucid intervals between lyrics, the young French leftists who grew up in the left-wing atmosphere did have to wonder if any of these large and stirring self-conceptions meant anything at all. To join a youth group and stage a few street brawls against the bad guys was a more-or-less normal pastime of young boys and even girls everywhere, with or without revolutionary slogans. But the adults had gone through hell. The young kids of the fifties were going through what came to be known as the Glorious Thirty—thirty years of uninterrupted economic expansion in France, a huge accumulation of national wealth: capitalism's grandest moment. It was true that democracy in France during the postwar decades was not entirely stable or reliable. The French empire was getting violently dismantled in different parts of the world, and this turned out to be a pretty brutal experience in Indochina and Algeria.

Someone in France in those years could always point to the short-run calamities, and make a pretty convincing claim that conditions were, all in all, wretched, and the nineteen-fifties and sixties were merely a continuation of the horrors of the nineteen-thirties and forties. But in the long run, this wasn't true. And so, the young militants in the sundry revolutionary tendencies chanted the chants and meanwhile noticed that, compared to the adults, they were leading lives of bourgeois privilege. The left-wing elders delivered finger-wagging lectures on how grateful the young people ought to be. These lectures demoralized an entire generation. And the young leftists ended up feeling, in stabs of painful self-accusation, a keen sense of their own unworthiness—a tortured recognition that the grown-ups were heroes, and the young people were fakes. This was an unbearable recognition to make—unbearable to some people, anyway.

Young Kouchner, following in the paternal path, enrolled in medical school, and at the same time, enlisted in the Communist Student Union. He flourished. He wrote literary criticism for the Communist student magazine, *Clarté*. His first essay was an appreciation of *Catcher in the Rye* by J. D. Salinger—a slightly subversive topic for a Communist magazine, given that France's Communists tended not to love America's culture. Kouchner became renowned for his stentorian singing voice. The Communist Student Union loved those old songs. And yet, the more lustily the students sang, the worse they felt—every stanza a dazzling new demonstration that some people, the adults, were magnificent, and other people, the students, were not. Régis Debray was one of Kouchner's friends in the Communist Student Union, and, in later years, Debray described these feelings with a sharper acuity than anyone else. The Glorious Thirty was glory's defeat, Debray observed. The militants who had fought in Spain or in the Resistance were the Series A generation. The militants of their own generation, his and Kouchner's, had to recognize that, by contrast, they were strictly Series B. They were the generation of the second rate—the less-than-Malraux, less-than-Camus generation. The students were *résistants* who had nothing to resist. They pretended to resist, even so, and pretending merely aggravated their self-doubts. They dreamed, therefore. They went to the movies.

At the end of 1958, Fidel Castro and Che Guevara and a handful of comrades overthrew the dictatorship of Fulgencio Batista in Havana. No one knew, at first, what the Cuban revolutionaries intended to do, once they had come to power. But, the months went by, and Fidel and his comrades slid visibly to the left, in a Soviet direction. A substantial number of Cubans fled the country. And, at the beginning of 1961, a group of those disgruntled exiles, right-wingers for the most part, together with an occasional left-wing anti-Communist, staged a military invasion at the Bay of Pigs, backed by the United States, with the hope of setting off a general insurrection. Fidel and his government fended off the invasion without much difficulty. Even so, this was a scary moment for the Cuban Revolution. And, in these circumstances, a tremendous excitement went bubbling through the zones of the student left in many parts of the world and especially in Paris. The reason for this excitement might not seem obvious. Cuba was far away, and the disputes between Cuba's revolutionary leaders and Cuba's exiles and the American government might have seemed of no special concern to young people hanging out in the cafes around the Sorbonne—a parochial quarrel of the Western hemisphere, without universal implications.

But the students, some of them, did see a universal implication. The fighting at the Bay of Pigs seemed to them a new outbreak of an older war, and this was easy to identify. It was the Spanish Civil War, the war of revolutionaries versus fascists, suddenly bursting into renewed flame in the far-away Antilles. A good many republican veterans from Spain had taken refuge in the Soviet Union after Franco's victory, and, by 1961, a number of those exiled republicans were already showing up in Havana to renew the struggle, literally singing songs from the Spanish war. The Soviet leaders in Moscow gave Havana their support, just as, in the thirties, they had supported the Spanish Communists. The scenes of solidarity in faraway Cuba offered a living proof that, in spite of every conventional belief, the days of the International Brigades and the French Resistance were not, in fact, at an end, and the past was the present, and the lyricism of long-ago was the lyricism of today. Or perhaps today's lyricism was superior to yesterday's. The young people in Kouchner's wing of the Communist Student Union gazed at the adults of their own party with awe, but they did rather wish that France's Communists would give up on the old Stalinist orthodoxies. The young people wanted a fresher, more appealing, more modern Communism—something less refrigerated, more human. Italian Communism seemed to them fairly appealing, all in all, but, then again, Cuban Communism, even more so. A warm tropical breeze appeared to be wafting outward from the socialist Antilles. Some people liked to imagine so, anyway.

In France, no one was more outraged by the invasion at the Bay of Pigs than Kouchner and Debray, and the two of them marched off to the Cuban embassy on the Avenue Foch in Paris and, in the spirit of the International Brigades, volunteered to fight in Cuba. The attachés at the embassy responded diplomatically.

211

"We are noting your request . . ." This meant no. Even so, these two young militants from the Communist Student Union had already made the crucial generational discovery—the discovery that, in later years, untold numbers of other people would likewise make, in a thousand versions. It was the discovery that history was not yet at an end. The Series B generation did not have to remain Series B. Both of those young men, Kouchner and Debray, took this discovery pretty seriously, too, and each of them fashioned his own response, and put a lot of creativity into that response—and the consequences for everyone else, for many thousands or millions of people around the world, turned out to be, in both cases, pretty big.

Debray refused to be discouraged by the embassy attachés, and he made his way to New York, hitchhiked to Miami, and crossed the strait to Cuba, even without an official invitation. He enlisted in the campaign to teach literacy to the Cuban masses in the countryside. He toiled in this campaign for two months, spent another few months in Cuba, and then another year and a half touring Latin America. This was more than an adventure in student vagabonding. In Venezuela, Debray hooked up with the Marxist guerrillas, who were trying to overthrow the Venezuelan government (which, at the time, happened to be at least nominally social democratic—but this did not faze the Marxist revolutionaries). The Venezuelan guerrillas, in Debray's phrase, were a *maquis*—the word that used to apply to the Resistance in France. He wandered into other countries, and wrote up these experiences, and his essays demonstrated quite a lot of skill, for a young man.

Everything that was lacking in the political culture of the student movement in the United States in the nineteen-sixties—an easy familiarity with the history and doctrines of the revolutionary left—seemed to be at Debray's fingertips: the history of August Blanqui and the French revolutionary conspirators of the nineteenth century; the doings of the Paris Commune and sundry uprisings across the continent; the collected resolutions of the first six congresses of the Communist International; the history of the Shanghai commune of 1927 and the Canton commune of 1928; the battle plans of the Spanish Civil War. Then again, Debray's education was entirely modern, too. At the Ecole Normale Supérieure, Althusser, the Communist philosopher, drew his motto from Lenin, "Marxism is all-powerful because it is true"—a motto of sheer fanatical delirium. Under this motto, Althusser in his seminar concocted a marvelously peculiar revolutionary doctrine, superscientific and faintly Catholic at the same, closer to anthropology than to anything Marx might have recognized. These teachings, as well, shaped Debray's imagination—Althusser's lesson that Marxism could be rendered flexible and creative and up-to-date.

Sartre published one of Debray's essays in *Les temps modernes* in 1965. Che Guevara visited Algeria that year, and a copy of the magazine fell into his hands. Che was in Algeria to work out the details of a complicated bit of hugger-mugger, according to which Cuba was going to export sugar to Algeria; the Algerians were going to re-export Cuba's sugar to Communist China; the Chinese were going to respond by shipping to Algeria weapons from the United States that had been found in Korea, during the Korean War; the Algerians were going to forward the American weapons to Cuba; and the Cubans were going to hide the weapons in containers of olive oil and smuggle them across the Caribbean to the Marxist guerrillas in Venezuela. In this manner, the Venezuelan guerrillas could arm themselves, without risking the difficulties that might fall upon their heads if Soviet weapons were discovered in their hands. (Debray has told the story of this deal in his political memoir, *Loués soient nos seigneurs*, or *Praised Be Our Lords*). Such were the undercover trade relations among the vanguard nations of the Third World revolution. And, as Che labored over these intricate arrangements, he glanced at Sartre's magazine and discovered Debray's essay. Debray was only twenty-four years old, but, soon enough, he found himself invited back to Cuba, this time as the guest of Fidel himself—housed in luxury at the grandest of Havana hotels, freed of every money concern, ushered about from one extravagant event to the next.

Many years later, after he had given up his Communist beliefs, Debray worked as a foreign policy adviser to President Mitterrand, and this meant that, in his memoir, he was able to compare Fidel to Mitterrand, one head of state to another; and the comparison was telling. A normal leader goes home in the evening and enjoys a private life. Mitterrand was a normal leader (doubly so: he had two families). But Fidel, in Debray's recollection, had abolished private life. Fidel was a monomaniac of his own revolution. He was a *latifundista*, rul-

214

ing his island nation like his own hacienda, attending to the tiniest details. Here was a premodern politician. He was a *condottiero* from out of the Middle Ages, with a strictly medieval sense of himself—an autocrat who, like all true autocrats, never laughed in public, or even in private. Fidel was the champion of the spoken word, instead of the written word, and in this way, he stood in the tradition of the European fascists, and not of the Communists. Debray recalled a visit to Cuba by Alberto Moravia, the Italian novelist. Moravia listened spellbound to Fidel's orations, and concluded that attending a mass rally in Havana afforded the pleasures of Communism and of fascism at the same time—the satisfaction of applauding for Communism's social goals, while savoring the extravagances of fascist oratory, Mussolini-style. But Debray, in those days, looked on Fidel and on Cuban Communism with no such feeling of irony.

Debray went through military training in Cuba. On the firing range one day, he was instructed by Fidel in person. Fidel pointed out the virtues of the Kalashnikov automatic rifle, the AK-47. "Today with the AK-47, three men have the same fire power as a company at the start of the century," Fidel said. "This means that three men can begin a war!" Fidel's whole purpose in inviting Debray to Cuba was to convince Professor Althusser's brilliant young disciple to work up this simple insight into a grand revolutionary theory—into essays that could stand next to the pamphlets of Lenin, or could even surpass Lenin and advance the revolutionary project into the age of Latin American socialism and Third World insurgency. Debray duly produced his *Revolution in the*

215

Revolution?—the very title of which signified an intention to go beyond Lenin and make a revolution in the revolution, and yet, to do so with the humble tentativeness of a question mark. Debray accepted Mao's notion that peasants, and not just workers, could make a revolution. He threw in Fidel's insight about AK-47s. And, adding a few other salts and spices, he came up with the military-revolutionary theory that was conventionally known as Guevarism, though it was Fidel's theory, too.

Debray explained that an absurdly tiny number of guerrilla fighters, a microarmy, could penetrate into a jungle somewhere and set up a base for themselves, which, in the language of Che and Fidel, was called a foco. And, having established the foco, the microarmy could launch a revolutionary war. The guerrilla fighters did not have to wait until social conditions were propitious. They could create their own social conditions. They did not have to rely upon the support of a Marxist political party. The guerrillas themselves could establish themselves as the nucleus of a new kind of political party, whose heart and soul would be military, instead of political. They could win support among the campesinos by treading a cautious and somewhat ambiguous path—by avoiding too much contact with the campesinos, and by holding meetings in remote villages only at the point of a gun, so that, if the forces of repression swept down upon the village, the campesinos could honestly claim to have been the victims, and not the supporters, of the guerrillas. In this fashion, the tiny guerrilla army could draw support partly by terrorizing the campesinos, and partly by articulating their grievances, and slowly transform itself into a mass party-army, more

216

rural than urban, more peasant than proletarian, more military than political. And such a party-army could seize state power, eventually.

Fidel dispatched his finest officers and comrades into the jungles of Latin America and Africa to organize their microarmies and begin the revolution along these lines; and, of those resolute people, Che was the first of the first. Che tried repeatedly, in the Congo, in Argentina, and in Bolivia, to establish his focos and launch the war. He never got anywhere at all. The Bolivians and the CIA finally tracked him down and killed him. And yet, for all of Che's failures, something in the Guevarist idea proved to be well-adapted to Latin America. The campesinos in quite a few regions inhabited (and still inhabit) a political culture so primitive and so isolated from the rest of society that utter strangers could, in fact, arrive from nowhere, and proclaim their doctrines, no matter how arcane or bizarre, and attract followers through an ambiguous mixture of persuasion and coercion, and launch a war. This has happened repeatedly in modern Latin American history.

The only problem with this strategy was that, if Guevarist militants armed with automatic weapons could penetrate into the jungle and start a guerrilla war, so could anyone else, given that success or failure had very little to do with the ultimate goals and intentions of the campaign. In Peru, a Maoist philosophy professor led the Shining Path, whose ideas were infinitely more brutal than anything that Che or Fidel had ever contemplated; and Shining Path became an enormous force, for a while, radiating madness at every moment. The Marxist militants of Colombia, without any backing from Fidel, achieved even greater successes, apparently without much of a well-developed program at all, and with the support of relatively few intellectuals. In the Mexican tropics, still another professor of philosophy, Subcomandante Marcos, launched his much more gentle guerrilla movement in the name of postmodernist doctrines of several sorts, which evolved over time unto such matters as transgender liberation; and Marcos, too, enjoyed success, for a while. Then again, large numbers of people launched guerrilla wars in the name of anti-Marxism and anti-leftism, too, and these people, the right-wingers, likewise discovered the satisfactions of automatic weapons, with the final result that, for every left-wing guerrilla in Latin America, there was a right-wing guerrilla. Right-wing triumphs canceled out left-wing triumphs, and lasting revolutionary victories proved to be impossible to achieve, or at least to sustain, except in Cuba. But this logical conundrum in Guevarist guerrilla theory was not obvious at first.

Debray ferried secret messages between Che and Fidel. In Bolivia, he also carried a gun, and took part in an ambush and scouted out terrain, though he pretended to be a journalist. When Che was finally tracked down and killed, in 1967, Debray was arrested, and was lined up against a basement wall, with six rifles pointed at him from ten paces. He ended up serving a sentence in a Bolivian jail. And yet, as he stewed in prison, his intellectual influence blossomed very quickly into something huge, all over the world. Fidel constructed a cult of Che the hero and martyr, and succeeded in spreading this cult to all points. And Debray's *Revolution in the Revolution?* stood at the heart of the revolutionary cult, or rather, at its brain—the Marxist doctrine that gave meaning to those dashing photographs of Che and the posters and the wall slogans. Fidel published *Revolution in the Revolution?* in an edition of three hundred thousand copies—and that was merely the Cuban edition.

Four years later, when Debray was freed, he discovered that he had become a world figure—not quite a symbol, the way Che in death had become a symbol, but, even so, a revolutionary theoretician whose every word was taken as holy writ by militants of the armed left or would-be armed left almost everywhere in Latin America and in many other places, Europe included. Debray went from his Bolivian jail to Chile, to be received in triumph by the Socialist president, Salvador Allende. And then, at last, Debray, the hero, returned to France—to the France that had meanwhile gone through May and June 1968. Revolution was on everyone's lips, and Che's image on every wall, in some neighborhoods. Debray should have cried out in joy at these developments. But Debray was a flesh-and-blood man and not merely a theory-generating machine, and four years in prison had changed his outlook, and when he returned home, he found that he was seriously out of step with everyone else. Almost everything about the post-'68 left-wing agitation in Europe struck him as slightly amiss. He thought that young people were making a big mistake with their cult of Che. The iconic photos of Che showed a sweet-looking man, but Debray thought the photos were misleading. Che in life was a hard, not a soft. The posters of Che seemed to symbolize, in the minds of the left-wing students, a spirit of rebellious freedom—the anti-authoritarianism of 1968. But Debray knew very well that Che was not a champion of rebellious freedom.

In Debray's definition, Che was "a partisan of hardcore authoritarianism." Debray knew that Che, and not Fidel, introduced the forced-labor camps into Cuba, back in 1960, at the start of the revolution. It was Che who militarized everyday work in Cuba with his vocabulary of "brigades," "contingents," and "battles." Che, too, was a man who never laughed—fully the master of himself, metaphysically possessed by his own ideas. As for the student uprisings in Europe, why, Debray could hardly take those events seriously. Professor Althusser had always been an enemy of left-wing "spontaneism," and the '68 uprisings were spontaneism run amok, and Debray remained Althusser's faithful student. Besides, everything that Debray knew from the left-wing past told him that, in any genuine revolutionary upheaval, blood must be spilled; and in Europe in 1968, this had not happened, except in a small way. He was struck by what he called, in a mordant phrase, "the absence of human sacrifice." The uprisings seemed to him an "anarchist psychodrama"—an uprising of petit-bourgeois brats, who lacked the courage to pick up guns and make a real revolution. To be sure, any number of enraged leftists in those years tended to agree with this hard-nosed analysis, which was why the new, post-'68 microarmies enjoyed as much support as they did. But Debray was too much the practical man to suppose that anything useful was going to come from European guerrilla movements. The magical properties of the AK-47 were not going to achieve a damn thing in the campesino jungles of Western Europe. Anyway, he was already beginning to entertain new thoughts entirely.

These new ideas had come to him during his prison years—the period in which, as he later wrote, he "became free," intellectually speaking. He took a long time to gather the courage to express the new ideas—a full twenty years, in the case of his judgment about Che. Still, he finally blurted out his honest beliefs. Debray believed that Che went into the Bolivian jungle for purposes other than victory. Debray believed that Che's truest intention was to lose. To be killed. Che's spiritual battle against the world and against himself required his own death, This was Debray's terrible secret—the truth that he had slowly recognized and had even more slowly decided to reveal. Then again, Debray began to suspect that Che was not alone in this suicidal desire. Maybe the larger desire for revolution in the modern world, Debray began to think, will someday appear to be an episode in the history of the desire for death. Maybe revolution and suicide had somehow drawn close to one another. The vast popularity of the cult of Che in so many places around the world took on a slightly creepy look, from this point of view.

But Debray was thinking of many more people than Dr. Guevara. He thought about President Allende in Chile, who killed himself with an AK-47 in the course of General Pinochet's coup, in 1973, and about Allende's daughter, Beatriz, who killed herself three years later, in

Cuba. He thought about Professor Althusser in Paris, who committed a kind of suicide by murdering his wife in 1980—a period in which, as Debray noted, quite a few French Marxists committed suicide. Debray never bothered to glance across the Rhine at his own comrades in Germany—a characteristic omission, on the part of a French intellectual. But it's obvious what he would have seen, if only he had bothered to look. For what was the history of the German revolutionary movement in the nineteen-seventies, if not a history of people on the verge of suicide, and beyond the verge?—even if no one has ever been able to rule out the possibility of official murders. The prison suicides, if they were suicides, of the Red Army Fraction's leaders, the death of one revolutionary comrade after another, the grisly panache, the riots that broke out in the aftermath of those prison deaths—these things did seem to celebrate a cult of human sacrifice. This was the meaning of Gerhard Richter's paintings.

And if Debray had glanced across the ocean at the United States? In his memoir he nodded in passing at America's Black Panther Party—this same party which had attracted so much admiration on the German left, and all over the world. The Black Panthers' leader was Huey Newton, the Supreme Servant of the People, as he liked to style himself. Huey Newton made his own contribution to the literature of revolutionary theory—his own version of *Revolution in the Revolution?*, except that Newton's manifesto was called *Revolutionary Suicide*. There was the suicide of Abbie Hoffman, the author of *Revolution for the Hell of It*. Suicide was "the apotheosis of the loser," in Debray's phrase, and, in one country after another, these people, the suicides, were the militants who had staked everything on the planetary revolution—the left-wing heroes who, in different ways, had been leaders of the worldwide movement of which Régis Debray had served as a principal theorist. And these people had lost.

Debray in his memoirs gave a few thoughts to the jihadis of the Islamist revolution, too. These people seemed fairly recognizable to him, and this was because the jihadis' love of suicide was not at all an expression of some weird anthropological quirk in Muslim society or a medieval legacy of Islam. Not at all—jihadi suicide was the height of modernity. But Debray's focus was on the Western left, and not on the revolutionary Islamists.

III.

Back in 1961 at the Cuban embassy in Paris, Debray refused to be discouraged, and he pushed onward to Havana. But Kouchner took no for an answer. Kouchner returned to medical school. This was not because he had given up on revolutionary politics. Over the next few years, Kouchner agitated on behalf of the Algerian independence fighters, and he even took a few risks on their behalf and lent the keys to his room to militants from the Algerian underground. Right-wing bombs began to go off in Paris, and Kouchner volunteered to join the left-wing guard protecting Simone de Beauvoir's apartment—a likely target of the right-wing terrorists.

Kouchner kept up his passion for revolutionary Cuba, too. In 1964 the Communist Student Union organized an expedition of French students to Cuba, and Kouchner signed up for the trip. He managed to wrangle an interview with Fidel and even got himself photographed together with Fidel, a characteristic feat on Kouchner's part—already notorious, among his friends, for his outsized ambitions and pushy habits. Kouchner positively boasted of these traits. In one of his essays for *Clarté*, the student magazine, he described himself as Rastignac—the young hero in Balzac's *Human Comedy* who burns with idealism yet also with desire for worldly success: the left-wing social climber par excellence. "Rastignac in 1963 is a Communist," was Kouchner's defiant, self-promoting phrase.

In Cuba he encountered Che on a couple of occasions. Che was minister of finance, and Kouchner saw him at the ministry, puffing cigars and eying the girls. Kouchner put a question to Che: why not hold elections in Cuba? Che dismissively replied by saying, look, that's what they do in the United States. (Or so Kouchner told me—though in an earlier version of this story, which you can find in *Génération* by Hervé Hamon and Patrick Rotman, the same exchange took place between Kouchner and Fidel). Che, in any case, seemed less attractive than Fidel—less human. Still, Kouchner remained, on balance, Che's admirer. Kouchner wrote his medical thesis on the nutritional diseases of starving Africans, and he dedicated it to Dr. Ernesto Guevara, the Argentinean man of medicine— one doctor's homage to another.

In the long conversation that Kouchner and Cohn-Bendit published in 2004, *When You Become President*, the two would-be presidents paused to discuss the 1968 uprisings and what had come out of those events. Cohn-Bendit was aggressively unrepentant. Bakunin and Durruti, the anarchist gods, still excited Cohn-Bendit's enthusiasm. "All revolts are excessive, unjust and sometimes blind," he said. "But finally, what fine times we lived through! What human warmth! What a liberation of speech, of our bodies, of our sexual and intellectual appetites!" Cohn-Bendit was sick and tired of getting blamed for every deplorable social trend that had come to afflict modern society. The Fischer affair of 2001 still weighed on him. He was seething, still, over the absurd accusations. To get smeared, and in such an ugly fashion! For that matter, Cohn-Bendit still shook his head in wonder at Régis Debray for having denounced the '68ers as petit bourgeois brats, back after he had returned from his Bolivian prison. An "anarchist psycho-drama"—ha! Kouchner asked, as a kind of game, what kind of funeral did Cohn-Bendit picture for himself. Cohn-Bendit answered instantly, "The Rolling Stones. I want people to sing 'Satisfaction' at my tomb." He was laughing at himself, to be sure, and yet not entirely. He wanted his ashes scattered on the Boulevard St.-Michel. He wanted to remain in capital-H History *ad vitam aeternam* as the spirit of May '68.

Kouchner, too, looked back on '68 with a satisfied pride. He took part in the marches and demonstrations, and, afterward, he absorbed those experiences into his picture of himself: a '68er, tried and true. He felt an instinctive fondness for anyone else who, around the world, had played a role in the uprisings—a '68er's warmth for all the other '68ers (except that Kouchner couldn't abide the French Maos). He was proud of having lent his automobile to Cohn-Bendit for the ill-fated trip into Germany. And what were the consequences of those long-ago uprisings, in Kouchner's estimation? Many a good thing—in the field of medical services, for instance. Doctors, in the past, used to occupy a lofty place on the social pyramid, and patients, a lowly place, and these hierarchies had served medicine badly. But the uprisings of 1968 radiated an antipathy for social hierarchies of every kind, and the antipathy swept the world of medicine. In the decades after '68, doctors, as a result, began to look on themselves less arrogantly than before. Doctors began to treat their patients more sensitively. This was progress.

But Kouchner remained a little skeptical on some other outcomes of the uprisings and the countercultural spirit. Maybe his own leftism always retained a few habits and assumptions of a slightly earlier age, pre-'68—a leftism that insisted on being practical, more concerned with measurable consequences, less interested in mere attitudes and styles. The countercultural antipathy for social hierarchies swept across the school system, too, beginning in 1968, and the authority of teachers was weakened. This, in Kouchner's view, had proved to be a disaster, at least in some of the schools—in the immigrant working-class neighborhoods of France, especially. Or so he argued—though Cohn-Bendit insisted on refuting his every claim. Kouchner argued that, because of the counterculture, people had come to look on science with suspicion. Cohn-Bendit, the bike-riding Green, was a friend of alternative medicine, and an enemy of nuclear energy and of genetically altered foods. But Kouchner was a man of science.

Kouchner felt that alternative medical approaches were downright harmful, sometimes, if only because they inhibited people with cancer and other serious diseases from getting themselves examined quickly enough. Kouchner was loath to dismiss nuclear power. He worried about pseudoscience. Maybe Kouchner was more like Debray than anyone might have imagined, and shared a bit of Debray's contempt for the petit-bourgeois brats. Kouchner had never wanted anything to do with the post-'68 impulse to build microarmies in Western Europe, though not because he felt an aversion to extreme risk and self-sacrifice. It was just that, like Debray, he found himself gazing in other directions entirely—away from Europe and its New Left reveries, away from the dreams of a European revolution, and toward the Third World.

In 1968, Kouchner thought about Nigeria. A ghastly war had broken out in the Nigerian province of Biafra in 1967. The war was a local affair, without any meaning for other people around the world—a war that was not an episode in the titanic struggle between Soviet Communism and American capitalism, nor a chapter in the magnificent struggle between Third World liberation and colonialist oppression (though some people in France saw in it a struggle between the Francophones of Africa and the Anglophones). Here, in any case, was a violent event that could not be described as the Spanish Civil War. And yet, the Biafra war was proving to be a humanitarian calamity. The Spanish Civil War produced six hundred thousand deaths in three years, a horrific statistic; but, in Biafra (as Hamon and Rotman point out, in their *Génération*) this figure was surpassed in three months. The Red Cross set out to organize a rescue mission, and, since Kouchner had passed his exams by then and was already a full-fledged medical practitioner, he volunteered, on a whim. This time, his offer was accepted. It was September 1968. In the eyes of his own, more militant comrades in France, the decision to go work for the Red Cross in faraway Africa must have seemed fairly absurd. A do-good enterprise—just when the tocsin of capitalism's final demise was about to sound in the streets of Europe's capitals!

Kouchner set off for Nigeria, even so, and waved goodbye to his left-wing friends. And yet, something about the spirit of May and June followed him to Africa, as if stuffed among his medical supplies. The Red Cross, he discovered, was a rigid institution. Red Cross volunteers were required to remain strictly neutral in all political and military disputes. The volunteers were sworn to keep mum, too—to say not one word about who might be to blame for a humanitarian disaster, and who might be the victims. Neutrality and silence were sacred principles for the Red Cross, and this was because the Red Cross insisted on observing the larger principles of international law. Red Cross volunteers entered war zones with the permission of legitimate states; and legitimate states demanded discretion; and the Red Cross was not in the business of challenging legitimate states.

Kouchner toiled in Biafra with three other doctors—a fellow Frenchman, a Yugoslav, and a Guatemalan. All four of these doctors were committed to their medical work, yet all four also happened to come from left-wing backgrounds, and they drew on their political instincts to make a few observations about who was to blame, and who were the victims, in Biafra. The Nigerian government was to blame, they concluded. The victims were the Ibo tribe. In Biafra, as they judged it, the government was pursuing a policy of ethnic extermination. (Later on, some people in the humanitarian movement came to question whether the Nigerian government had pursued any such policy—but Kouchner had seen exactly what was going on and never doubted that a deliberate program of extermination had been put into effect.) But the Red Cross wanted nothing to do with these kinds of judgments. The Red Cross wanted its volunteers and workers to bite their tongues, just as Red Cross workers had always done in the past, and to keep to their humanitarian tasks. Even during World War II, when the Red Cross workers learned about the Nazi gas chambers, they had kept their mouths shut, and this was, for them, a matter of sacred obligation.

So Kouchner and the other doctors in Biafra went about their medical duties, and muttered to themselves about the events before their eyes and about the code of neutrality and silence. And when Kouchner got back to France, he did what no Red Cross worker was supposed to do, and rushed into print with news of what he had seen—the disasters inflicted on the Ibos by Nigeria's government, and the deplorable role played in these horrific events by the British and the Soviet Union, both. His report aroused very little attention. Still, by saying anything at all, Kouchner had already mounted a one-man insurrection against the Red Cross—one more '68-style uprising against the hierarchies of command-and-obedience in a well-established institution. During the next years, Kouchner embarked on still other medical missions: to Peru, to Lebanon during the civil war, to Bangladesh. By the time he returned from this last expedition, he had seen enough. The Red Cross was a law-abiding institution, and Kouchner's sympathy for law-abiding institutions was limited. He and a handful of fellow-thinkers decided to organize a little group of their own, a minuscule alternative to the Red Cross, with more radical principles—not a respectable, legal, establishment organization like the dowdy old Red Cross, but an outlaw group, more aggressive and nimble in its humanitarian activism, less humble, less obedient: a rebellious mini-organization.

Kouchner's idea was to create an emergency humanitarian group capable of reacting to crises around the world quickly and flexibly, and yet capable also of reporting on whatever the volunteer workers might happen to see. A medical organization that could act, and could also speak; devoted to health, and also to truth. A more political Red Cross—a Red Cross willing to identify the political realities that create humanitarian crises, in the belief that humanitarian disasters do not have to be the destiny of mankind. Kouchner and his little circle called their new organization Doctors Without Borders. The new organization was action-oriented. A devastating earthquake flattened the city of Managua, Nicaragua, in 1972, and Kouchner's brand-new Doctors Without Borders rushed to the site—their very first mission. In Paris, the ultras of the revolutionary left, his own friends, could only sneer at this sort of do-good operation and go on plotting their ridiculous microwars—the plottings that, in France during that same 1972, led to the New People's Resistance and the kidnapping of the Renault executive and a few other brushfires of left-wing violence, in the guerrilla spirit.

And yet, in those years, the one person in France or anywhere else in Europe who succeeded in putting together an organization that genuinely resembled a reasonably effective, large-scale, long-lasting guerrilla unit was, in his nonviolent fashion, Dr. Kouchner. Guevarist revolutionaries all over the world, following the doctrines laid out in Debray's *Revolution in the Revolution?*, wanted to take a handful of highly trained left-wing cadres from the law schools and the universities and send those people into the jungles and mountains, in order to establish their military focos. This was precisely what Doctors Without Borders proceeded to do, except without the military aspect. Kouchner's organization recruited people out of the hospitals and the medical schools, and sent those brave souls into the most impenetrable corners of the world. Only instead of carrying AK-47s, they carried medical bags, in order to serve the poor and the oppressed.

The political difference between Kouchner's emergency medical focos and Debray's revolutionary guerrilla focos was not always clear in the early years. In Guatemala, a Guevarist movement launched a guerrilla war against the ruling oligarchy, and Debray, who was a friend of the Guatemalan guerrillas, looked on Kouchner as a reliable comrade and arranged for him to lend a hand. Kouchner duly arrived in Guatemala and, through Debray's contacts, joined up with the guerrillas and performed his medical duties. Kouchner, in those days, was running a sort of medical wing to the worldwide guerrilla movement. Doctors Without Borders offered a medic's addendum to *Revolution in the Revolution?*

Still, after a while, Kouchner began to distinguish a little more clearly between his own missions and the Guevarist revolution. The New Philosophers in France asked their questions about Communism, and Kouchner was perfectly capable of seeing that, on this topic, the New Philosophers were on to a truth, and their old-fashioned left-wing critics were unable to respond, and Che Guevara had nothing to offer the world's poor. This could not have been an easy recognition to make, for a man like Kouchner. To have grown up in the bosom of the Communist movement, only to discover that Communism was a grand mendacity; to discover that he himself had spent many years of his own life upholding a political lie; to discover that his old comrade Régis was wrong on every point—yes, this was a fearsome discovery to make. But, all right, Kouchner accepted the indisputable. His own emphasis had always been medical, anyway, and not Marxist. And so, without breaking his stride, he accepted the New Philosophers' condemnation of Communism, and he kept up his humanitarian missions into the Third World, even so—these missions that were no less dangerous than any guerrilla struggle, no less frightening, no less difficult, but which had the great virtue, in contrast to a Communist insurgency, of refusing to lie.

New Philosophy got its start in 1974, and, in that same year, Kouchner undertook a mission to Iraq. The Baathists were already in power, though Saddam Hussein had not yet risen to the top. The Baathists were massacring Kurds. Kouchner and his comrades set out on a thousand-kilometer trek on horseback from Turkey across the border into Iraqi Kurdistan. He and a couple of other Frenchmen were bombed by the Baathist army—a terrifying event, rendered more bitter by the fact that, as Kouchner knew all too well, Baathism's helicopters and missiles were built in France. This was not his only flirtation with danger in Iraq. Some eighteen years later, in the aftermath of the first Gulf War, when Saddam launched a new series of massacres, Kouchner returned to Iraqi Kurdistan for another mission, and this time barely escaped getting assassinated. He switched from one automobile to another—only to watch the first car get blown up. Over the decades, Kouchner went through a lot of experiences like that during his many months, adding up to years, in the war-zones of Iraq, Lebanon, Liberia, Kenya, Somalia, Sudan, Nigeria, Vietnam, Afghanistan, the Balkans, Nicaragua, El Salvador, and Guatemala. The cult of heroic action? Nobody in Europe was more heroic. The spirit of selfless dedication, the commitment to the super-oppressed, the noble qualities that so many people imputed to Che Guevara? Kouchner embodied every aspect, except for the aspects that, in Che's version, were murderous,

233

tyrannical, and mendacious. Kouchner's project was a Guevarism of the rights of man.

Cohn-Bendit questioned Kouchner closely on these many dangerous expeditions. Cohn-Bendit wondered if Kouchner wasn't drawn, in a perverse way, to danger and risk—if he wasn't attracted by death. Tales of danger-courting heroes and the risk of annihilation did seem to keep cropping up in Kouchner's conversation. "Can you tell me, my dear Bernard, why?" This was a reasonable question. Anybody who reads Debray's rueful commentaries on the life and motives of Dr. Guevara would have to acknowledge that morbid and complicated impulses are not exactly rare in modern times, and more than one doctor may well have found an allure in what is doomed to defeat.

Kouchner responded by quoting the French philosopher Vladimir Jankélévich, one of the heroes of the Resistance. Jankélévich said, "Adventure is the risk of death." Jankélévich wanted to live every new moment with an intensity—"the minuscule adventure of the coming minute." Kouchner cited Alexandre Dumas. He was D'Artagnan, M.D. He was playful.

Cohn-Bendit persisted: "You are one of the men who has seen the most wars on all continents. Maybe more than Napoleon. Are you sure you don't like war?"

"I don't like war," Kouchner replied. "I like to make war against war—a variation that the psychoanalysts will note, I hope, in favor of my lucidity." Great warriors, he emphasized, had never fascinated him. "But I admire the great resisters." That was his explanation, finally. Resistance inspired him. He was, in his maturity, the same person he had been as a boy. He knew who his heroes were—the people "who struggle for the defense of a minority," or, as he said, "for the conquest of liberty." The kind of people who struggle to protect victims like his own grandparents—the Jewish grandparents who could not find a proper place to hide, back in 1943, when little Bernard was four years old. He was on a mission against injustice.

He did have to wonder how to describe this mission in political terms, though, once he had given up on Marxism. He looked to Glucksmann on this point (and Glucksmann, in turn, looked to Václav Havel's guru, the Czech philosopher, Jan Patočka). Glucksmann wanted to speak about a new kind of humanism, something modest and a little gloomy—a "humanism of Bad News," which Glucksmann distinguished from some new utopian Gospel of Good News. A "humanism of Bad News" meant a humanism that aspires to undo the worst, without trying to achieve the best. A humanism without a fanaticism. This impulse fit the new medical-humanitarian movement. But what would this mean in practice—a humanism of Bad News? What were the political implications? This question had to be answered as soon as Kouchner launched the most famous of his missions, the Boat for Vietnam, in 1979. This particular mission was not much different, in practical terms, from any of his campaigns in the past. And yet, this time, because Glucksmann and Bernard-Henri Lévy and some other intellectuals mounted a public campaign on Kouchner's behalf in Paris, and because the young intellectuals recruited the old intellectuals, and Aron and Sartre got involved, the mission attracted a lot more attention.

And the Boat for Vietnam sailed at once into a sea of controversies unlike anything that Kouchner had ever had to face in the past.

Some of these controversies touched on strictly humanitarian issues. Masses of extremely vulnerable people in Vietnam, in their panicky effort to escape the Communists, were racing into the South China Sea, and there was a danger that Kouchner, in trying to rescue these people, might end up encouraging still more desperate Vietnamese to set to sea, which would only feed the disaster, instead of helping to quench it. (This, to be sure, was an old and unsolvable conundrum for any humanitarian campaign: the problem of how to aid the victims without encouraging the victims to persist in victimhood, and without encouraging new people to plunge into victimhood, and without leading faraway observers in other countries to conclude that every last humanitarian challenge had been met. And I could go on, listing the bad results that can easily derive from the best of humanitarian intentions. But I don't have to do so—David Rieff has already done this, in his embittered study of these conundrums, A Bed for the Night.)

Other controversies touched on personal and bureaucratic matters. There was Kouchner's penchant for self-promotion. A number of his colleagues in Doctors Without Borders came to feel that, after their many years of risky and heroic missions together, they had seen Bernard's face in the newspapers one too many times. The man was "publicity-crazy," in Rieff's phrase—though, from Kouchner's viewpoint, publicity was the gasoline that kept his humanitarian organization chugging ahead. Then again, some of Kouchner's critics complained that, in lining up the famous intellectuals to campaign for his mission, he had transformed a pure-minded humanitarian effort into a trendy extravaganza, and the Boat for Vietnam had become, as the sardonic wits liked to say, a Boat for St.-Germain—meaning, the fashionable Left Bank in Paris. These controversies piled one on top of another, and, in the end, Kouchner decided to resolve the issue simply by walking away from his angry friends at Doctors Without Borders and by starting up a rival organization all his own, Doctors of the World, where he could publicize himself to his heart's content—a minor split in the humanitarian ranks, which seems not to have done any damage to the larger cause.

But the sharpest and most vehement arguments over the Boat for Vietnam were ideological and political, and these disputes, the doctrinal quarrels of circa 1979, touched on some pretty fundamental questions. Kouchner's mission in East Asia was meant to save lives, and yet the mission could easily be interpreted as an intervention into the affairs of a sovereign state, the People's Republic of Vietnam. The Boat People were citizens of the People's Republic, and the People's Republic had by no means granted permission to Kouchner or to anyone else to go trolling in the sea for the purpose of rescuing the enemies of the People's Republic. By what right, in the name of what international accord, could Kouchner go ahead with such a mission? He invoked a higher right, but, to be sure, scoundrels on the wrong side of the law always invoke a higher right. In France, a number of people on the left—not the new-style humanitarians but the old-school traditionalists—saw in Kouchner's mission a graver problem, too. This expedition of his may have been humanitarian, whether or not it was legal. But was this expedition, judged by left-wing standards, "progressive"?

Everybody on the left acknowledged the scale of suffering in the Third World, and in Indochina, especially. But the orthodox left clung to a fairly specific interpretation of these sufferings and their origin, and, according to this interpretation, the ultimate blame rested on Western imperialism: the imperialism of the United States, especially. And if imperialism was the problem, what was the solution? Anti-imperialism. And who were the leaders of the anti-imperialist cause in Indochina? These leaders were the Communist parties, like it or not, and this remained the case even if, in one country or another, the Communists behaved a little brutally.

If anyone had conducted a poll of world opinion in 1979 (an impossible thing to do, but I am speculating), the orthodox left-wing interpretation of misery in Indochina would very likely have enjoyed the support of a large majority of people, outside of the United States and the Soviet bloc and perhaps a few other places. Certainly an overwhelming majority of the world's intellectuals would have defended the Communist liberation movements of Indochina, and would have done so with a real vehemence. To anyone who harbored those ideas, the notion of rushing to the rescue of Communism's enemies in Vietnam could only have seemed blatantly and unmistakably reactionary—a retrograde humanitarianism that might succeed in rescuing a few people but was also bound to inflict a political blow on Indochina's best hope for progress in the future, namely, the Communists. In France, some people on the left were already listening to the New Philosophers, and these people lined up with Kouchner and his humanitarian missions, and it was fairly astonishing that Sartre, in the final chapters of his life, chose to be among them.

But a much larger number of intellectuals and journalists, together with the left wing of the Socialist Party in France, not to mention the Communist Party, wanted nothing to do with retrograde humanitarianism and foreign interventions into the internal life of Communist Vietnam. These people, the traditional leftists, wanted to know where this sort of intervention was going to end. This was a reasonable question. For if Kouchner was doing a good thing by sailing the seas of East Asia in a rented ship with six doctors (followed by a few other ships, after a while), why stop there? Why not launch rescue missions on a much larger scale, with more than a rented boat? The debate on this theme arose in France, but it spread right away to the United States and aroused a lot of polemical energy, too.

The exact manner in which this particular French debate migrated to America was something that no one could have predicted, except by noting that, in the history of ideas, nothing is predictable. The crucial role was played by Joan Baez, the singer. There was a lyricism of the nineteen-thirties and forties left, and Joan Baez was, all by herself, the lyricism of the nineteen-sixties left. She lifted her voice, and hearts pounded, and this was true not just in the United States. In the seventies, at the height of her success, the vagaries of life led her to France, where she spent a lot of time, and in France, too, she had her fans. One of those people happened to be Debray, who has described in his memoirs the pleasure he derived one day from listening to Baez serenade the elderly heroine of the Spanish Civil War, La Pasionaria, the mythic Communist orator—one revolutionary woman serenading another, across the generations.

Apart from singing, though, Baez also did some listening (as she has described in her own book, *And a Voice to Sing With*, back in 1987). She followed the French debate over Communism, Marxism, New Philosophy, Indochina, and all the rest. She gazed at the scenes of boat people flailing about in the South China Sea. She was horrified. And, in 1979, she wrote a letter to the Vietnamese Communists, apologizing for America's actions in the Vietnam War—yet also requesting an improvement in human rights. That was a novel thing to do, for someone with a golden history in the American peace movement. She wrote a second letter, a little sharper, requesting improvements once again. This time, she asked some of her comrades from the American left to sign, and a number of people did—Nat Hentoff, I. F. Stone, Allen Ginsberg, and quite a few others, the independent souls.

And now, at last, the debate broke out in the American left, on the far left and among the liberals, both. A great many people looked at Joan Baez's protest and were beside themselves with indignation. A condemnation of the human rights situation in Communist Indochina—by Americans? By the very people whose armed forces had wreaked so much damage on Indochina? The orthodox militants of the American left took out a full-page ad in the *New York Times* to express their righteous wrath. Dave Dellinger, the Christian pacifist, condemned her—Dellinger, the single most influential organizer of the American antiwar movement at its height, in the late nineteen-sixties and early seventies. From Dellinger's perspective, Baez's letter to the Communist leaders was genuinely ominous—a step toward a new imperialism. And perhaps something in this argument was not entirely absurd. In 1979, Jimmy Carter was in the third year of his presidency, and he was groping to come up with a new kind of foreign policy, something different from the policies of the Nixon administration that had preceded him.

Carter had already taken a few steps in this direction. It was Carter who seized on the concept of human rights and elevated it into one of the main concerns of American foreign policy. He established a new bureau in the State Department, and he put the bureau under the responsibility of an officer grandiosely called the assistant secretary of state for human rights and humanitarian affairs. And, with this bureau up and running, the Carter administration and its assistant secretary took to banging the table on behalf of human rights and humanitarian issues all over the world—not just in the Soviet bloc but in Latin America, too, and even in countries whose kleptocrats and dictators might have expected a bit more gratitude from the fickle United States. This sort of human-rights crusading aroused a good deal of anxiety on the conservative right, among the old-fashioned "realists," the old Nixon hands, who figured that Carter was undermining some of America's more reliable friends around the world. (And, to be sure, the reliable friends began to tumble from their thrones: the dictator Anastasio Somoza in Nicaragua, the shah of Iran . . .) And the policy proved upsetting to quite a few people on the orthodox left, as well. Chomsky published his political magnum opus in 1979, *The Political Economy of Human Rights*, in two volumes (written with Edward S. Herman), expressly for the purpose of unmasking human rights as a cruel hypocrisy in the service of imperial rapacity.

Carter's foreign policy, in short, attracted enemies on every side—which ought to have made clear, at least, that he was up to something new. And then, like everyone else, Carter watched in horror as masses of Vietnamese fled into the sea; and he examined his own moral conscience, and I suppose that he glanced at the state of American public opinion, too, where he would have seen the debate over Joan Baez and her protests. He ordered the Sixth Fleet into action. The American navy went about scooping up the boat people. This was not like Bernard Kouchner sailing around with half a dozen kindly doctors. And, with Carter's order to the fleet, the whole quandary of a human-rights policy and of humanitarian action in the modern world, the enormous tangle of unresolvable questions about foreign interventions and their justification and purposes and consequences—all this, our modern predicament, floated majestically into view.

To everyone all over the world who had spent the previous fifteen years laboring to get the American military out of Southeast Asia, in the keen belief that Western imperialism and especially the United States posed the greatest of all dangers to poor people everywhere—to everyone who still clung to that august and deeply felt opinion, the spectacle of America's navy trolling the seas in order to rescue the enemies of Vietnamese Communism was bound to seem profoundly repulsive. But did U.S. imperialism really pose the greatest of dangers? Mightn't the Communists pose a danger of their own—as demonstrated all too obviously by the flight of thousands of unhappy Vietnamese into the sea? Maybe the power of the United States, with its navy and everything else, was a force that could be harnessed to good purposes, as well as to bad ones—depending on circumstances, and on the choices of the people in power, and on the demands of democratic opinion. Maybe the strength of the strong was not, by definition, a crime against the weak. Maybe power was a tool that, decently employed, could do a world of good for the most oppressed of the oppressed, just as, in the past, the power of the big Western countries had all too systematically done worlds of harm. Maybe Western strength and imperialist oppression did not have to be synonymous.

This was the new possibility in the field of human rights and humanitarian action, the grand-scale alternative view of world politics that had merely been hinted at by the tiny cadres of Doctors Without Borders and Kouchner's new Doctors of the World and a few other people—the Che-like adventurers with their medical bags and their non-Che-like ideas. If a rented ship from France was a good idea, the Sixth Fleet was a better idea.

This logic was undeniable. At least, Kouchner seemed to think so. People with power, Kouchner began to say, had a right to intervene in other societies, under certain conditions—a right, in spite of the sacred mandates of international law and the inviolability of borders. There was a right to intervene on humanitarian grounds, and to do so "without borders." More than a right—there was, in Kouchner's word, a "duty." A moral duty to use power to rescue the vulnerable. A duty to use this power wherever people were in desperate need. A duty for wealthy and powerful countries not to stand by, fat and happy, while the rest of the world went to hell. Or, to put this entire argument the other way, the supremely oppressed had a right to be rescued, no matter what the theorists of anti-imperialism or the defenders of the inviolability of borders might say.

None of this was entirely unprecedented in the history of ideas. The ancient left-wing principle that used to go under the name of internationalism showed no concern at all for the integrity of duly constituted states. "Workers of the world" meant workers without borders. But whether Kouchner's new theory of humanitarian intervention had remained faithful to this left-wing provenance or had evolved into something new, perhaps an idea beyond any of the conventional ideologies, neither left-wing nor right-wing nor any-wing—this was a murky question. Kouchner sometimes wondered about this. Were left-wing motives the best of all motives that anyone could have? He noticed a few oddities in his experience as a humanitarian militant, and he commented on these oddities to Cohn-Bendit.

Kouchner had gotten to know quite a lot of medical volunteers and humanitarian workers, his own comrades over the years—the people who served side by side with him, at risk of life and limb, in the world's most dreadful hellholes. A good many of these courageous volunteers came from respectable left-wing backgrounds like his own and were happy to see the impudent, anti-authoritarian spirit of '68 radiating from the words "without borders."

And yet, for all the '68ers and repentant Communists and newly liberalized anarchists in the humanitarian ranks, Kouchner noticed that most of the people toiling at his side in one dangerous mission after another over the years came from backgrounds of a rather different sort. And what were these very different backgrounds? They were religious. Kouchner pointed this out to Cohn-Bendit, and refrained from drawing any conclusion. A few comments about Jimmy Carter, the pious Christian, might have been apropos here. But, having made this observation, Kouchner had nothing else to say, and neither did Cohn-Bendit—quite as if the two of them, in contemplating the humanitarian enthusiasms of people from religious backgrounds, had tiptoed to the edge of their political understanding, and could only pause and wonder about what might lie beyond. For what exactly is the urge that leads some people, and not others, to devote themselves to the cause of the oppressed in faraway places, and to push aside the many sophisticated arguments that may stand in the way of doing so, and to risk their own necks? What is the inner force, the pressure, that prompts some people to commit themselves to this kind of life? There is a left-wing answer to this question, but there are other answers, too, and Kouchner and Cohn-Bendit, for all their experience and virtues and courage, were not the right men to come up with those other answers.

CHAPTER FIVE:
THE '68ERS AND THE TRAGEDY OF IRAQ

I.

Mostly Kouchner and Cohn-Bendit discussed the Iraq crisis and what to do about it—the issue that had been tearing apart their wing of the European left ever since late 2002 and early 2003. Kouchner did have a few thoughts on this topic, not just because of his background as a militant and a medical volunteer. He had become, by that time, an old hand at government service, chiefly because of his years as minister of health, but also because of one additional experience, which dated back to the nineteen-eighties. François Mitterrand may have been a devious old bird, but socialism, in the Mitterrand version, always made room for romantic and revolutionary impulses of several kinds (romantic idealism was Mitterrand's most devious stroke of all); and one of those impulses prompted him to bestow on Kouchner an almost whimsical title. This was Secretary of State for Humanitarian Action, a magnificent-sounding office which was placed under the auspices of the foreign minister—an inspiration that Mitterrand could only have drawn from Carter and the U.S. State Department's new assistant secretary for human rights and humanitarian affairs. Kouchner, as secretary of state for humanitarian action, wielded only a modicum of power. President Mitterrand was not about to dispatch the French army to wage full-scale war against Serbian nationalists in the Balkans; and neither was he about to send Dr. Kouchner to wreak mayhem in remote corners of the Third World in the name of all that was good and decent.

Still, Kouchner did have his modicum of power, thanks to Mitterrand, and he put the modicum to constructive use. Humanitarian actions under the tricolor of France duly sallied forth into Africa. Some of these official interventions were no more impressive than the Boat for Vietnam, even if they could claim to be official actions. In Liberia in 1990, Kouchner stumbled on a warehouse filled with some thirty-five hundred terrified Francophone Africans, who were about to be massacred by their enemies. He got on the phone to Paris and requested a ship from the French navy. The navy had no intention of sending a ship. Kouchner called up his old contacts from the Boat for Vietnam campaign and rented a ship of his own, and, in his official capacity, he denominated the ship a vessel of the French Republic. And he and France's rented ship sailed away with the endangered French-speakers.

A cynical observer might dismiss these African adventures of Kouchner's as little more than French imperialism for the postimperial age. Or someone could look on these missions as too little, too late—shoestring operations that could have done a lot of good, if only they hadn't been shoestring. Even so, the secretary of state for humanitarian action racked up some achievements, and one of these achievements was in the field of law. The Carter administration in the seventies tried to build a legal foundation in sundry international accords for the new human-rights policy, and France's secretary of state for humanitarian action did as best he could to lay down legal precedents for humanitarian intervention. In 1988 Kouchner, together with the jurist Mario Bettati and a few colleagues, drew up a resolution for the UN General Assembly, asserting the right to intervene into one country or another in case of natural disasters or some other dreadful emergency. This resolution was passed. It was General Assembly Resolution 43/131—the very first expression in international law, as Kouchner judged it, of a victim's right to be represented by someone other than his own government.

Two years later Kouchner managed to get another resolution approved by the General Assembly. This was Resolution 45/100, asserting a right to create "humanitarian corridors" to aid the victims: one more intrusion into the sacred autonomy of sovereign states. A blow against borders. At the end of the first Gulf War, in 1991, Kouchner helped draw up still another resolution, this time addressed to the Security Council, calling for military intervention into Iraq on behalf of the Kurds. France proposed the resolution. The Security Council voted its approval, and the intervention duly took place—a historic event in the annals of international law. In this fashion, the legal record in favor of humanitarian interventions grew ever larger, until, by Kouchner's count, some 350 resolutions had eventually been passed.

Kouchner's appointment as the United Nations administrator in Kosovo in 1999 followed more or less logically from these activities. His years at the Ministry of Health gave him a proper administrative background. But he was appointed also because, in France, the political class had come to recognize that Kouchner, their own man, the medical D'Artagnan, had pretty much invented the concept of humanitarian intervention as something more than a once-in-a-blue-moon exceptional act, and had popularized this idea, and he had even succeeded in rendering the idea modest and demure by clothing it in international law. The NATO intervention in Kosovo, the '68ers' war, was, in the last analysis, Dr. Kouchner's war. Chirac had succeeded Mitterrand by that time, and Chirac talked up Kouchner to Kofi Annan at the UN; and Annan appointed Kouchner to take over from the NATO armies and administer Kosovo in the name of the UN. Kouchner presided over a staff of several thousand people in Kosovo—the "most ambitious project the UN has ever undertaken," in Michael Ignatieff's account. Kouchner said things like, "The fascists must not prevail." Here was La Pasionaria. And this experience, too—Kouchner's antifascist years of command at the UN headquarters in Pristina, from 1999 to 2001, commanding his team of '68ers—shaped his view on Iraq in the prewar months.

He came at this question from a perspective very much like Michnik's. He wanted to ask, who really has the moral authority to call for military interventions against this or that dictatorship around the world? Who has the right? And, like Michnik, Kouchner figured that moral authority rests with the dictatorship's victims. Kouchner felt that he understood the victims in Kosovo pretty well. He did not love those people. He and the UN team and the NATO soldiers labored hard on behalf of oppressed and miserable Kosovars of every ethnic persuasion; and, even so, the ethnic haters went on hating. The sheer number of ethnic groups in Kosovo was scarcely to be believed—Muslim Albanians, Orthodox Serbs, Roman Catholic Serbs, Serbian-speaking Muslim Egyptians, Ashkalis (Albanian-speaking Muslim Gypsies), Goranis (who are Albanian-speaking Christian Gypsies), and even a group of people who were pro-Serbian Turkish-speaking Turks, in testament to the marvelous richness of human experience; and each of those mini-ethnicities stewed in its own pot of resentment and pursued its specialized vendettas. Victims were victimizers, in Kosovo. People got murdered left and right. And, on all sides, the annoying, unlovable, and sometimes detestable victims reserved a special indignation for their own saviors, the UN administrators and their NATO enforcers.

There were Kosovars who felt outraged not to be receiving better salaries from their international benefactors, and Kosovars who felt indignant at being made to wait for travel permits. Kouchner had to rub his eyes in astonishment. The nerve of these people! And yet, he recognized that, at some level, most of the Kosovars did see in NATO's intervention and in the UN protectorate their own salvation. Mad hatreds and ideologies may blind entire populations twenty-three hours a day, but sooner or later the twenty-fourth hour rolls around. And with these Kosovo experiences in mind, Kouchner wondered, what were the Iraqis likely to think about a potential foreign intervention into their own benighted homeland? Bush was plainly headed toward a military confrontation with Saddam. How did the Iraqis look on such a prospect? With eagerness? Or were they recoiling in horror at the very notion of heathens, pagans, imperialists, Zionists, Crusaders, and oil-plunderers pushing their way into Iraq?

In December 2002, when the debate over the impending invasion was reaching its highest pitch, Kouchner ventured into Iraq to see with his own eyes what the Iraqi attitudes might be—his third trip to the country. He visited the Kurdish north and questioned everyone he met, and he described their responses to Cohn-Bendit in *When You Become President* (as well as in a second book, *Les guerriers de la paix*, or *The Warriors of Peace*). The Kurds had been fighting against the Baath dictatorship for more than thirty years by then, and during all that time, they had begged repeatedly for a foreign intervention. Kouchner made his way to the exact spot where the Baathists had tried to assassinate him, back in 1992. He visited the zones where the Baathists had carted off Kurdish women and sold them into prostitution in the Gulf countries. He traveled to Halabja for a return visit—to the town that Saddam had gassed (using, as Kouchner recalled with more than a little bitterness, weapons made from French and German materials, and helicopters built by the French and the Americans). He learned something that might have surprised a great many people. The Iraqis in 2002 were afraid of Al Qaeda.

Kouchner was perfectly aware that, all over the world, people had listened to the Bush administration fulminate about the dangers of a secret alliance between and Saddam and Al Qaeda. He knew that, all over the world, entire publics had come away convinced that Bush was an atrocious fabulist, and no such alliance existed. But the Iraqis told Kouchner about precisely such an alliance, or what they concluded to be an alliance, between Saddam and a group called Ansar al-Islam, which was Al Qaeda's affiliate in Iraq (and the ancestor of what became, after the invasion, a number of splinter groups affiliated with Al Qaeda). In 2002 Ansar al-Islam was already battling against Saddam's worst enemies, the anti-Baathist Kurds. Ansar al-Islam was growing stronger, too. Hundreds of bin Laden's militants had fled Afghanistan after the overthrow of the Taliban, and some of those militants had turned up in Iraq and had taken their place in Ansar al-Islam.

The newly energized organization was seizing villages and converting them, Taliban-style, to the glory days of the ancient caliphate. Fantasists of the seventh century were wandering around the village streets, brandishing their scimitars. Here was the "realm of pure myth," in Nafisi's phrase. Ansar al-Islam tried to assassinate one of the Kurdish leaders in Iraq, Barham Salih, a few months before Kouchner's visit. (Salih became famous for making a dramatic speech to the council of the Socialist International, in Italy in January 2003, pleading for left-wing solidarity, and, indeed, for an invasion—the single most forceful statement of the left-wing interventionist position.) And yet, the Iraqi Kurds, for all their fear of Al Qaeda, were chiefly afraid of Saddam. Quaking in fear, actually.

It was impossible for Kouchner to penetrate into Iraq's Arab zones because of the dictatorship (and because of Saddam's demonstrated habit of trying to assassinate Bernard Kouchner). Instead, he went to Iran to speak with Iraqi Shia who were living there in exile. Nobody in modern history has massacred more Arabs than Saddam Hussein, and most of the massacred Arabs were Iraqi Shia—two hundred fifty thousand of them, by Kouchner's estimate (though the standard American estimate was three hundred thousand). This had led to certain feelings. And to each of these Shiite exiles in Iraq, just as to each Iraqi Kurd, Kouchner put the same question: "Do you really want the American war?" And each new person, as he reported to Cohn-Bendit, looked him in the eye and said, "Why are you waiting to fight at our sides? Why are you waiting to get rid of Saddam Hussein?" The responses reminded him of Wolf Biermann, the German '68er, the songwriter and hero of the antitotalitarian cause in East Germany.

Biermann was old enough to recall World War II and the American bombings. And Biermann recalled his mother's reaction: "I learned from my mother that there are bombs that rescue." Kouchner pointed out to Cohn-Bendit that, in Kosovo in 1999, a great many people had tended to reason along those same lines. Kosovars didn't want to be bombed; and yet wanted the United States to start bombing. Visiting Iraq and Iran in December 2002, Kouchner came to think that a vast number of Iraqis had arrived at pretty much the same degree of schizophrenic confusion. They were frightened of war. Yet they wanted to be rescued—not from Saddam's weapons of mass destruction, but from Saddam himself. They wanted to be rescued from Al Qaeda's militants and affiliates. And they had a right to be rescued. In Glucksmann's phrase, these people had the "right to D-Day."

On the other hand, as Kouchner judged it, not every D-Day ought to require a D-Day-like scale of operations. The key to success, in his analysis, was to keep everyone among the big Western powers focussed on a single goal, and this had to be the overthrow of the Baathist dictatorship. The Western powers had to be solid as a rock on this one point. Every last gesture and syllable from the lips of the Western powers ought to have been designed to convince the Baathist leaders that Saddam's days in power were numbered, and no miracle at the last minute was going to salvage the dictatorship—no maneuver by the UN or foreign-policy initiative by a powerful country. If only Saddam could be convinced of his own impending defeat, maybe he would scuttle away peaceably, in order to keep his wealth and save his family. Or maybe his more reasonable generals, if any such people existed, might feel encouraged to take their chances and stage a coup d'état. Or the generals might scuttle away themselves, and the regime might collapse. These were attractive possibilities—nonviolent ways of bringing the dictatorship to an end. But none of these best-scenario possibilities was going to congeal into reality if the Western powers showed even the slightest weakness or hint of dissension among themselves.

And if Saddam stayed put and no one mounted a coup? The next step might well have to be military, but not on a giant scale. Precision bombing strikes and a few other military actions had succeeded in pushing Milosevic's army out of Kosovo in 1999. And more: the NATO bombings undermined Milosevic's standing back home in Serbia, and his cronies gradually deserted him,

255

and his enemies grew stronger, and, after a while, Milosevic's enemies managed to stage a genuinely peaceful revolution in Belgrade and overthrow him. Kouchner wanted to try similar methods in Iraq, a series of graduated steps, in the hope that one or another of those ever more forceful measures would ease Saddam out of power, without having to resort to anything as violent and risky as a full-scale invasion. Give less-than-war a chance, was his idea—though the only way to do this convincingly was to brandish the certainty of all-out war as the only alternative. Kouchner belonged to a bipartisan, left-and-right political club in France called the Club Vauban, and, in the name of this organization, he and another club-member composed a manifesto under the slogan, "Neither War nor Saddam," advocating these graduated measures. The manifesto emphasized how despised was Saddam, among Iraqis. "Why does everyone pretend not to know that more than 80 percent of the Iraqis are hostile to Saddam Hussein?" This figure referred to the fact that Kurds accounted for 20 percent of the Iraqi population, and Shia for perhaps 60 percent, and there were Christians, too, and other groups, and some of the Sunni Arabs likewise hated Saddam—making for a percentage, all in all, that had to be higher than 80. This manifesto ran in *Le Monde* during the first week of February 2003—a few days before Fischer's confrontation with Rumsfeld in Munich.

II.

Only, by then, everything was already going to hell, from Kouchner's point of view. He was already furious—judging, at least, from what he went on to write during the next year. He was furious at his own government, in Paris. Bush and the United States had been putting ever more pressure on Saddam and had been making it ever more obvious that, unless Saddam caved, the invasion was guaranteed to go ahead. The French should have done everything possible to make these American threats look ever more fearsome.

Instead, Chirac's French foreign minister was running around the world actively campaigning against the American policy. Kouchner was convinced that, by agitating so energetically against the American invasion, French diplomacy was only sustaining Saddam in his fantasy that somebody, somewhere, was going to rescue his regime. This was a disaster. The no-war policy was the enemy of the less-than-war possibility. After the invasion, when the American investigators had finally managed to interview Saddam and some of his generals in their prison cells, we learned that, until the last moment, Saddam did imagine that, because of objections in the Security Council, the United States was not going to invade. This was Kouchner's fear entirely—what he had warned against in his manifesto in *Le Monde*.

Then again, Kouchner was furious at the Bush administration. The whole style of the American administration rubbed him the wrong way. On this point, too,

Kouchner was of one mind with Michnik. The official American arguments for war made no sense to him. He understood the larger strategic issues at stake. He spoke about Arab extremism and not just about the dangers posed by this or that particular organization or political party. He knew that something ambitious had to be done, not just in Iraq but with an eye to transforming the entire region. Chatting with Cohn-Bendit, Kouchner pointed out that gentle and conciliatory approaches had made no progress at all in coping with the extremist currents in the past. He was furious that Bush didn't make the pure humanitarian case. The argument for war against Saddam, in Kouchner's eyes, resembled the argument for war against Milosevic, except that, compared to the Serbian nationalists, Saddam was worse, by far. Some opponents of the war make the case that, as the years went by, Saddam's boot had begun to tread less heavily on Iraqi necks, and the dictatorship was no longer the dreadful atrocity that it had been, in the past; and war was no longer justified. Kouchner saw this differently. Saddam staged an election in 2002 and triumphed with 100 percent of the vote—which, in Kouchner's eyes, ought to have shown the world that, in darkest Iraq, there was no room whatsoever for political opposition, nor the slightest hope for political alternatives in the future, nor anything but fear, torture, murder, poverty, demagogy, and paranoia: the ruin of an entire society.

So why didn't the Bush administration rest its case on human-rights and humanitarian grounds? Kouchner was genuinely puzzled by this. He judged that a human-rights and humanitarian argument would have carried a weight in Europe, politically speaking. Kouchner and Michnik—to cite only those two men—were some of the most admired figures anywhere on the continent. There is such a thing as moral prestige, and these men embodied it. That was why Cohn-Bendit argued with them in such a friendly and ingratiating style, and with such conspicuous respect—never for a moment challenging their motives or their ideological bonafides. Why didn't the Bush administration, in trying to drum up a few European allies, look to these people and their arguments—to the dissident heroes and the admired humanitarians? Why not make at least a cursory effort, a gesture, to bolster those people's standing and popularity and persuasiveness in Europe? The Bush administration made no such effort. But then, why not, at the very minimum, put a bit more emphasis on human rights at the UN? Kouchner pointed out to Cohn-Bendit that, despite what the American state department may have imagined, a human-rights approach enjoyed quite a lot of support at the UN.

In December 2002, the General Assembly voted a resolution condemning human rights in Iraq—Resolution 57/232, which was adopted nearly unanimously. This did not have to be a meaningless gesture. The whole trajectory of thinking at the UN, over the course of the nineteen-nineties, had led ever more steadily in the direction of Kouchner's "right to intervene." In 2001, after the terrorist attacks, Kofi Annan and the UN were awarded the Nobel Prize, and, in his acceptance speech at Stockholm, Annan spelled out the new thinking. "Today's real borders," he said, "are not between nations, but between powerful and powerless, free and fettered, privileged and humiliated. Today, no walls can separate humanitarian or human rights crises in one part of the world from national security crises in the other." Here was precisely the logic for the invasion of Iraq, declaimed with the deep solemnity of a UN Secretary General at a Nobel Prize ceremony. The logic was to end the tyranny of the extremists in Iraq as part of a larger campaign to bring about the downfall of extremist currents throughout the region: a human-rights intervention that was also going to be a national-security intervention.

Why didn't the Bush administration seize on that kind of thinking and make a fuss over Resolution 57/232—and, on that basis, call for Saddam's final overthrow? But this was outside the realm of possibility, in Washington. During the whole period after 1989, the worldwide human-rights movement and the worldwide humanitarian movement had veered in ever more militant directions, until the UN had responded with speeches like the one that Annan delivered in Stockholm. "Without borders" had become the concept of the hour. But the Republican Party in the United States had remained pretty much indifferent to these developments. The Republicans, most of them, had sunk into a nationalist isolation and simply could not understand the shifting mentality in the NGOs or at the UN. The Republicans did believe in borders. Bush himself, having run for president as an opponent of the Kosovo war, could hardly be expected to sing a song of human rights and humanitarianism in connection to Iraq—at least, not without undergoing a philosophical transformation. And so, the administration never managed to understand that, within the UN and among the sundry do-good NGOs, quite a few people might have turned out to be America's allies, if only America had presented a case on grounds of human rights and humanitarianism.

Kouchner was beside himself about this. He preferred Tony Blair. In Kosovo, when Kouchner was still the UN administrator, Blair arrived on a state visit, and the two men fell into what appears to have been, in their eyes, a lively and fascinating discussion of the ever pesky question of who was going to foot the bill for British patients in French hospitals. During the build-up to the Iraq war, Blair spoke about Saddam's weapons and even led the British public to suppose that Saddam's weapons posed a terrifying immediate threat—in forty-five minutes, no less. This was, in Kouchner's word, a "lie." And yet, as he observed, Blair knew very well that, in regard to Iraq, the real argument for intervention rested on something larger. A journalist in the know (Peter Stothard, formerly of the London *Times*), reported that, in Blair's private mutterings as he paced around the office, the prime minister had left no doubt whatsoever that tyrants worried him more than weapons. Blair chose to keep those thoughts to himself. Why was that? Kouchner knew why. It was because the antipathy for Bush among the British public was overwhelming, and antipathy was going to trump any kind of human-rights or humanitarian argument. And it was because the British, following the French example, had never really comprehended the meaning of September 11—had never entirely appreciated the dangers posed by the extremist currents in the Arab world. Kouchner was beside himself over these things, too—beside himself that Tony Blair, who knew better, had failed to cope more skillfully with these vexing political difficulties.

But mostly Kouchner fumed at the Americans, and fumed still more once the war had gotten underway. By the time that he and Cohn-Bendit sat down to ruminate over the good old days of the sixties for their *When You Become President*, the Americans had already rolled into Baghdad. The two or three weeks during which Donald Rumsfeld had seemed to be a military genius had come and gone, and the months were passing, and the immensity of the American blunders had become unmistakable. And Kouchner was dumbfounded. In Kosovo, he and his UN team had recognized right away that security was the number one key to everything else. And there was a number two key: the delicate matter of guaranteeing the personal dignity of everybody in an occupied society. The big problem facing the UN administrators in Kosovo had been what to do with Kosovo's ethnic-Albanian nationalist guerrillas—the Kosovo Liberation Army. The nationalist guerrillas emerged from the war against Milosevic with the deluded impression that somehow their own tiny ragtag army, and not NATO, had driven the Serbian soldiers out of the province; and the victors expected to reap the spoils. Kouchner and his UN colleagues had to come up with clever ways of dealing with those deluded people in their triumphal euphoria.

To disband the Kosovo Liberation Army would have made no sense at all. The nationalist guerrillas, offended in their pride, would have gone on fighting, crazy as that would have been. Kouchner and his team came up with the idea, then, of retaining the Kosovo Liberation Army, and reorganizing it into a National Guard, American-style—the Kosovo Protection Corps—which was going to be less than a full-time army, yet would dole out military prestige and a dependable salary to its soldiers. Reorganizing the guerrillas into the brand-new Kosovo Protection Corps was never going to untangle the million problems of Kosovo. And yet, this very clever maneuver accomplished what political maneuvers are generally supposed to accomplish, which is to buy time. Why didn't the Americans try something similar in Iraq? Why dissolve the Baathist army? Why not merely reorganize it, and keep on paying the soldiers, and let them retain their prestige, and, in this fashion, buy a little time to come up with deeper solutions to the problems of Iraq?

Kouchner was amazed that the Americans failed to protect the government buildings in Iraq; amazed that no one guarded the hospitals; amazed that America's soldiers made themselves so remote from the ordinary Iraqis—though, to be sure, this was how the American military had behaved in Kosovo, too. Kouchner knew very well that progress in disastrous situations can only come from face-to-face encounters with the everyday population. In his time in Kosovo, he had taken the trouble to learn to speak somewhat in Serbian. He orated in Albanian. He picked up a bit of Roma. He ran hair-raising risks to make himself a familiar face to the ordinary Kosovars—someone whom the people felt they could trust. He stood in front of angry crowds and announced bad news, when the news was bad. The Kosovo Albanians demanded information about their disappeared. Kouchner took it upon

263

himself to tell them, face to face, that their disappeared were dead.

Why not approach the Iraqis in a similar fashion—respectfully, honestly, in a style that was sober, friendly, and personal? Why not study a little Arabic? Rulers from outside can perfectly well establish a relatively decent relation with liberated populations, if only they take the trouble to understand the people and present themselves properly, or so Kouchner believed. He knew that, in the UN bureaucracy and even in the American government, quite a few people had already demonstrated a talent for administering faraway regions. Not every American was an Ugly American. His own team in Kosovo was bursting with capable and selfless people, a magnificent team. Including some Americans! Why didn't the American viceroys in Iraq draw on people like Kouchner's team from the start?

His Gallic nostrils flared. He detected the unmistakable odor of executive incompetence. His phrase for the American administrators in Iraq was "obtuse dogmatism"—a damning phrase, given Kouchner's experience and enthusiasm for overthrowing Saddam. He could not understand the American treatment of Grand Ayatollah Ali al-Sistani, the Shiite leader in Iraq—the most influential person in the country. The American viceroy, Paul Bremer, never managed to meet Sistani. Kouchner was dumbfounded yet again. Iraq wasn't Bremer's country—it was Sistani's. The Americans blamed the ayatollah for refusing to meet with them, but Kouchner knew very well that, with a proper approach, any reasonable person will eventually yield to an insistent suitor. Sergio Vieira de Mello of the United Nations succeeded in meeting Sistani. The ayatollah was approachable. But, by the time the Americans made a serious effort, Sistani had already been offended, and it was too late.

Kouchner was apoplectic. And yet—this was interesting—he was not in despair. He figured that, fiascos and all, the intervention was going to be for the best, in the end. "You'll see," he told Cohn-Bendit, "history will say that the Americans liberated the Iraqis, whatever the future may be, even if they did it poorly." That was an impressive thing to say, given the scale and amplitude of Kouchner's experiences around the world. He was quite sure of his opinion. He said, "The Americans have led a legitimate war on the basis of bad and false reasons, and, unfortunately, without the international community. In the long run, they will win, even so—but badly."

He thought about the European peace movement. The mass marches against the war, the placards, the slogans, the chanting crowds—every last aspect of this movement reminded him of the grossest errors of the left-wing past. "In our generation," he told Cohn-Bendit, "antiwar marches used to offer protection to the worst Stalinist regimes, the most frightening massacres, and because of this, I wouldn't let myself take part anymore—nor would you, Danny. God knows how often we heard people shout, 'Down with Bush!' But I didn't hear even the tiniest cry, 'Down with Saddam!' And let's not even mention—or rather, we had better mention—the anti-Semitic incidents. . . ."

Cohn-Bendit tended to agree with this condemnation, though his tone was milder. For that matter,

Kouchner himself sometimes softened his tone. Kouchner happened to attend a peace march in Boston before the war, and he noticed right away that America's peace movement was a bit more attractive than anything he had seen in Europe. "I found myself in the middle of a crowd of Democrats, sympathetic types, and not idiots. But when they demanded that America not intervene, they were doing exactly what Saddam wanted them to do." Kouchner's thoughts drifted back to France. The mild tone evaporated. "And then, there was this scandalous statistic, this poll—33 percent of the French preferred Saddam's victory to Bush's!"

Cohn-Bendit objected, "That was a statistic which turned up in one poll, and never again."

"You're wrong," said Kouchner, "they came up with it twice."

Kouchner was astonished by the failure of so many people on the left to see the larger grandeur in the interventionist idea, even in its peaceful versions. His idea was to establish the rudiments of a global social democracy, to call it that—though he didn't have any particular phrase to sum up his larger vision. He had developed a plan for worldwide health insurance, at an extremely primitive level, which could be offered at a cost of $34 per person per year (a sum that he derived from Jeffrey Sachs, the American economist). A minuscule amount. Perhaps even this tiny amount was out of reach, given how many people stood in need—yet, even so, Kouchner wanted to begin. This was globalization conceived in a positive light—a globalization of political rights and social benefits, and not just of markets. Maybe some of

Kouchner's ideas on themes like this overlapped with the dreams and aspirations, the socialist nostalgias, of the antiglobalization movement. But the antiglobalizers did not recognize that power and wealth were needed to proceed with this kind of program.

Kouchner had no patience for those people, the antiglobalizers. He regarded them as incoherent. He sneered—and here he lost Cohn-Bendit. The antiglobalizers, in Cohn-Bendit's view, might well have made a few incoherent demands. But social protest movements are always a little unruly and excessive, and what the hell. Cohn-Bendit remembered all too clearly how the older generation used to sneer at his own mass demonstrations, and he had vowed never to do anything of the sort, once he had achieved the august status of a left-wing elder himself. Cohn-Bendit figured that, for all their flaws, the antiglobalization demonstrators were raising valid issues, and he was pleased—quite as if, in his eyes, the antiglobalizers were the heirs to his own 1968. Or so he suggested. Kouchner did his best to sympathize with Cohn-Bendit's paternal benediction. Okay, maybe the demonstrators had succeeded in bringing this or that important issue to public attention, and this was good. Kouchner made the concession.

But he could not get himself to respect these demonstrators. To go mill about the streets, chanting nonsensical slogans—what was this? Kouchner believed in action—in taking things into your own hands, and not just stamping your feet and demanding that someone else go do something. He was a Guevarist still, in his reformed fashion. He believed in risk. He thought big. He was a visionary. Anyway, he was a doctor. The antiglobalization rioters running amok in the streets of perfectly safe and wealthy cities like Seattle or Genoa—who were these people, in comparison to the volunteers who risked life and limb on behalf of the NGOs or the United Nations in the remotest jungles and deserts on earth? Really, the antiglobalists were zeros, in Kouchner's estimation. Do-nothings in romantic costumes. He seemed barely able to restrain himself from calling them petit bourgeois brats.

He had put together yet another NGO, this one called *Malades sans frontières*, or Patients Without Borders, to launch his program for worldwide health service. He had managed to persuade Chirac to back the new organization, together with the Socialist leaders in France. Kouchner had raised money from bankers. His new group had gone into Africa and begun to work, trying to construct local health organizations. Why didn't more people on the left recognize what it means to take action on behalf of the poor and the oppressed? "Direct action" was the anarchist ideal. Here was direct action. Global responsibility? Here it was. The logic for over-throwing Saddam descended from precisely this larger idea, in his judgment: solidarity with the oppressed, responsibility, action. Why didn't more people on the left view the war in that light?

But Kouchner's argument about Iraq mostly focused on a specific reality, and this was the scale of the disaster in Iraq under Saddam's rule. The grimness of the human landscape in Iraq, together with the plea for help that so many Iraqis had been making for so many years, sufficed to justify the invasion, even without reference to worldwide principles. Yet where were the champions of the humanitarian cause, the human-rights militants, who should have responded to these pleas? Kouchner wasn't concerned about the orthodox left—the traditional left that had always been wrong about totalitarian movements, the left that pictured America as the fountain of evil, the left that had never wanted to overthrow Milosevic, the left that, in February 2003, was perfectly content to march in the streets side by side with the supporters of Saddam and the wildest of Islamist totalitarians, as masses of people had done in the giant antiwar demonstrations in Paris and London. Kouchner didn't give a damn about the anarchist rioters at the antiglobalist demonstrations, either, even if Cohn-Bendit obliged him to mutter a sympathetic word or two. He cared about the human-rights and humanitarian militants. Those people, his own comrades, where were they?—the people who, during the Balkan war, had played such a noble role in calling for a NATO intervention? The people who had grown infuriated over Srebrenica—what had happened to those people, to their social consciences, to their rebellious spirit?

In France, a handful of intellectuals stood up to call for the overthrow of Saddam, even if they gagged at Bush and his clumsiness. Kouchner saluted Pascal Bruckner (who nearly writhed at the very thought of Bush), and the filmmaker Romain Goupil (one more '68er, from the Trotskyist ranks), and perhaps two or three others. Kouchner saluted Glucksmann, his fellow-thinker on questions of intervention ever since the Boat for Vietnam—Glucksmann, who, in his indifference to public opinion, went poring through Bush's speeches, looking for the passages that might be fairly reasonable. These were the intellectual heroes of France. Their numbers were pitiful. Not even a faction: a clique. Kouchner could have turned his gaze to other countries, and he would have found similar people to salute all over the world—Biermann and the philosopher Hans Magnus Enzensberger in Germany; Michnik and a good many of the old dissidents from the Slavic east; a variety of Blair's foreign-policy supporters, on the left and right, in the English-speaking countries; Mario Vargas Lllosa and still other people in the Spanish-speaking countries; and so forth, from one region to the next. And yet, these people added up to a pretty small minority among the world's intellectuals. Kouchner was right about this. In the case of Kosovo, in 1999, a lot of people in the Western countries had eventually come around to lending their support to what was, in the end, an American war. But, in the case of the Arab world in 2003 and afterward, there were still a great many people who figured that, if a giant wrong was crying out to be righted, wasn't this the Palestinian issue?

Kouchner did think the Palestinians had been wronged. He had worked on their behalf for decades, ever since the Lebanese civil war—just as he had worked on behalf of the Algerians, even earlier. But it was strange that, in regard to truly the largest of horrors and injustices in the Arab world, so many high-minded people preferred to avert their eyes. The tenor of Kouchner's comments on the intellectuals and human-rights and humanitarian militants suggested pretty plainly that, in his judgment, a huge number of people had betrayed their own best principles—had done this out of anti-American spite, or out of loathing for Bush, or who knows why, but they had done it. A dismaying situation: America, in its maladroit fashion, had just succeeded in overthrowing the worst tyranny of modern times, and the world's intellectuals were virtually quivering in indignation that such a thing had taken place. What did Kouchner feel about Cohn-Bendit, then? By Kouchner's logic, Danny Cohn-Bendit should have been marching at the head of a parade, calling for the overthrow of Saddam.

Cohn-Bendit did call for Saddam's overthrow, actually. It was just that, in Cohn-Bendit's estimate, the proper way to overthrow Saddam, as he explained, was to maintain a multilateral pressure, and help the Iraqis themselves overthrow their own dictator, someday. Kouchner could hardly take this seriously. Cohn-Bendit's program was a nonprogram. A make believe. Kouchner didn't point a finger, though.

III.

Instead, in his amiable way, he talked with Cohn-Bendit about someone else, and this was Joschka Fischer. The two of them analyzed Fischer's three-piece suits. What were these supremely dignified and conservative suits about?

Cohn-Bendit observed that, for Fischer, three-piece suits and bodyguards were his "monk's habit"—proper costumes for a foreign minister. "When I speak to him about his outfit, Fischer always responds, 'These are my work clothes. If I don't wear them, I won't be recognized by my peers.'" Cohn-Bendit gave this some thought, and figured that, on balance, it was better to remain a humble politician like himself—a "simple" caucus leader for the Greens in the European parliament, with no need to deck himself out in diplomatic regalia. But then, this difference between himself and Fischer, between his own modesty and Fischer's superambitiousness, went back a long way.

Cohn-Bendit recalled the moment when he and Fischer first decided to go into ordinary politics. It was 1978, a mere two years after the Meinhof riots. The two of them and Cohn-Bendit's future wife were sitting around the table, talking about their prospects. The libertarian-spontex revolution was finished, and they knew it. Cohn-Bendit wanted to join the nascent Green movement.

Fischer said, "You're right, we should join the Greens. But, in order to have an influence over how this party-movement evolves, one of us is going to have to be a candidate for the Bundestag." This seemed true enough. On the other hand, anyone who ran for office was going to have to do a lot of glad-handing among the Green activists.

"It's not for me," Cohn-Bendit said. "But if you want to do it, I'll back you."

So he and Fischer made a pact. Fischer did the politicking, Cohn-Bendit endorsed him, and Fischer got himself elected. He was a Bundestag representative from Hesse. In this fashion, Fischer became the genuine politician, the one with big-time personal ambitions. But this involved accepting a politician's way of thinking and speaking.

"To reach a certain level of power in a party," Cohn-Bendit observed, "it's necessary at some moments not necessarily to lie but, in any case, not to say the truth. You keep quiet, you let things go. When he was climbing his way up through the Greens, Fischer was always calculating. He spoke only when he was sure of having the right effect. Otherwise he kept quiet. There's no point in being peremptory and wanting to push yourself on people when you don't have a majority."

Fischer bided his time, waited until his own popularity had grown, and only then did he act.

Cohn-Bendit explained, "That's how he became the most admired political man in Germany"—though Cohn-Bendit sometimes considered that Fischer's cautiousness was a mite excessive. In his oratory, for instance. Cohn-Bendit sincerely believed that Fischer's speeches would be livelier if only he wouldn't take so much advice from the chancellery—a suggestion which Cohn-Bendit offered in a frank and friendly spirit, from one pal to another.

Kouchner, too, wondered about those three-piece suits. "I've lived interesting moments with Joschka Fischer before and after he became Germany's foreign minister. But I think that he began to lose his way with his three-piece suit." What did this mean, though—to lose his way? Kouchner didn't explain. He had no desire to criticize Fischer, at least not openly. Kouchner was himself a politician, after all, and Fischer was his ally on most matters, maybe his biggest ally on the European continent. Kouchner pulled back. "I've never taken his three-piece suit seriously," he said, on afterthought. "I know the Joschka who is underneath the suit. I've been close to him in Strasbourg, Frankfurt, Paris, and other places, and we have in common our history of being activists and militants—qualities that are ever more rare in the political parties."

Kouchner sympathized with Fischer over his problems in political life. Kouchner knew very well that Fischer's popularity in Germany had exposed him to lies and calumnies from the second-rate press, and even from the first-rate press. He remembered the attacks on Cohn-Bendit's moral character, too—the scandal season of 2001. For that matter, Kouchner had run into his own hail of wild and dreadful accusations, lately—in his case, something about an oil company in Burma, where he had foolishly left himself vulnerable to attack as a corrupt politico of the lowest sort: an unscrupulous, fake humanitarian, secretly offering his benedictions for sale to the highest bidder. The journalists were gleeful about these attacks. The Burmese oil scandal taught Kouchner a lesson about public persecution, and he gazed at Fischer and at Cohn-Bendit, his brothers-in-politics, and pangs of solidarity for the wronged and the hanged throbbed in Kouchner's comradely heart.

And yet, and yet—what about those three-piece suits? Kouchner remembered one day when he was still the UN administrator in Kosovo. He traveled to Berlin and visited Fischer at the foreign ministry and was dismayed by the gray politicos in his entourage and by the wooden quality of the man's language. "I looked at the three-piece suit of this former ultra-radical and I understood that he had chosen a road that allowed him to rise higher than me in the political hierarchy." Maybe there was a note of jealousy here, or of personal distaste. Kouchner went on, "You're not going to talk me out of this idea that three-piece suits are a way of separating yourself from other people."

But the upsetting point, to Kouchner, was mostly a matter of principle. How could it be, after all, that Fischer had responded to the Iraq crisis the way he did? That was the question lurking behind those jabs at the three-piece suit. Fischer: a man with an upstanding background as revolutionary militant. A man who had lived his life by asking, *résistant* or *collabo*? A man who had learned about Srebrenica and had firmly responded by saying, "No more Auschwitz," and had pushed Germany to take action. From Kouchner's point of view, it was hard to understand why this same Fischer would have turned against the interventionist logic now, in the crisis over Iraq—Fischer of all people, the impudent rebel against despots and dictators of every sort. Kouchner suspected that, like Tony Blair, Fischer had kept his eye on the polls, and this was natural. But there had to be more to Fischer's response than political opportunism, there was obviously more, the tremble in his voice at Munich made this indisputable—and none of this was mysterious, not really.

Cohn-Bendit had laid out the reasoning, after all—Cohn-Bendit, the least opportunistic of all politicians. The several arguments about multilateralism, the United Nations, and international law, the worries about American "Bolshevism" and ineptitude, and about the sorry consequences that were likely to unfold in the Arab and Muslim world—those were substantial arguments, whatever Kouchner might think of them. Anyway, Fischer spoke up on his own account. During those same months in late 2003 and early 2004 when Kouchner and Cohn-Bendit were preparing their *When You Become President*, Fischer delivered a couple of speeches dealing with Iraq and the transatlantic crisis. And these speeches—at Princeton University in New Jersey in November 2003, and at the annual Munich security council, the one in February 2004—spelled out his thinking.

It's true that Fischer's speeches tended to roll by like enormous freight trains, each phrase dragging along the next like a row of box cars, with each new phrase constructed as if by committee: an endless series of foreign-policy "initiatives," "declarations," "programs," "processes," and "systems." Fischer spoke about "the Partnership for Peace program," the "declaration on a common future," the "EU/NATO Mediterranean process," "a system of regional security cooperation based on transparency and verification," and so forth, endlessly. "In order to succeed," he said (in his speech at Munich in 2004), "the European Union, the US and Canada should, in view of this major challenge to our common security, pool their capabilities, assets and projects to form a new transatlantic initiative for the Middle East"—which could only mean that something called a "new transatlantic initiative" had been launched, presumably replacing a previous transatlantic initiative, and the new initiative, whatever it might be, was going to generate its own committees, partnerships, declarations, systems, processes, programs, subinitiatives, capabilities, assets, and projects.

Cohn-Bendit had put his finger on this problem exactly—Fischer was leaning too heavily on the chancellery for his speeches. But was this entirely bad? Maybe Fischer was a step ahead of Cohn-Bendit on this particular matter. Watching those formulaic phrases roll by, you could imagine that, in choosing his phrases and hitching them together, Fischer had taken into account the efforts and views of any number of hardworking consultants and officials in the Berlin ministries—such that every time he delivered a speech, the toilers in government ministries all over Berlin could look up from their work stations and identify with sober pride the very phrase that had sprung from their own memos and committee deliberations. The speeches were dull, but the speechmaker was popular, and this was because every new sentence tumbling from his mouth was more than a sentence: it was a coalition.

Besides, the meaning of those clunky phrases was clear enough. Fischer addressed the weapons-of-mass-destruction argument about Iraq, and soberly noted that, in the rush to war, the weapons inspectors had never been allowed to complete their business. Fischer thought that Germany's refusal to participate in the war had already been validated by subsequent events. He thought that multilateralism was the key to effectiveness. He endorsed the UN, though he acknowledged the UN's imperfections. He considered that, without the legitimacy of a UN resolution and international law, the war in Iraq was going to be made still more difficult, and the results were very likely going to be disappointing.

Fischer considered that, by fighting in Iraq, America had fallen into a terrorist trap. He emphasized the importance of winning the peace, but, then again, he seemed to think that winning the peace wasn't really possible. He promised that, if NATO ever chose to play a role in Iraq, Germany would not stand in the way—though he also specified that German troops were not going to participate. Anyway, he doubted that NATO could be of much help. His pessimism was unshakable. He did want to see progress between the Israelis and Palestinians, though. The sincerity of Fischer's concern for Israel's security was unusual in Europe, something truly distinctive. But each of his other points was fairly conventional—popular positions for any politician to adopt in Germany and in France and in quite a few other European countries, too, especially in the Western half.

If anything was surprising in Fischer's argument, it was only that, in assembling his many careful phrases, he seemed to have overlooked almost completely the kind of reasoning that Kouchner and other people had been proposing ever since the crisis got underway—quite as if Fischer's single audience had become the foreign ministers and defense ministers of the Western countries, the Powells and Rumsfelds and their counterparts in each country, without regard to his old comrades, the reformed rapscallions of the revolutionary left. From a viewpoint like Kouchner's, it was well and good that Fischer stood up to defend the United Nations. Kouchner himself was devoutly enthusiastic for the UN. And yet, Fischer never seemed to reflect that, if only Germany and France had stuck together with the United

States during the early months of the crisis, the UN would have ended up stronger, instead of weaker. And what about Kouchner's argument that a European insistence on standing shoulder to shoulder with the United States might have persuaded Saddam to give up without a fight, or with only a token fight? Fischer didn't even bother with this argument.

But the oddest aspect of Fischer's speeches was something else. At the heart of Kouchner's argument about the war and the larger crisis stood his picture of Saddam's dictatorship. In Fischer's speeches, a picture of the dictatorship never seemed to appear. Fischer said, "The federal government feels that events have proven the position it took at the time to be right"—meaning, presumably, that the weapons inspectors had discovered no weapons, and the invasion had played into the terrorists' hands, and a lot of people were getting killed for no good purpose. All this did seem to be true in the short run—with the long run yet to be decided. Still, the invasion had made some other discoveries. The stories about Saddam's son torturing Iraq's Olympic athletes and about women college students getting raped by the Baathist elite—these were anecdotes. They turned out to be innumerable. Every family in Iraq seemed to have a trove of these anecdotes, all to themselves. The invading armies found their way to a large number of mass graves. These were more than anecdotes. A grave was discovered containing what were said to be the remains of two thousand members of a single clan, the Barzanis. The country was studded with Srebrenicas. The economic sanctions on the Baath regime (together with the missile attack by Clinton, back in 1998) may have crushed Saddam's weapons programs, but sanctions had also crushed the middle class and the poor.

The failed electric lines symbolized the failed society. The oppression, fear, and poverty, the wretched state of the culture, the brutalized tone of some of the religious leaders, the paranoid conspiracy theories, the crowds in some of the Sunni districts chanting in a mood of sheer delirium their hatred for Jews and their love for Saddam—every aspect of Iraqi life turned out to be uglier, sadder, and more squalid than anyone had imagined. The country had been demolished, one psyche at a time. This—in a land where the middle class had once flourished, and Baghdad was once a jewel of world civilization, and the Baghdad Philharmonic had performed. No weapons of mass destruction; and yet, mass destruction. The invading armies discovered the rubble of more than three decades of totalitarian oppression. What was the point in having a militant background like Fischer's if the discovery of these dismal and infuriating realities seemed to register hardly at all on his official oratory?

To be sure, Fischer earnestly wanted the invasion to succeed, once the war had gotten underway, and he said so repeatedly, in his speeches and interviews. He said, "We have to win the peace together because otherwise we will lose together." He said, "We are in agreement that the coalition's efforts must be successful. The forces of violence and terror in Iraq must not win the upper hand." He sounded emphatic. Germany had even undertaken a number actions to help out in Iraq. Germany had agreed to forgive Iraq's debt. German officers were training a few hundred Iraqi soldiers and policemen—though the training was taking place in the United Arab Emirates, where the German trainers did not have to worry as much about protecting themselves. The Germans were playing their part in the larger war on terror. They were helping to guard the Strait of Gibraltar. The German navy was patrolling the seas off East Africa. A couple thousand German soldiers took up positions in one of the military sectors in Afghanistan. This was not a small contribution. The process that had begun in Kosovo had not ended in Kosovo. The era of postpacifism had arrived in Germany, and German military forces traveled hither and thither around the world in the interest of peace and freedom and self-defense. These were Green achievements—Fischer's, above all.

Even so, his speeches on Iraq were gloomy and a little distant—the speeches of a man who seemed less than engaged in this particular struggle. A short while before he addressed the 2004 Munich conference, a group called Ansar al-Sunna (one of the Qaeda affiliates that descended from the original Qaeda group in Iraq, Ansar al-Islam) launched a suicide bomb attack in the Kurdish city of Erbil. More than a hundred people were killed. Fischer in Munich expressed his sorrow. His "heartfelt sympathy"—a human sentiment. "We are appalled by the horrific terrorist attacks." Only, the man who was appalled did not appear to be infuriated, not even rhetorically. And yet, who were those victims in Erbil? They were Kurdish fighters—some of the truest, most tested anti-Baathists of Iraq. The Kurdish militant in charge of maintaining good relations with Israel (a good many of the Kurdish democrats felt a sympathy for Israel) was among the victims—a man with much to offer the people of Iraq. And what were those Kurdish militants fighting for—viewed from the standpoint of European, not to mention German, history? This was obvious. *Résistant*, or *collabo*?—wasn't this the question that had driven Fischer's generation from the very start? Those murdered people in Erbil, weren't they the *résistants*, and didn't this reality merit something more than a formulaic sympathy?

But the Iraq War was a delicate issue in Germany, and perhaps Cohn-Bendit was thinking precisely of this sort of circumstance when he commented, in regard to Fischer, that in politics, "it's necessary at some moments not necessarily to lie but, in any case, not to say the truth. You keep quiet, you let things go." Or perhaps Fischer kept a rhetorical distance from the Iraq War because he, too, was apoplectic about the American leaders. He distrusted their values and honesty and competence (or, at least, he gave that impression, without leveling any accusations). He knew that Donald Rumsfeld had never been a partisan of nation-building. The neocons struck him as strange—the topic of neoconservatism made him want to discuss the old-fashioned Trotskyist instinct for secret maneuvering. He thought the humanitarian interventionists were naive about the American leaders. Then, too, it may be that, in his middle age, Fischer had become pessimistic about the Arab world. Back in 1986, during his debate with Glucksmann, he had doubted that giant changes were going to overtake the Soviet Union; and during the Iraq crisis he harbored a similar skepticism about the Middle East. Anyway, he was frightened of setting off a clash of civilizations. He thought that if France and Germany had joined the United States and Britain and their allies in the invasion of Iraq, the entire enterprise would have ended up looking like a Christian Crusade.

IV.

Still, Fischer made one other argument in these speeches, and this was eye-catching. He spoke about the illusion of world peace that had clouded so many people's minds after the collapse of the Soviet bloc. He spoke about the "End of History" and the euphoric belief that grand-scale conflicts were a thing of the past and that Europe's peacefulness was the world's—these many dreamy ideas that had flourished amid the dot-com boom and the "culture wars" of the nineteen-nineties. And yet, all the while, something that he chose to call a "new totalitarianism" (oddly echoing Rumsfeld's accusatory distinction between the two Europes, "New" and "Old") was gathering strength. And what was this new totalitarianism? It was "Islamist terrorism and its inhumane jihad ideology"—the totalitarianism of Al Qaeda and the Taliban and similar groups. Now, someone might wonder why, if Fischer had wanted to speak about totalitarianism in the Muslim world, he didn't offer a few additional comments about the Baath, given that, from the perspective of conventional political theory, Saddam's regime was instantly recognizable as a genocidal party-state in the twentieth-century style.

But, all right, Saddam and his crimes and doctrines were a settled matter on the German political scene, and Fischer was not going to utter one syllable that might put into question the policies of his own government. So he spoke, instead, about Muslim totalitarianism in its Islamist branch—and this was fairly remarkable, given how many people in Europe continued to look on Islamist terrorism merely as an anthropological weirdness, or as an expression of social resentment, or as a demented version of old-fashioned religion, or as an Israeli creation, or as anything at all except a modern ideological temptation, familiar to Europeans. Fischer hit the "totalitarian" note, even so, and, by speaking in this way, he conveyed the unavoidable suggestion that something about radical Islamism did, in fact, merit a modern description. The new totalitarians were obviously never going to conquer the world, and in this respect were less ominous than the Stalinists and Nazis (even if Ayatollah Khomeini and the more radical Islamist revolutionaries considered that world conquest was a proper goal). Nor were the new totalitarians ever going to rival the power of Nazi Germany or the Soviet Union (unless they got hold of the wrong weapons).

Even so, the modern Islamist movement had already managed, during the last quarter century, to produce deaths by the million in a variety of countries, and because the word "totalitarian" seems to drag the word "genocide" behind it, like a dead horse, Fischer's new rhetoric hinted at this dismal reality. By hitting his "totalitarian" note, Fischer hinted at one other thought, as well. This was the obvious and unavoidable idea that people in the liberal and democratic countries had a duty to put up a struggle, just as liberals and democrats had done against the against the "old totalitarians" of long ago—the obvious implication that, if totalitarianism was the problem, resistance was the solution.

"Notwithstanding the controversy about the war in Iraq," Fischer said in his Munich speech in 2004, "we have long shared the view that following 11 September 2001, neither the US nor Europe and the Middle East itself can tolerate the status quo in the Middle East any longer." This was a pretty sweeping statement. It meant that Fischer rejected the policeman's view of Islamist terror—the idea that, with a handful of well-chosen arrests or the dismantling of a small number of underground cells, the problem could be solved. He thought that people in the Middle East had gotten stuck on the road to a modern society, more or less the way that Germans, too, in the past, had gotten stuck. And so, he advocated a subtle and complicated fight against the new totalitarianism—a program to bring about some fairly big changes in the Middle Eastern political atmosphere, to transform what had now become intolerable. In spite of his own skepticism. World security, in his analysis, depended on something deeper than a globalized economy.

"It depends," he said at Princeton, "even more on the globalization of fundamental values, such as human rights, respect for life, religious and cultural tolerance, the equality of all human beings, of men and women, the rule of law and democracy and a share of the blessings of education, progress and social security." On the principles of modern liberal democracy, in short. "Positive globalization is the real strategic response to the deadly challenge of a new totalitarianism." Fischer wanted to tiptoe carefully through the Middle East with these ideas, in order not to awaken any memories of the imperialism of the past. And yet, positive globalization remained his goal—the globalization that he defined as liberal democracy and civic sanity. He sounded like Bernard Kouchner in these remarks. Positive globalization was positive globalization, no matter how you sliced it. Something huge, even revolutionary.

The evolution that had led so many people from the radical leftism of the sixties to a liberal intervention in the Kosovo War, the evolution of the leading '68ers from revolutionary leftism to liberal internationalism—this evolution seemed to have ended in a dispute over the Iraq crisis in 2003, with Cohn-Bendit and Fischer and a major portion of left-wing opinion adopting a cautious reticence on the Iraq War, and Kouchner and Michnik and other people among the old '68ers remaining more steadfast. But anyone who paid attention to Fischer's speeches and his discussion of the new totalitarianism and the need for positive globalization could only have concluded that, between the cautious Fischer and his more militant comrades, the gap was not so vast as all that. There was a tactical divide, but not really a philosophical divide. And these speeches of Fischer's raised an interesting question about the antitotalitarian left in Europe and its relations to the Bush administration.

Fischer expressed his ideas about a new totalitarianism and positive globalization beginning in November 2003, in his speech at Princeton. During that same month—thirteen days earlier, as it happened—Bush delivered a speech of his own, addressed to the National Endowment for Democracy. The mainstream press in the United States paid very little attention to Bush's speeches, by and large, and this was a mistake, considering how keenly ideological was his administration. This speech, too, the one addressed to the National Endowment for Democracy, came and went without much commentary, except in a *New York Times* column by William Safire. This was an important speech, though. As I judge it, the speech in November 2003 marked the turning point in Bush's thinking—the moment in which, much more clearly and consistently than before, he embraced, at least in his rhetoric, a philosophy of democratic idealism, and in a fairly radical style. Naturally, Fischer's Princeton speech and Bush's National Endowment for Democracy address differed pretty dramatically. Fischer at Princeton was not about to lob any provocative accusations at the United States. He failed to accuse America of "Bolshevism," the way his mischievous friend Cohn-Bendit had done, and said nothing at all about "obtuse dogmatism," the way Kouchner had done. The man in the three-piece suit knew how to keep his tone even and friendly. He accused no one of being an asshole. And yet, in a slightly elliptical fashion, he did offer some definite criticisms. He warned against presenting any hint of paternalistic attitudes toward the Arab world, and warned against missteps. No one could have doubted that, in Fischer's estimation, the United States had screwed up badly in Iraq and was continuing to screw up, with doleful consequences for the entire world.

But, then again, Bush in his address to the National Endowment for Democracy likewise acknowledged a few screw-ups. Bush, too, made clear that, over the years, the United States had stumbled badly, and on a massive scale. He said, "Sixty years of Western nations excusing and accommodating the lack of freedom in the Middle East did nothing to make us safe—because, in the long run, stability cannot be purchased at the expense of liberty." Bush's phrase was "Western nations," but everyone knew which was the principal Western nation. This was a not a small remark. In this single sentence, Bush proposed a larger, more encompassing criticism of American policy than anything that Fischer had suggested, or, for that matter, Cohn-Bendit and Kouchner. In Bush's picture, America's mistake added up to more than a series of blunders. The entire policy had been in error from the days of Franklin Roosevelt (whose achievement was to establish an alliance with the kingdom of Saudi Arabia) until the first years of his own administration. A multigenerational systematic mistake. And what was the worst and ugliest moment in that sixty-year run of error?

Bush didn't say, and didn't have to say. Everyone knew. The worst and ugliest example of "excusing and accommodating the lack of freedom in the Middle East" surely had to have been the moment in 1991 when Bush's father, as president, had called on the Iraqi Kurds and Shia to rebel against the Baath, and then had abandoned the rebels to their fate. Surely the ugliest moment in America's history in the Middle East were those months after the first Gulf War when the Baathist forces went about liquidating entire populations—and the American Armed Forces watched, and did nothing. Nonintervention in the face of mass slaughter—that was the bottom, morally speaking. This was an extraordinary admission from an American president, even if the admission was not quite spelled out in full.

Bush the Younger went on: "As long as the Middle East remains a place where freedom does not flourish, it will remain a place of stagnation, resentment, and violence ready for export. And with the spread of weapons that can bring catastrophic harm to our country and to our friends, it would be reckless to accept the status quo. Therefore, the United States has adopted a new policy, a forward strategy of freedom in the Middle East." So Bush, too, proposed an ambitious program, not just for one country or a single disputed border, but for the entire region.

The wartime schism that sundered the United States from the general public in Western Europe took place even so, and was bitter and costly—took place in spite of the amazing fact that, on one side of the ocean and the other, a good many people, on the left and on the right, the ex-student revolutionaries of the nineteen-sixties and the people who had always despised the student revolutionaries of the nineteen-sixties, had in different ways inched their way to some of the same conclusions about the deepest of dangers in the modern world, and the deepest of solutions.

"Neither the US nor Europe and the Middle East itself can tolerate the status quo in the Middle East any longer," were Fischer's words in November 2003. "It would be reckless to accept the status quo," were Bush's, a few days earlier. Fischer proposed "the globalization of fundamental values, such as human rights, respect for life, religious and cultural tolerance, the equality of all human beings," and so forth. Bush proposed "a forward strategy of freedom in the Middle East." Two speeches, given in the same month—with both speeches advocating what could only be called a revolution.

I don't want to overinflate the significance of speechmaking. Bush at the National Endowment for Democracy announced more clearly than ever before his conversion to what is called, in the American political language, Wilsonianism—the doctrine of Woodrow Wilson, who wanted to make the world safe for democracy. But Bush's conversion was raw, naive, and partial, and was hardly shared by some of the tough-guy warriors in his administration—which meant that Bush was never likely to wield these newfound ideas with much agility or consistency, and was always going to contradict himself, and was never going to persuade his more skeptical critics of his own sincerity. As for Fischer and Germany's foreign policy—well, the government in Berlin belonged ultimately not to Fischer but to Schröder, whose own ardor for the ideals of liberal interventionism had never been especially great. Germany was not about to abandon its short-term interests in Russia and China and in the arms bazaars of the Middle East just because of a couple of speeches by the foreign minister. Besides, with the right combination of action and inaction, the German diplomats could always launch the sort of campaign for Middle Eastern democracy that might aim at achieving a grand success six hundred years from now. In short, oratory is not reality. (Hegel was wrong.) Even so, something here cried out for notice.

The political schism that broke out between Europe and the United States in 2003 exacted a pretty severe damage on the war in Iraq (by persuading a lot of people that America's overthrow of Saddam was illegitimate; by presenting insuperable barriers to any Muslim country that might have wanted to join the American effort; by allowing Saddam's supporters to continue believing that somehow the Baathists would ultimately triumph; by allowing a great many people to persist in the belief that terrorist massacres in Iraq represented an anticolonial struggle; by preventing the power of world opinion and especially European opinion from entering into the anti-totalitarian side of the war; and so on). And yet, the Atlantic schism, for all its dismal consequences, was never as deep as sometimes appeared to be the case. This was a political schism, but not in every respect a philosophical schism. Fischer had been for several years the most admired politician in Germany. Kouchner was never going to become the president of France, but had been for a long time, according to the French polls, the single most admired politician in his own country. These two men, having gone through fairly similar political trajectories, had arrived at fairly similar views of the modern crisis, and this viewpoint of theirs was not so different from Tony Blair's. And all three of these leaders of the antitotalitarian left in Europe had ended up more or less in accord with at least one of George W. Bush's multiple aspects—the Wilsonian face that Bush presented at the National Endowment for Democracy and in some of his other speeches.

Skillful and clearheaded leaders ought to have been able to bring together these people, the consistent or inconsistent Wilsonians of the world, at least sufficiently to keep the Atlantic alliance from fraying as badly as it did. A bit of diplomatic skill might even have produced an altogether different political landscape at the outset of the war. Was Kouchner really so foolish in supposing that, if only the Bush administration had presented a liberal and humanitarian argument, the UN might have been persuaded to overthrow Saddam? I cannot judge. But I know that Fischer, in conversation with me, said something that was roughly consistent with Kouchner's argument. Fischer remarked that, after September 11, the American officials could have come to Europe (meaning, France and Germany) and proposed a vast strategic campaign to transform the larger Middle East, beginning with Afghanistan, and proceeding to Iraq, and including a Palestinian-Israeli settlement. If the Americans had proposed such a thing, and if they had seemed honest and aboveboard, the Europeans might have responded by saying, no, let's do Afghanistan first, and Palestine-Israel second, and Iraq later on. And if the Americans had insisted on Afghanistan first, and Iraq second, the Europeans—well, they might have gone along.

But the Bush administration did not know its own mind. The Bush administration made no such presentation in Europe or anywhere else, except in a few offhand ruminations to journalists in Washington that attracted very little attention. The administration chose to bully the allies instead and to hammer on the famous points that turned out, later on, to be false. And, afterward, when the false arguments had dropped away and the liberal and humanitarian logic of the war had begun to loom much more prominently—when the people of Afghanistan had chosen to show, in truly substantial numbers, that democracy was an Afghan aspiration, and the people of Iraq had shown that democracy was likewise an Iraqi aspiration, and the astounding elections had taken place in Afghanistan in October 2004 and in Iraq in January 2005, when the oppressed had arisen at least sufficiently to speak and had said, "We want to live in a democracy"—when all this had taken place, the American administration was still in no position to speak about totalitarian dangers and liberal goals. Entire publics felt burned by Washington and were in no mood to listen. In Washington nobody took the trouble to straighten out this particular problem. Perhaps nobody in Washington really cared about public opinion in the zones of Old Europe or in other parts of the world where Europe still had influence, which was pretty much everywhere. Nor did anyone in a position of power in Europe present a superior, alternative strategy—a large, well-planned campaign to roll back the totalitarianism of the Muslim world. By the spring of 2005, Fischer was already saying that he regretted not having done precisely that. Too late—much too late! The left-wing alternative was not to be. And so, the schism took place, and healed only partly in the next couple of years, and the inconjunction between Mars and Venus may have played a role in these developments. But astrological influences were not the crucial factor. Political ineptitude was in the saddle, and rode mankind.

V.

The invasion of Iraq was a tragedy from the start. The "obtuse dogmatism" of the American government that Kouchner spoke about turned out to be military and not just administrative, political, ideological, diplomatic, and rhetorical. In the first days of the invasion, in March 2003, the American forces went vaulting ahead at lightning speed, dashing toward Baghdad and not fretting too much about the irregular units and Baath militia along the way—the Fedayeen Saddam in their black uniforms, who kept on fighting even as the Americans raced along in their astonishing armored vehicles. And no one seemed to pause and wonder about these behind-the-lines fighters or to ask why they were putting up such a stubborn and even suicidal fight.

A passage in Makiya's *Republic of Fear* bears on this mysterious question. Makiya explains that, if the Baath militia drew on a political tradition in Iraq, it was the legacy of the Futuwwa Youth, from the nineteen-thirties. The Futuwwa Youth was an Arabist movement, organized as a paramilitary force, which drew its own inspiration, in turn, from the Hitler Youth of Germany—a lightly armed and somewhat disciplined organization, dedicated to the ideals of racist nationalism, the irrationalist cult of violence, and worship of the leader. In mentioning this colorful historical precedent (and in having cited repeatedly the Nazi inspirations), I don't mean to reduce the history of

Baathist politics in Iraq to an imitation or mirror of Europe from its darkest decades. Baathism, like any mass political movement, has its local idiosyncrasies and autochthonous elements. Modern totalitarianism may have arisen in Europe and may have spread from there to the world, and yet, other regions and cultures have proved fully capable of generating their own bad ideas, and even worse ones. Still, in the case of Iraq, the inspiration that led from the Hitler Youth to the Futuwwa Youth to the Fedayeen Saddam should tell us something about those disastrous first days of the 2003 war.

The top figures in the Bush administration in 2003 were not without experience in presiding over the invasion of a foreign country and the overthrow of its leader. In 1989, under the administration of Bush the Elder, a number of those same officials organized the American invasion of Panama and the arrest of Manuel Noriega, the Panamanian dictator. Noriega was a demagogue and populist, and he knew how to whip up his supporters with a Latin American nationalism and an appeal to social justice. He wielded his own paramilitary irregulars, the Dignity Battalions, who intimidated his enemies and even tried to frighten away the administration of Bush the Elder. The American warplanes flew overhead, even so, and American troops came floating downward onto Panama City beneath their fluffy parachutes, and crowds of Panamanians cheered and applauded the invaders, thrilled to be liberated from their own dictator. (American interventions do get received that way, sometimes—just to show that Michnik's theory about U.S. disasters in Latin America is not invariably correct.) And, on the streets beneath those descending parachutes, the scary and ferocious Dignity Battalions faded away. I can imagine that, among the people who drew up the plans for invading Iraq in 2003, those Panamanian experiences might have led to an expectation that Iraq's Fedayeen Saddam were likewise going to fade away, and all dictators are alike.

Saddam's fighters turned out to be true believers, though. And what did they believe? They believed that infernal imperialists and Zionists were trying to destroy the Arab nation; that cosmically sinister conspirators had launched the attack against them; that Islam and its ultimate destiny was at stake. Crowds in the Sunni streets chanted, "Our blood, our souls, we sacrifice for you, Saddam." Baathism, it is said, went into an ideological decline many years ago, but these elements of the Baathist idea do not seem to have gone into decline. These were precisely the paranoid beliefs that Baathism has shared with the Islamists, for all the differences between those doctrines. People who clung even halfway to these particular beliefs were not going to wilt in the face of the cosmically sinister conspiracy, even if the cosmic conspirators went whizzing by in their Bradley fighting vehicles.

The Iraqi militants who clung to these views were already inculcated in the delirious ideals of suicide martyrdom. The radical Islamists positively revered suicide bombings and were famous for doing so. But Saddam, too, had done his best in the years before the invasion to promote that same ghoulish cult of suicide, and not just by paying Palestinians to blow themselves up (though it must be said that Saddam had distinguished himself in this particular area of foreign aid). Before the invasion, Saddam paraded the Baathist army through the streets of Baghdad, and a number of Saddam's troops ostentatiously marched by in their natty suicide-bomber uniforms—just to show that Baathists, too, were preparing to blow themselves up. The hard-bitten militants of the Baath, together with the most radical of the Islamists, were definitely going to fight on, then, no matter how many military vehicles from the United States rolled by. This was precisely what the Bush administration, in planning the invasion, had failed to understand. Here, finally, was the terrible blunder foretold in the White House National Security Statement of 2002—the blunder that derived from supposing that totalitarian doctrines and modes of behavior were no longer a force in the world, and that modern dangers stemmed, instead, from "rogue states," which is to say, from rabble-rousing gangsters like Manuel Noriega.

And so, the American military penetrated into the Iraqi interior, in the eager expectation that Baathists and Al Qaeda's affiliates and supporters all over Iraq were going to sink into despair at the mere spectacle of American technology (that was the meaning of "shock and awe") or at the sight of foreign troops desecrating Saddam's palaces. Jay Garner, the first of the American viceroys in occupied Iraq, had himself photographed slouching in an arrogant pose of barbarous American informality at one of those magnificent and ghoulish palaces. (From that slouching pose to the sinister fun-and-games at Abu Ghraib was but a step—each of those photographs communicated contempt for the Iraqis.)

But the Baathists and radical Islamists were neither shocked nor awed, and launched their guerrilla insurgency, doubtless following plans drawn up before the war. And the American military, or at least the top brass, failed to recognize what was happening. A very small number of Americans and British soldiers were killed in those early days, and the small numbers appeared to be, in the eyes of the American analysts, militarily insignificant. Here was the delusion.

Among those early casualties was Michael Kelly—the journalist who had written so glibly and nastily about Fischer in the *Washington Post* a few weeks earlier. Kelly traveled to Kuwait to cover the invasion for the *Post* and the *Atlantic Monthly* and was assigned a journalist's "embedded" slot among the Third Infantry Division. The Third Infantry led the way into Iraq, and the Sixty-ninth Armored Regiment led the Third Infantry, and Kelly took his place in the Sixty-ninth, riding in a Humvee. After a very few days the unit reached the outskirts of Baghdad, and the Humvee came under fire and swerved to get away, and tumbled into an irrigation canal. Kelly and the driver (whose name was not reported) were killed. Dozens of journalists have been killed in the wars of recent times, which has made the job of war correspondent rather more dangerous, statistically speaking, than the job of soldier. And yet, Kelly's death was, I think, somewhat unusual, and not just because, in Iraq, he was the first American journalist to be killed. His lofty position in the American press, his nimble prose, the many achievements that were already his, and the prospects before him—all of this made Kelly the newsprint equivalent of an army general and not just a grunt. Generals stay out of danger, normally. Not this general. Kelly was forty-seven, and he had two young children.

It is natural to wonder why he chose to ride in the Humvee with the Sixty-ninth Armored—why he didn't let other journalists run the dangers of frontline reporting and assign himself, instead, the easier and probably more influential assignment of composing think-piece commentary back home in the United States. I cannot answer this question with any intimate knowledge of the man. But some things are not mysterious. The columns that he wrote in March 2003, in the days immediately before the invasion, showed that, like the army chieftains and the Bush administration as a whole, Kelly imagined that everything was going well in the preparations against Saddam. The forebodings that many other people had felt, the warnings about impending disaster that were proposed even by people who were eager to see Saddam overthrown, the European fears that Americans, in Fischer's phrase, did not know how to play "chess"— these fearful thoughts seemed to pass Kelly by, judging from his columns.

Kelly worried about Saddam's chemical and biological weapons—the weapons that, later on, turned out no longer to exist. But Kelly spoke to U.S. Army officers in Kuwait, and the officers assured him that, if Saddam let loose these terrible weapons, the army was well-prepared to cope. Kelly duly acquired his own chemical warfare suit, with special goggles to replace his newsman's nerdy eyeglasses. He was impressed by the American military's up-to-date gadgetry. He took note of the superior systems of communication, armor, and weapons. He was confident of the American training. Some of his columns from Kuwait on these themes are excruciating to read, in retrospect—columns as delusionary as anything said by Richard Perle to Cohn-Bendit in their debate back in Washington during those same prewar weeks.

Kelly interviewed the commanding general of the Third Infantry. The general was self-assured. Kelly was euphoric. He wrote, "It is remarkable enough that the United States is setting out to undertake the invasion of a nation, the destruction of a regime, and the liberation of a people. But to do this with only one real military ally, with much of the world against it, with a war plan that is still, by necessity, in flux days before the advent, with an invasion force that contains only one fully deployed heavy armored division—and to have, under these circumstances, the division's commander sleeping pretty good at night: Well, that is extraordinary.

"A victory on these terms will change the power dynamics of the world. And there will be a victory on these terms."

This was the mood. The Washington elite had worked itself up into the kind of hysteria that manifests itself as manic self-confidence. At the start of the American Civil War, in 1861, spectators from the Washington of those days departed the city to observe the first Battle of Bull Run from a hilltop, in the expectation that Union troops were going to put an end to the Southern secession in no time at all—and those Washingtonians of 1861 had everything in common with the Washingtonians of 2003. Or maybe every war starts off on that sort of note—in the belief that you and your own cause are immortal, and God or History or the latest gizmo is on your side. And so, in March 2003, the American military drove into Iraq, protected by the imaginary armor of those dreamy illusions. And the difficulties began—the small-scale harassments from fanatics behind the frontlines, plus a bit of resistance from Saddam's regular troops. After three days, a major said to Kelly, "This is much tougher than anticipated."

Kelly was a good reporter and noted everything down. He wrote: "What actually happened in the first three days was a surprise and made the American advance significantly more difficult and dangerous."

But he was not about to bail out. He did have a good deal of experience in dangerous circumstances, which he had acquired over the years. He had spent five weeks in the Gaza Strip, a dangerous assignment. He went to the Balkans and spent a couple of months in the region around Bihac, in Bosnia, when Bihac was under siege by the Serb nationalists. He thought about death, and about risk. He wrote, "If the citizens and defenders of Bihac had not come to more or less comfortable terms with death, they would become overwhelmed, and unable to summon the wherewithal to fight for their lives. Accepting death, it turned out, was indispensable to defeating death."

But Kelly's principal experiences with death and risk came during the first Gulf War, in 1991—the experiences that he described in his book, *Martyrs' Day*. He was in Baghdad before the war and remained there when the Americans bombs began to fall. His knees shook. His girlfriend, whom he later married, was in Tel Aviv, working for CBS. Kelly went to join her; and Saddam sent Scud missiles to bomb Israel. Kelly ventured into Iraqi Kurdistan. He spent eight days hitchhiking with the pesh merga, the Kurdish anti-Baath militia, and this, too, proved to be a terrifying experience.

He was affected by the people he observed in these different places. In Israel in 1991, the public was issued gas masks, in case Saddam's Scuds turned out to contain gas, and chic Israeli women conspired to transform their gas masks into stylish fashion accessories. Kelly admired their pluck. In Kuwait City he observed a different kind of experience. He arrived in Kuwait after Bush the Elder's coalition had driven the Baathist army back into Iraq, and he was overwhelmed by the Kuwaiti tales of killings, tortures, and robberies. He learned about rapes conducted with a peculiar cruelty in front of a woman's family in order to make the entire family a victim—the kind of thing that Kouchner discovered in Kosovo and described in his *Warriors of Peace*. But I think that Kelly was struck with particular force by his experiences in Kurdistan—by the mountain people wandering through their moonscapes of leveled villages and cinderblock ruins. He visited a resort town that Saddam had gassed and napalmed in 1988 (back when the Baathist army did have these weapons) and had blown up with TNT. He met with a man in his ruin of a home and examined his napalmed arms.

Kelly visited Halabja, where weeds and shrubs were growing over the concrete ruins and the demolished buildings. He spoke with a doctor in Halabja, just as Kouchner had done. Kelly spoke with a young underground writer, a Kurdish intellectual who turned out to be a fan of Dumas, Solzhenitsyn, and García Márquez. The Kurdish intellectual told Kelly that, back during a moment when Saddam had lost control of the big Kurdish city of Sulaimaniya, free speech briefly went into bloom. The Kurdish intellectual brought out a newspaper, which unfortunately lasted only a single issue, before Saddam and the Baath restored the dictatorship.

"I wrote the whole thing myself, and we made copies of it on a mimeograph machine," this man explained. "I wrote about important things, about the function of censorship in a fascist structure and the nature of democracy versus the nature of the totalitarian state." Fascism, totalitarianism, democracy—those were the Kurdish intellectual's words, these very specific political terms that so many people in other parts of the world have not wanted to apply to a non-European place like Iraq. The Kurdish intellectual commented about Gárcia Márquez: "Magic realism is very good for addressing the most important thing about Iraq, the losing of the sense of rationality."

And then, Kelly, having enjoyed his discussion of free speech and García Márquez and fascism, made his way out of Halabja and its ruins, and found that he had caught a pretty serious illness. He lost fourteen pounds. Kurdish militants rescued him and brought him to a doctor, who fitted him out with an intravenous tube.

It's easy to imagine that Kelly's experiences in Halabja and his conversations about fascism had everything to do with his insistence, in early 2003, on riding back into Iraq in a Humvee of the Sixty-ninth Armored. Or maybe Kelly was motivated by a narrow literary impulse. On the printed page, Kelly seemed most at home when he could write about big topics—about death and the meaning of life. About extreme oppression. About the fighters who tried to fend it off. About resistance, and about collaboration. By contrast, his columns about Clinton's sex life, or about Clinton's animal-like aides, or about the admirable qualities of Bob Dole's inarticulate and noble demeanor, banged on a tiny drum, and Kelly banged too hard, given the petty scale of his themes. Too much anger, too much indignation, went into his quarrelsome columns, even if now and then he got off a clever remark. His column on Fischer in February 2003 was one of these excessive commentaries—a piece that seemed to have been written by someone with too much furor and too little time, and who therefore ended up hurling tiny insults.

But on the sufferings of the Kuwaitis, on the oppression of the Kurds and their resistance, on the decision that some people make to risk death in order to survive—on these themes, Kelly composed his sentences with a sense of gravity. War journalism was on his own scale. I can imagine that he rode into Iraq with the Sixty-ninth Armored because he was confident that, in time, he would have something important to report, just as he did during the 1991 war, and he expected to see scenes of horrendous oppression and inspiring resistance, and expected to sound some deep notes in reporting on these scenes. And why was Kelly drawn to these big themes? In one of his columns he mentioned in passing that his father had fought the Nazis; but Kelly went on to specify that his father did not, in contrast to so many other elders of the World War II generation, guilt-trip his privileged children.

Kelly did not grow up, as so many of the young people of the New Left had done, consumed with the need to prove himself by mimicking the heroics of his elders. He did not seem afflicted with a psychological complex about the antifascists of his parent's generation. Nor did Kelly draw his values from the moralistic youth movements of the left. He grew up Catholic in what appears to have been a conventional American style—Catholic with a sharply defined sense of right and wrong that did not derive from a teenage reverence for the heroes of the Spanish Civil War and the French Resistance.

A background in the left seemed to strike Kelly as positively repulsive—judging, at least, from his column about Fischer. He criticized Fischer precisely for having come out of such a background and for having failed to overcome its limitations. Kelly's criticism of Fischer was the opposite of Kouchner's, in this respect. Kouchner, with his jabs at the three-piece suit, worried that Fischer had outgrown the values of his left-wing past—and Kelly worried that Fischer had failed to outgrow the values of his left-wing past. Opposite criticisms—and yet, the opposite criticisms amounted to the same thing, in the end. Kelly was an American with conservative instincts who had felt a need to go to Halabja and meet the victims, and Kouchner was a Frenchman with left-wing instincts who had felt a need to go to Halabja and meet the victims. And each of those men had somehow arrived at a similar view, crisp and well-defined—quite as if the petty questions of left and right mattered very little, compared with the truly enormous questions of hatred for tyranny and solidarity with tyranny's victims.

Not a hair on Kouchner's head was hurt during the invasion of Iraq, but this was a matter of luck. Kofi Annan somewhat reluctantly dispatched his most experienced and skillful people into Baghdad after the invasion, and Kouchner was sooner or later supposed to be one of those UN officials. His appointment was already a fait accompli, at least in his own account. He had made the rounds in Washington, preparing for his responsibility; he had dined with Rumsfeld (who seemed to Kouchner full of illusions); he was confident that quarrels between Bush and Chirac were not going to weigh against his appointment, and the Americans were going to accept him in Baghdad, just as they had done in Pristina. He waited for Annan to say the word. Meanwhile, Annan sent de Mello to set up the mission—de Mello, the Brazilian diplomat who had preceded Kouchner to Pristina, too. Annan dispatched a few other people from Kouchner's old Pristina team, as well—Jean-Sélim Kanaan, Fiona Watson, and Nadia Younès, with whom Kouchner had been especially close. Iraq was a difficult assignment, and these were some of Annan's best people.

Together with a number of other colleagues, these people set up a headquarters for the UN in Baghdad, at the Canal Hotel. On August 19, 2003, the hotel was blown up by a suicide truck-bomb. Every one of those individuals from Kouchner's team—de Mello, Kanaan, Watson, and Younès—was killed, together with nineteen other people. Another one hundred fifty were wounded.

(One of those nineteen dead, I must report, was a college classmate of mine, Arthur Helton—a veteran of the 1968 uprising at Columbia University who hadn't been especially political at the time but who grew up to become one of America's most heroic human-rights lawyers, a man who battled for the rights of Vietnamese Boat People, Haitian refugees, Palestinians, and refugees from around the world. At the moment of the explosion, Helton and his colleague Gil Loescher were conferring directly with de Mello. Arthur Helton was the author of a book called *The Price of Indifference*. Loescher was devastatingly wounded, but survived.) Who ordered that suicide attack? For that matter, who was behind the ambush that had killed Michael Kelly and his army driver back in March? Kouchner paused over this question, at least in regard to the Canal Hotel bombing, in *The Warriors of Peace*.

"Who killed our friends?" he asked. He answered carefully: "Not moderate Islam, which I love and which teaches us a great deal about the link between generations and the art of life. Instead, it was the intolerance and religious extremism that I call Islamic fascism—the false virilities, the unalterable taste of certain people for the power of dictatorship."

And what were those UN people and NGO volunteers, the idealists, doing in Baghdad? Kouchner proposed an explanation—his own explanation, an account of his own thinking, even if some of his friends in Baghdad might have phrased these concepts in a slightly different fashion. Kouchner wrote, "In September 1933, at the League of Nations, a German Jewish citizen, Mr.

307

Berheim, protested against the Nazi pogroms. The representative of the Reich, Joseph Goebbels, declared, without being chastised: 'Sirs, a man's house is his castle. We are a sovereign state. Let us do as we intend to do with our socialists, our pacifists, and our Jews.' And the Nazis did as they intended . . .

"The Shoah took place, and those who knew, didn't protest. After the conflict of 1939–45, our generation wanted to react. And thus was created—with the war and torture in Algeria, with Vietnam, with the convulsions of Communism, then the beginnings of Amnesty International—what André Glucksmann called a 'humanism of Bad News.' We didn't want to see any more pictures of killings before we rose up in opposition. Ever since the nineteen-fifties, we were on the alert against injustices and massacres on five continents, inside the borders of recognized states. We were done with mere indignation and powerlessness.

"Intervention—the word was frightening, it seemed synonymous with rape. But nothing is more consensual, so long as intervention always responds to a cry for help." Rape, consensualness—these were preposterous words. Still, it was clear enough what Kouchner meant to say. He wanted to be a *résistant*, not a *collabo*—even if resisting meant shoving international law aside for a moment, and pushing his way across the borders of some other country. That was his reasoning, and he gave this reasoning a label, and the label was generational: "Our generation wanted to react."

In this one passage, Kouchner defined the moral logic of the people with backgrounds like his own—the logic of the people who had gone into the streets in the nineteen-sixties and early seventies and had fought their battles, sometimes foolishly; the logic of people who may have deluded themselves for a while with fantasies about Che Guevara or the PLO or some other guerrilla mania, and yet who, after a while, righted themselves; the logic of people who had come to realize that intervention in the Balkan atrocities of the nineteen-nineties was the fulfillment of their own ideals, of their belief in a modest "humanism of Bad News." This one little passage of Kouchner's amounted to a generational manifesto.

But it may be that, with the suicide bombing of the UN mission in Baghdad, the airy concept known as "our generation" finally ceased to exist. Millions of people had gone through the left-wing experiences of the sixties, and a distinct cluster of the most prominent and irrepressible of those people had drawn some very similar lessons and had traveled more or less the same path, from 1968 to NATO and the Kosovo War. By the summer of 2003, some people in the generational cohort still favored the principles of liberal intervention in a militant spirit, and were not about to be put off by George W. Bush; and other people, without dissenting on philosophical grounds, wanted to be more cautious and respectful of international law, and were frightened by Bush. But if there was any chance of bringing those two groups together, this possibility got blown up by the truck-bomb in Baghdad. The truck-bomb killed the very people whose job would have required them to labor night and day to reconcile the American-led overthrow of the dictator with the principles and legalities and political realities of the UN—a reconciliation that would have brought together, as well, the more militant '68ers with the more prudent and cautious '68ers, the antitotalitarian left with the antitotalitarian left.

The story of the generation of 1968 ended there, surely. In Baghdad in August 2003. Nobody else was likely ever again to speak about "our generation" and its mission—not in regard to the generation of '68, anyway. Cohn-Bendit's imaginary '68ers' International, the worldwide cohort that he had pictured back in the nineteen-eighties in his book *We Loved the Revolution So Much*, did come into existence, for a while, in the nineteen-nineties, and Kouchner and some of the people in his group in Pristina were the International's action team. The team was gone, now. Or, if some such team did exist somewhere, if some group of people still pictured themselves as a political generation because of a distinctive twist or impulse in their passion for social justice and freedom—if any such cohort existed (and surely such cohorts existed, they had to exist, history produces these groups willy-nilly; they already existed among the aid workers and the hard-suffering soldiers around the world, the people fighting for human rights, the people who were fighting against all odds for a democratic revolution in the Middle East), the members of that cohort were going to be a little younger. Maybe a lot younger—a new generation entirely. And the younger generation was going to have to find its own way of thinking.

The language of political morality that had come out of the shadow-driven childhoods of the nineteen-forties and fifties was surely too old, by now, for use by anyone younger. Maybe the language that came out of those long-ago childhoods had always been too emotional, anyway—a distortion introduced by shadows too dark even to imagine. The new generation was going to need a new way of speaking, then—a new language for talking about some very old and wrenching and unresolvable arguments. About resistance, and collaboration, to begin with. About totalitarianism, and antitotalitarianism. About liberal and humanitarian intervention—about the humanism of Bad News. And the new generation was going to need its own way of speaking about the tragedies that descend all too fatefully upon the people who struggle against tragedies— upon those people especially: the risk-takers. The resisters.

INDEX

315

INDEX

90531878R00208

Made in the USA
Middletown, DE
24 September 2018